L. B. Roberts
London Jan

THE MUSLIM CREED

THE MUSLIM CREED

Its Genesis and Historical Development

A. J. WENSINCK

FRANK CASS & CO. LTD.
1965

Published by Frank Cass & Co. Ltd.,
10 Woburn Walk, London, W.C.1
by arrangement with
Cambridge University Press.

First published 1932
Second impression 1965

Printed in West Germany
E.C.M.

CONTENTS

PREFACE

A general survey of Muslim dogmatics may be found in various works on Islam; there are also in existence translations of single creeds and monographs dealing with special aspects of the problem. But there would appear to be a want of a comprehensive study of the historical development of Muslim dogmatics, and this book, consisting for the most part of translations of, and commentaries upon, the creed in its various forms, is designed to supply that want.

Since the treatment is historical rather than systematic, the work does not pretend to be a handbook of Muslim dogmatics, but it is hoped that the first five chapters may serve as a systematic introduction to the subject.

It is with genuine gratitude that I acknowledge my indebtedness to the late Sir Thomas Arnold, Professor H. A. R. Gibb, of the University of London, and Mr S. C. Roberts, Fellow of Pembroke College, Cambridge, without whose help it would have been impossible for me to prepare the book for the press.

A. J. W.

LEIDEN
March 1932

CHAPTER I

Introduction

A creed may take various forms: it may consist only of a few words or may be a whole treatise; it may be a doxology, a short phrase, or a work on dogmatics. This is as true of Islam as it is of Christianity; moreover, in both religions the short formula is anterior to the creed, which in its turn is anterior to the treatise on dogmatics.

This sequence is based on the historical development of the two religions. Apart from the various brief expressions in which the fervour of the earliest Christians and Muslims was embodied, formulae were required by the Faithful not for their own private use, but to distinguish them from the surrounding world; they were needed as a confession of faith, a challenge, and an invitation. To those in whom sympathy with the new faith had been kindled, this formula was the confession by means of which they could proclaim their new-born feelings. Creeds, on the other hand, that is, enumerations of the articles of belief, are not in the first place addressed to the world of non-believers, but to the dissenting children of the mother church; they owe their origin to the necessity, felt by the orthodox community, of vindicating the truth in the face of sects and heretics, and it is only when the theoretical foundations of the faith have been prepared by discussions and controversy that theologians begin to write treatises in which they expound the creed of the community, exposing the roots of scripture, tradition or reasoning, which underlie it.

Generally speaking, the earliest type of the Muslim confession of faith, namely, the phrase or sentence, is found in Tradition (*ḥadīth*), that is, the literature which has assumed the form of *Logia Muhammadis*, though it is, in fact, a mirror of the history of Muslim ideas during the first century A.H. In Tradition we find the earliest discussions and definitions of faith and Islam, of faith in its relation to works, of the pillars of Islam, of eschatology.

Tradition also contains the germs of the second type, namely, the collections of the articles of belief, which in the history of Christianity are called creeds. Just as in Christianity some articles of the creed originated in the controversies with heretical bodies or sects, so in Islam, in which councils were unknown, the views held by Khāridjites, Murdjites, Ḳadarites, Mu'tazilites, Djahmites and Djabrites, gave rise to discussions, which, when the atmosphere had cleared, were condensed by the doctors of the church into summaries of the orthodox faith; these in their turn served as bases of commentaries by later doctors. We possess several of the so-called *'aḳīda*'s (creeds) and also commentaries upon them. Of special importance is the collection printed in Haidarabad in 1321 A.H., which contains (*a*) the Fiḳh Akbar I, ascribed to Abū Ḥanīfa, with a commentary; (*b*) the Fiḳh Akbar II, also ascribed to Abū Ḥanīfa, with a commentary by Abu'l-Muntahā; (*c*) the Testament (*Waṣīya*) of Abū Ḥanīfa, with a commentary by Mollā Ḥusain ibn Iskandar al-Ḥanafī; (*d*) the *Ibāna 'an Uṣūl al-Diyāna* of al-Ash'arī, with three appendices by later authors.

These works are of special importance, since in their background we can discern the discussions with the sects and the relations with the dogmatics of Christianity and with Hellenistic philosophy; here we are at the fountainhead of that Muhammadan scholasticism, which for centuries was destined to supply the wants of medieval and post-medieval thought, and to be rejected by very few, if any, thinkers of the period.

After the first half of the tenth century A.D., in which the Fiḳh Akbar II probably originated, several doctors composed creeds of a more or less varying structure. Gradually the polemical side, which at the outset was directed against heresies, disappears to make room for scholastics. Such was the origin of the type of the popular catechisms like those by Abū Ḥafs ʿUmar al-Nasafī, Abu'l-Barakāt al-Nasafī and al-Sanūsī.

al-Ashʿarī's *Ibāna*, the fourth important work in the collection just mentioned, forms a transition from the creed to the dogmatic treatise. It contains an exposition of the orthodox faith,[1] followed by a number of chapters on separate questions, in which the orthodox view is defended against deviations to the left as well as to the right. This work, probably the earliest of its kind, is the forerunner of larger works by well-known theologians such as al-Ghazālī, al-Baiḍāwī, al-Īdjī and al-Sanūsī.

Besides the *Ibāna*, al-Ashʿarī wrote another work which was destined to become a primer, having a distinct character of its own; this was the *Maḳālāt al-Islāmīyīn*, a work on Muhammadan sects, which was followed by similar works from the pens of later writers such as ʿAbd al-Ḳāhir al-Baghdādī, Ibn Ḥazm and al-Shahrastānī.

It may be asked why no reference has been made to the Kuran as a source of information on this subject. An answer cannot be given in a few words, but it can be given in a negative form: the Kuran does not proclaim a compendium of faith that could serve as a characteristic description of Islam, either in contrast with other religions, or as a means of distinction from the peculiar doctrines of the sects. In the same way the creeds of the Christian church could not be directly taken from the New Testament. Nevertheless, the Kuran contains the elements of the *shahāda*.[2]

It must be remembered that Judaism, Christianity and Islam, in presenting themselves before an unbelieving world, emphasized, each in its turn, the unity of God and the resurrection of the dead. These are the points which are foremost in the records of the Jewish martyrs who

1 Pp. 7–13.

2 The "confession of faith" or the "two phrases", viz. "I witness that there is no God but Allah" and "I witness that Muhammad is Allah's Apostle".

suffered death at the hands of the Syrians and the Romans,[1] as well as in the Acta of the Christian martyrs who were put to trial before the Roman prefects. Furthermore, they formed the nucleus of Muhammad's preaching at the beginning of his career, when he had to face the scepticism of the Makkans, who did not believe that their scattered bones would be quickened and had no wish to learn about the approaching Day, depicted by Muhammad in such vivid colours.[2] Afterwards, when Arabia had embraced Islam, it was no longer necessary to lay stress on this point.

The idea of the unity of Allah does not occupy so large a place in the earliest parts of the Kuran; later, however, it occurs many times. Sura cxii has become very popular in the Muhammadan world: "Say, He is one God; God the everlasting. He begetteth not, and He is not begotten, there is none like unto Him". Still, these verses have not the form required for a brief phrase, nor are they elaborate enough for a creed. The first sentence of the *shahāda* occurs, though not literally, in sura ii. 256, where it is only one out of many equally impressive sentences. It is the "verse of the throne": "God, there is no God but He, the living, the self-subsisting; neither slumber seizeth Him nor sleep. His, whatsoever is in the Heavens, and whatsoever is in the Earth. Who is he that can intercede with Him, but through His own permission? He knoweth what is present with His creatures and what is to befall them; yet nought of His knowledge do they comprehend, save what He willeth. His throne reacheth over the Heavens and the Earth and the upholding of both burdeneth Him not, and He is the High, the Great". It is clear that this verse does not possess the characteristics of a creed any more than sura cxii. Nor does sura xxvii. 26: "God! There is no God but He, the Lord of the glorious throne"; nor sura

1 Cf. II Maccabees.

2 Cf. Snouck Hurgronje, "Une nouvelle biographie de Mohammed" (*Revue de l'histoire des religions*, tome xxx, Paris, 1894), p. 149 *sqq.*; also in *Verspreide Geschriften*, I. 339 *sqq.*

xxviii. 88: "And call not on any other god with God; there is no God but He. Everything shall perish, except His face. Judgment is His and to Him shall ye return".

In the second and third periods of Muhammad's preaching in Makka, his chief aim was to prove the truth of his cause, to win over his opponents and to confirm his adherents in their faith, by narratives of how in the olden times Allah had sent Apostles and Prophets to other communities, who had scorned them, but were severely punished for their unbelief. The position of Abraham, Moses, Hūd, Ṣāliḥ and Jesus, as described in these suras, is really the same as that of Muhammad in Makka; they were Apostles of God like himself. "Moses, the Apostle of the Lord of the worlds,"[1] "Ṣāliḥ, the Apostle of God,"[2] "Jesus, the Apostle of God,"[3] occur side by side with "Muhammad, the Apostle of God".[4] Muhammad's rank, it is true, is high, but there is no trace of a unique position. Even in a passage belonging to the Madina period, the Christians are admonished to give up the doctrine of the Trinity and to believe in God and His Apostles:[5] "O people of the Book, overstep not the bounds in your religion, and of God speak only the truth. The Messiah Jesus, son of Mary, is the Apostle of God, and His word which He conveyed into Mary, and a Spirit proceeding from Himself. Believe, therefore, in God and His Apostles, and say not: There are three gods. Forbear, it will be better for you. God is only one God". It may be remembered here, that, according to Caetani,[6] Muhammad never tried to convert Jews or Christians.

In other passages of the Kuran Muhammad emphasizes his own apostleship: "Say to them, O men! Verily I am unto you all the Apostle of God, Whose is the kingdom of the Heavens and of the Earth. There is no God but He! He maketh to live and He killeth! Therefore, believe on

1 Sura xliii. 45.
2 Sura xci. 13.
3 Sura lxi. 5 *sq.*
4 Sura xlviii. 29.
5 Sura iv. 169.
6 *Annali*, 23 A.H., § 50, note 1.

God and His Apostle".[1] Here indeed is the quintessence of Islam and here are the ideas expressed in the two sentences of the *shahāda*. But the characteristic form is lacking.

According to Sale and others, the words "I am unto you all the Apostle of God" mean that Muhammad here extends his mission to mankind in general. This extension would, however, contradict other passages of the Kuran, such as sura iv. 169, in which Muhammad calls himself one of the Apostles, their "seal", it is true,[2] but not different from them in other respects. Just as the Apostles were sent to their *umma*'s, so he, as the Arabian Prophet, was sent to Arabia. In this connection it is important to consider the term *ummī*, one of the favourite epithets Muhammad gives himself in the Kuran. Later writers usually explained this term as meaning "illiterate" and connected it with the problem of Muhammad's ability to read and write. *Umma* conveys the meaning of "people". When the term is used in a religious sense it means community; in a profane sense it is ἔθνος and *ummī* is ἐθνικός. When Muhammad called himself *ummī*, he meant thereby that he was the Arabian Prophet of the gentiles, speaking to the gentiles to whom no Apostle had ever been sent before. His feelings are the same as those of Saint Paul, when he writes to the Romans: "I speak to you Gentiles, inasmuch as I am the Apostle of the Gentiles".[3] In the same sense Muhammad emphasizes that the Kuran is an "Arabian book" or an "Arabian verdict".[4] As representative of these ideas may be cited the opening verses of sura xliii: "Thus unto thee as unto those who preceded thee doth God, the Mighty, the Wise, reveal Himself. Is not God verily the Indulgent, the Merciful? But whoso take other deities as lords, beside Him, God watcheth them; but thou hast them not in thy charge. Thus have we revealed to thee an Arabian Kuran, that thou mayest warn the mother city[5] and all those around it".

1 Sura vii. 157 *sq.* 2 Sura xxxiii. 40. 3 Romans xi. 13.
4 Sura xii. 2; xiii. 37; xxxix. 29; xli. 2. 5 *I.e.* Makka.

This is a limited description of the field of Muhammad's mission. Moreover, it is improbable that he ever changed his view. In Madina the Jews, who should have rejoiced at his preaching, disappointed him. The consequence of this was not a revocation of the theory of the *umma*'s, but a revised and enlarged version, in the sense that Islam was represented as the true religion of Abraham which had been forsaken by the Jews. It is clear that in this revised doctrine it is not Muhammad who is raised to a higher level, but Abraham.

It is true that there are in the Kuran expressions that seem to cover a wider field. We have already seen an example of this in the verse: "Say to them, O men! Verily I am unto you all the Apostle of God".[1] None of these passages, however, seems to have been revealed after the Hid̲jra. Sura xxxiv. 27: "And we have not sent thee otherwise than to mankind at large, to announce and to warn", belongs to a passage, the tenour of which does not differ from that of the third Makkan period, that is, the time when Muhammad announced that the Arabic Kuran had been revealed to him, that he might warn the mother city and all those around it. It seems impossible to admit that the man who emphasized this idea should have regarded himself as a missionary to the whole world.[2]

The view that Muhammad conceived of his mission as a universal one is naturally derived from Muslim tradition. Here it reaches its most characteristic expression in the story of how Muhammad sent letters to the Great Powers of his time, the Emporor at Byzantium (Ḳaiṣar), the King of Persia (Kisrā), the Negus of Abyssinia (al-Nad̲jās̲hī), the Governor of Egypt (al-Muḳawḳis), inviting them to embrace Islam. These letters are, however, of a doubtful

1 Sura vii. 157; cf. Sir T. W. Arnold, *The Preaching of Islam*, 2nd ed., p. 29, where similar passages are discussed.

2 Cf. Snouck Hurgronje, *Mohammedanism*, p. 46, note, who emphasizes the misuse of the term *al-ʿālamīna* in the Kuran, and Buhl in *Islamica*, ii. 135 *sqq.* Of the limited sense of the term *al-nās* we shall find an instance, *infra*, p. 13, note 3.

authority,[1] if indeed they are not wholly legendary. Signora Dr. Vacca[2] is probably right in supposing that these and similar tales were invented to furnish the Prophet's *exequatur* for the conquerors who conducted the Muhammadan armies to the four quarters of the world.

It is clear that the solution of this problem is of some importance for our present subject, since it throws light on the statement that the Kuran does not contain a creed, nay, not even proclaims a brief phrase in order to serve as a spiritual standard of Islam, either in face of the non-Arabian world, or for the private use of the community.

Yet, just as the elements of the *shahāda* appeared to be present in the Kuran, so the elements of a creed are not lacking. In sura ii. 285 a kind of summary of Muhammad's faith is given. It runs thus: "The Apostle believeth in that which hath been sent down from his Lord, as do the Faithful also. Each one believeth in God, His angels, His Scriptures and His Apostles". Parallel to this verse is sura iv. 135: "O ye who believe, believe in God and His Apostle, and the Book which He hath sent down to His Apostle, and the Book which He hath sent down aforetime. Whoever believeth not on God, His angels, His Books, His Apostles, and on the last day, he verily hath erred with far-gone error". In other verses belief in Allah and his Apostles only is mentioned.[3] Yet the sequence "Allah, His angels, His Books, His Apostles and the last day" occurs again in some traditions and in some forms of the creed.[4]

The rather negative result of our inquiry into the contents of the Kuran with a view to a summary of Islam may be supplemented by evidence drawn from a different field. Apart from the letters said to have been addressed by Muhammad to the Great Powers of his age, we possess a series of documents of secondary authenticity, namely, the diplomatic documents in which Muhammad stipulated

1 Caetani, *Annali*, 10 A.H.

2 *Rivista degli studi orientali*, x. 87 *sqq*., esp. p. 106 *sq*.

3 iv. 151.

4 *Infra*, pp. 23, 188.

the conditions on which the tribe, family or private person mentioned in the superscription embraced Islam or entered into political relations with the State of Madina. A large collection of these documents has been inserted by Ibn Sa'd in his *Ṭabaḳāt*.[1] Others have been preserved in the works of Ibn Isḥāḳ, al-Balāḏhurī and al-Wāḳidī. They have been discussed by Wellhausen, Caetani[2] and J. Sperber.[3] These documents do not provide us with *prima facie* evidence; at best they may be termed good reproductions of the original pieces. This is shown by the fact that some of them occur in versions which vary in length according to the efforts of the author to adapt the document to the style of later Islam. It is clear that if any short phrase embodying the tenets of Islam had existed in Muhammad's time, it would have been used by him in these documents. The fact that it is not so used suggests that these documents are to some extent genuine.

In many instances the acceptance of Islam by a tribe or person is simply expressed by the verb *aslama*. Usually, however, to this general term a few special duties of Islam are added. In the letter to Ukaidir, "when he had answered the invitation to embrace Islam, having done away with Allah's rivals and the idols", the duties of Islam are summarized thus: "You are bound to perform the *ṣalāt* at its appointed time and to hand over the *zakāt* as it is incumbent upon you".[4] A similar summary of the duties of Islam is given in several of these documents.[5] In other cases Muhammad summons the person addressed "unto Allah",[6] or "unto Allah and His Apostle";[7] elsewhere the enumeration of the conditions of Islam is preceded by the general order to believe.[8] An illustration

1 Wellhausen, *Skizzen und Vorarbeiten*, IV. No. 3; *Ṭabaḳāt*, vol. I/II, ed. Mittwoch and Sachau, p. 38 *sqq.*

2 *Annali*, passim; also in *Studi di storia orientale*, III. 238 *sqq.*

3 *Mitteilungen des Seminars für orient. Sprachen zu Berlin*, vol. XIX/II.

4 Ibn Sa'd, No. 73; Sperber, *loc. cit.*, p. 58.

5 Ibn Sa'd, Nos. 87, 119, 124 *a.*

6 Ibn Sa'd, No. 140.

7 Sperber, *loc. cit.*, p. 14.

8 Ibn Sa'd, No. 46; cf. No. 29.

of the slight value of the wording of the documents appears in the fact that the last mentioned (Ibn Sa'd, No. 29) has suffered an alteration at the hands of al-Wāḳidī,[1] who replaced the words: "to those who believe, perform the *ṣalāt*, deliver the *zakāt* and are of good advice regarding the religion of Allah" by the *shahāda*: "who believes in Allah and confesses that there is no God besides Him and that Muhammad is His servant and His Apostle".

In a letter addressed to al-Mundhir, Muhammad says: "Who performs our *ṣalāt* and directs himself towards our *ḳibla* and eats what we have slaughtered, he is a Muslim".[2] Hilāl, the chief of al-Baḥrain, receives a letter which begins: "Peace and safety. I praise in reference to thee Allah, the one God, Who has no partner. I summon thee unto Allah alone, that thou mayest believe in Allah, and obey and enter the body of the believers. For this would be better for thee. Peace upon whomsoever follows the guidance".[3] In the letter to Nahshal ibn Mālik, he and his fellow-Muslims are described as "persons who have embraced Islam, perform the *ṣalāt*, pay the *zakāt*, obey Allah and His Apostle and hand over from the booty the fifth for Allah as well as the portion for the Prophet, and adduce warrants for their conversion and turn their backs on the polytheists; for such believe in Allah".[4] John, the chief of Aila, a Christian, may embrace Islam or pay the *djizya*; at any rate he must obey Allah and His Apostle; if not, Muhammad threatens to make war upon him, to kill the adults among his people and capture the children, "for I am the Apostle of Allah, in truth. I believe in Allah, His Books, His Apostles, and in the Messiah, the son of Mary, that He is the Word of Allah and I believe that He is the Apostle of Allah...".[5] Finally, mention may be made of

1 Translation by Wellhausen, p. 320, note 1, as cited by Sperber, *loc. cit.*, p. 19.

2 al-Balādhurī, *Futūḥ*, ed. de Goeje, p. 80 *sq.*

3 Ibn Sa'd, No. 41.

4 Ibn Sa'd, No. 61; cf. Nos. 90 and 142.

5 Ibn Sa'd, No. 45.

the story of the conversion of the clan Ḥāri͟th ibn Ka'b in Na͟djrān.[1] The document addressed by Muhammad to their chief is reproduced by al-Balā͟dhurī in a succinct form,[2] which does not, however, throw much light on our problem. Ibn Sa'd, in his description of the deputation of these people to Muhammad, does not mention the document. When they meet him, they "salute him and witness that there is no God but Allah and that Muhammad is the Apostle of Allah". Whether or no any historical value is to be attached to the report as a whole, the wording, which has simply been put down in formulae dear to later Islam, is certainly worthless as evidence. Ibn Isḥāḳ mentions Muhammad's letter to the chief of the deputation in such a lengthy form, with so many details of *fiḳh*, that its spuriousness seems quite certain.

This selection from Muhammad's letters and diplomatic documents could be supplemented by additional examples; but these would have even less importance from a religious point of view, and many of them would certainly be spurious. We may therefore consider the instances given above as significant of the limited importance of the religious aspects of Islam in Muhammad's relations with the tribes of Arabia.

Caetani has distinguished several stages of attachment to Islam as represented by several groups of Arabian tribes.[3] They quite possibly correspond to the actual facts in Muhammad's time. Similar degrees of islamization may also be recognized in the documents from which extracts have already been given. In any case, a compendious description of the duties of Islam fills only a small place when compared with the fiscal duties imposed by Muhammad on those who wished to live on peaceful terms with him. There is no trace of the religious enthusiasm of the early suras of the Kuran, or of the parenetic tenour of

1 Sperber, *loc. cit.*, p. 82 *sqq.* 2 Ed. de Goeje, p. 70.
3 *Studi di storia orientale*, III. 345 *sqq.*

later suras, which, although lengthy, can at once be recognized as the expression of Muhammad's personal feelings. Here, in letters to tribes and families not yet or scarcely converted, it would have been possible to preach Islam in an equally impressive way. Here also there would have been an opportunity for mentioning the brief phrase or the creed of Islam, if they had existed at all. But they do not appear; the only instance of the use of the *shahāda* is certainly spurious.[1] The reason is obvious: religion was here of secondary importance as compared with political and fiscal matters.

This view is confirmed by the attitude assumed by a large part of the "islamized" tribes after Muhammad's death. Caetani is right in his protest against rendering by "apostasy" the term *ridda*,[2] which had become current for an act that was rather of a political nature and probably also was an economic revolt. Obviously there was no desire to sever the religious bonds with Madina, since the bonds were too loose to be felt. The contracts concluded with Muhammad had been regarded by the tribes as being agreements made between themselves and the leader of the community in Madina; with his death the validity of these agreements had ceased. This view is the less surprising, since Muhammad had neglected to nominate a successor or vicegerent, or had deliberately refrained from doing so. No single man in Arabia could tell what would become of the community of Madina from the day when Muhammad should die. Could anyone expect that the numerous tribes would be willing to follow the doubtful authority of the new leader of a community entering a critical, or possibly fatal, phase of its career?

Nothing of all this appears in the Arabic sources. On the other hand it must be acknowledged that the catchword *ridda* is not used indiscriminately throughout this literature. In *ḥadīth* the attitude taken by Abū Bakr after

1 *Supra*, p. 11.

2 It may be emphasized that the terms *ridda* and *murtadd* only obtain their signification in later Muhammadan law.

Muhammad's death is by no means regarded as the only one possible for a Muslim. No less a person than 'Umar is represented as taking a different point of view, based upon a tradition. Is all this history or legend?

Here are some of the details: al-Nawawī, in his commentary on Muslim's collection of traditions,[1] says that the resistance of Arabia was of three kinds. There was unbelief in two groups, those who followed a false Prophet (Musailima, Sadjāḥ, Ṭulaiḥa, al-'Ansī) and those who gave up religion altogether. There was, besides, a third group, which refused to pay the *zakāt*; this group, however, did not renounce Islam.

This somewhat artificial division is apparently intended to justify Abū Bakr's attitude towards two of these groups, in that the first two are charged with unbelief, whereby they had forfeited any clemency. To us a distinction between tribes that desired to remain Muslim without paying the *zakāt*, and those who rejected Islam altogether, seems artificial. We should rather have drawn the line between those who followed religious or political adventurers and therefore turned their backs on Madina and Islam and those who cut the links with Madina, without associating themselves with any new religious leader. This latter group did not, in all probability, reject Islam; for their attachment to religion must have been too insignificant a fact. What they rejected was the *zakāt*.

It is the position of the latter group of tribes that is reflected in the standard tradition on the subject.[2] It runs thus: "When the Apostle of Allah had departed this world, and Abū Bakr had been appointed his vicegerent, and some of the Beduins had forsaken Islam, 'Umar ibn al-Khaṭṭāb said to Abū Bakr: How is it possible for thee to make war on these people,[3] since the Apostle of Allah has said: I am ordered to make war on people till they say: There is no God but Allah? And whoever says: There is no God but Allah has thereby rendered inviolable his

1 i. 102.
2 Muslim, *Īmān*, trad. 32.
3 *al-nās*, cf. *supra*, p. 7, note 2.

possessions and his person, apart from the duties which he has to pay. And it belongs to Allah to call him to account. Thereupon Abū Bakr answered: By Allah, I shall make war on whomsoever makes a distinction between the *ṣalāt* and the *zakāt*. For the *zakāt* is the duty that must be paid from possessions. By Allah, if they should withhold from me a string which they used to pay to the Apostle of Allah, I would make war on them on account of their refusal. Thereupon 'Umar said: By Allah, only because I saw that Allah had given Abū Bakr the conviction that he must wage war, did I recognize that he was right".

This tradition has been put in a form that might, at first sight, seem to claim for it some historical value. But such an illusion cannot last long. We are no longer inclined to believe that state affairs of the highest importance were decided by prominent personages after the manner of the later doctors of the law. The fact that the standard tradition occurs also in a more elaborate form is enough to show that we have here to do with materials that were prepared in later times with a view to questions that were then urgent. Like Muhammad's letters to the Great Powers, these traditions had to serve as Muhammad's *exequatur* for the *futūḥ*, the political expansion of Islam, and a theoretical basis for these was found in the division of the world into the territory of Islam and the territory that was not yet Muslim, but had to be islamized. The duty of bringing about this latter state of things was embodied in the tradition: "I am ordered to make war on people, till they say: There is no God but Allah".

In the foregoing pages, we have had occasion several times to point to traditions, which are put into the mouth of Muhammad, but were undoubtedly compiled in later times in reference to current questions and circumstances. It may indeed be argued that the main part of Tradition originated in this manner. Still, though we have failed to find some brief expression of the creed of Islam in the Kuran or in Muhammad's semi-official documents, we cannot put *ḥadīth* aside without first inquiring whether this literature may not contain some genuine utterances of Muhammad on the principles of Islam. There appears to be only one tradition on this subject that bears indubitable traces of an early origin. It is this: "When the tribe of 'Abd al-Ḳais[1] came to the Apostle of Allah, they said: O Apostle of Allah, we are a tribe from Rabī'a, between us and you is the abode of the infidels of Muḍar, so that we cannot reach you, except in the sacred month. Tell us what we have to do and what we may teach those who dwell farther off. He said: I give you four commandments and four prohibitions: faith in Allah; thereupon he explained this by the words, witnessing that there is no God but Allah; and that Muhammad is the Apostle of Allah; performing the *ṣalāt*, handing over the *zakāt*, paying the fifth from booty. And I prohibit the use of four things...". The four things enumerated are four kinds of vessels used for keeping wine and other drinks. It would be out of place to discuss this tradition in detail. The particulars concerning the four kinds of vessels have given the commentators some trouble—needless trouble, one may say, for, according to another tradition,[2] the prohibition was later revoked by Muhammad. These two circumstances seem to point to the antiquity of the tradition.

On the other hand, it must be observed that the words "thereupon he explained this..." have been added by people who were anxious to put the *shahāda* into the mouth of Muhammad in this passage. In the numerous versions of the *shahāda* similar extensions of the original short form are to be found.[3] It has even been forgotten that the commandments are declared to be four in number and that a fifth was added.[4] But this again seems to

1 Its dwelling-places were in the eastern part of the peninsula, cf. Caetani, *Annali*, 8 A.H., p. 178 *sqq*.

2 *E.g.* Muslim, *Aḍāḥī*, trad. 37; cf. *Handbook of Early Muhammadan Tradition*, s.v. *Vessels*.

3 Cf. *Handbook*, under the catchword *Vessels*, esp. Aḥmad ibn Ḥanbal, *Musnad*, iii. 22 *sq*.

4 Muslim, *Īmān*, trad. 24.

indicate that the tradition dates from a time when the characteristics of Islam had not yet been summarized as they subsequently were. An enumeration of four duties of Islam, such as occurs in our tradition—faith, *ṣalāt*, *zakāt*, the fifth from the booty—is in accordance with the style of Muhammad in his dealings with other tribes, as we have seen above.

Notwithstanding these indications of the early date of this tradition, it must be acknowledged that there are circumstances which render its connection with Muhammad doubtful. We must abandon, apart from the *s̲h̲ahāda*, some other terms, such as "the infidels of Muḍar"; and the reference to the teaching of Islam, for which these people show some zeal, does not come convincingly from the mouths of spokesmen who as yet knew hardly anything of Islam. Moreover, although the historical sources mention the deputation of ʻAbd al-Ḳais, they make no reference to the present tradition. Finally, the summing-up of the commandments and the prohibitions of Islam in two series of four items each betrays a later origin. Such enumerations were, as a matter of fact, popular with the generation that gave rise to the tradition of the five pillars of Islam. The present tradition is perhaps the earliest specimen of that kind.

CHAPTER II

The "Pillars of Islam" and the "Confession of Faith" (*shahāda*)

Would Muhammad himself have been prepared to condense Islam either into a brief phrase or into a creed? We have seen that apparently he did not desire to do so, either in the Kuran—though the elements of a simple creed are not lacking—or in his diplomatic documents, or, it seems, in his utterances. This is in accordance with his character. We may call him a Prophet, or a politician, or both; he was certainly no religious philosopher. Moreover, the change in his career brought about by the *hidjra* and its consequences, produced a change in his general attitude.

Muhammad's conversion, the awakening of his religious enthusiasm—still, in spite of all treatises on psychology and religion, a miraculous occurrence—conveyed the notion that he was elected to be the preacher to Arabia of the religion for which Judaism and Christianity had prepared the way in other lands. As we have seen, a large part of the Kuran is taken up with stories of the messengers of Allah, his predecessors in the world's history, all of whom preached the same doctrine under nearly the same circumstances. The belief in his own election, which he retained with a miraculous firmness, enabled Muhammad to endure scorn and disdain on the part of his fellow-countrymen, and finally he turned his back upon them, accompanied by a little band of followers, who believed in his God, his mission, and the revelations granted to him.

It was not long before his religious position in Madina became also that of a political leader. Here we have the amazing, but not unheard-of, spectacle of the genesis of a theocracy. Such a phenomenon, however, was certainly unknown in Arabia, and unexpected by Muhammad himself. The religious nucleus that was to be his *umma*, had now come into existence. It was no longer a vague historical reminiscence, such as it had been in the Makkan period, but a matter of fact that needed careful guidance and watchful statesmanship as well as daily bread. There was a considerable Jewish element which ought to have been ready to recognize the identity of Muhammad's gospel with their own. Could any hope of their adherence be entertained, in accordance with Muhammad's ideas of the place of Prophets and Apostles in history and of their being one in spirit and tendencies?

Events turned out otherwise. The Jews of Madina—three comparatively important clans—proved not to be disposed either to recognize the alleged identity or to look upon the newcomer from Makka as a second Moses. This was a severe blow to Muhammad. It threatened to overthrow a conception that had hitherto guided him in his religious career. But he took fresh courage by assuming that the Jews had forsaken their original religion, which had been that of Abraham; and Abraham is from this time onward called in the Kuran the originator of Islam, the builder of the sanctuary at Makka and the inaugurator of the rites of pilgrimage. Instead of Jerusalem, Makka became the palladium of Islam.

The first political consequence of the new state of things was that the Jews, who by their stubbornness in religious matters had become an alien element in the body of the Madina theocracy, had to be got rid of; the three clans were banished or done away with in the course of a few years. The second consequence was that the theocratic idea became strengthened. It is no longer the story of how earlier Prophets and Apostles had suffered at the hands of their contemporaries that forms the subject of the Madina revelations. We now find questions of law, military expeditions and booty, relations with the pagan tribes and regulations of religious rites taking the most prominent place; and the dominating point of view in the later portions of the Kuran is: obedience to Allah and His

Apostle,[1] just as it is in the diplomatic documents addressed to the Arab tribes. This is the real word of the theocracy of Madina as well as of the world-empire that was to come into existence within half a century. The enforcement of this obedience on the peoples of the Eastern world at the point of the sword was justified by the tradition: "I am ordered to make war on people, till they say: There is no God but Allah".[2]

What Muhammad and the rulers of Madina cared for above all was the theocratic idea. It has been observed that Muhammad even avoided regulating affairs once for all by revelations.[3] His cast of mind was not that of a lawgiver, or that of a philosopher; three centuries were yet to elapse before the juristic and theological system of Islam could be completely worked out. In the course of these centuries there would be occasion for it to formulate its creed. We must not seek to find it in Muhammad. Neither his nature, nor the course of his life, can justify us in expecting a creed from him.

Theory and practice, as they were developed during some decades after Muhammad's death, allowed the leading powers in spiritual matters to express the essentials of Islam in traditions of which the confession of faith (*s̲h̲ahāda*)[4] and the enumeration of the five pillars[5] of Islam are the most important. The collections of *ḥadīt̲h̲*—our chief source of information for the early development of the theology of Islam—have preserved a series of "sayings of Muhammad" which must be regarded as the outcome of the theological labour carried out by the generation of the Companions. These sayings are the forerunners of the

1 Sura iii. 29, 126; iv. 62; v. 93; viii. 1, 20, 48, etc.

2 *Supra*, p. 13.

3 Snouck Hurgronje, *Verspreide Geschriften*, I. 212; II. 71, 289.

4 "I witness that there is no God but Allah and I witness that Muhammad is the Apostle of Allah."

5 Islam is built on five pillars: faith, *ṣalāt*, *zakāt*, fasting in Ramaḍān and pilgrimage.

confession of faith and of the tradition of the pillars of Islam; they must therefore be considered first.

These traditions go back to a type that may be regarded as characteristic of the earliest phase of religions such as Christianity and Islam. The Roman centurion declares[1] that a word spoken by Jesus will be sufficient to heal his servant. Jesus marvelled at his faith, saying: "Verily, I have not found so great faith, no, not in Israel". The keeper of the prison in which Paul and Silas were imprisoned in Macedonia says to them: "What must I do to be saved?" The answer he receives is: "Believe on the Lord Jesus Christ, and thou shalt be saved, and thy house".[2]

When Muhammad was on one of his expeditions a Beduin[3] came to meet him, caught his camel by its rope and said: "O Muhammad, tell me, what can bring me to Paradise and keep me far from Hell?" At first the Prophet refused to give him an answer. Then he turned towards his companions, saying: "Verily this man is guided and is on the right way". Then, looking on the Beduin, he asked him: "What didst thou say?" When the man had repeated his question, Muhammad answered: "Thou shalt serve Allah, without associating anything with Him; thou shalt perform the *ṣalāt*, hand over the *zakāt* and keep sacred the bonds of relationship. Now let go the rope of my camel".[4] The parallelism between this tradition and that of the New Testament is obvious, and requires no comment. The tradition further contains some noteworthy indications of the development of Islam. The way to Paradise is a way of service. No special mention is made of faith; it is implied in the service of the one God. No essential difference is made between this service and other duties, except in so far as it is to take first place.

This suggests an early date of origin. As to the sequence of the other duties, *ṣalāt* and *zakāt* have their fixed place here as in Muhammad's diplomatic documents; to them

1 Matthew viii. 5–13. 2 Acts xvi. 30 *sq.*

3 The type of people who have neither civilization nor religion.

4 Muslim, *Īmān*, trad. 12; cf. 14.

is added the rigid observance of the bonds of relationship, an early Arabian virtue which was promoted by Islam. Later traditions strike it out of the list to make room for duties which are more essentially Islamic. In some of the diplomatic documents it is the handing-over of the fifth from the booty that comes after the *zakāt*.

The tradition, as has already been remarked, occurs in various forms. Here is a different one:[1] "Once there came to the Apostle of Allah a man from the people of Nadjd,[2] with dishevelled hair; we heard the humming of his voice, but we did not understand what he said till he was near the Apostle of Allah. Then he began to ask him about Islam. The Apostle of Allah answered: Five *ṣalāts* every day and night. He asked: No more? The Prophet answered: No, what is above this number, is supererogatory. Further, the fast of Ramaḍān. He asked: No more? The Prophet answered: No, what is more than that, is supererogatory. Further, the Apostle of Allah mentioned the *zakāt*. He asked: No more? The Prophet answered: No, what is above it, is supererogatory. Thereupon the man went away saying: By Allah, I shall add nothing, nor omit anything. Then the Apostle of Allah said: He is saved, if he keeps his promise".

Three points are new in this tradition: first, even the service of Allah is not expressly mentioned. Islam consists of ritual duties only. Secondly, *ṣalāt* is specialized: five prayers every day and night. It may be remembered that the number of five daily *ṣalāts* was fixed as the outcome of a long process, the beginnings of which can be traced in the Kuran, whereas the evidence of its conclusion is found in early tradition.[3] At any rate, the process was finished before the rise of the sects. Thirdly, the fast of Ramaḍān, which was imposed on Muslims early in Madina by revelation, appears here for the first time as one of the cardinal duties of Islam.

1 Muslim, *Īmān*, trad. 8; cf. 15.
2 The table-land of Central Arabia.
3 Cf. Caetani, *Annali*, 2 A.H., § 11 *sqq*.

It is not necessary to enumerate all the variants of the tradition. They are forerunners of the tradition of the pillars of Islam. The negative characteristics which they have in common are the absence of any distinction between the ritual duties and the inner relation of man to Allah, and the lack of a fixed summary of the duties of Islam.

These traditions are the immediate successors of the descriptions of Islam in Muhammad's diplomatic documents.[1] Theological thought made gradual progress; the examples discussed above represent only an early stage; still, they were the outcome of discussions and perhaps of differences of opinion. This conclusion may be drawn with some certainty from the promise of salvation to those who clung to the catchword without adding anything to it. In this way the hope was expressed that this formula would be the last word spoken on the question. The theologians of Madina could not have foreseen that Islam would have to go through a process of development for centuries, before it could reach a position that could be maintained throughout the Islamic Middle Ages.

It was the rapid course of events in the first decades following the death of Muhammad—the hostile attitude taken by the previously islamized tribes, the restoration of order by Abū Bakr and his generals, the splendid feats of arms under 'Umar, which were followed by the islamization of large parts of the ancient world—that made clear to the Companions, and to the pious generation of their successors, that the term "Islam" had obtained a temporal meaning. It seemed as if the narrow path, originally the only way by which the city of Islam could be reached, had been enlarged and paved and become an easy highway for the multitudes who came from all sides to embrace Islam.

In the Kuran the terms *islām* and *īmān* (faith) are synonymous; *muslim* and *mu'min* comprise the whole body of those who had escaped from Hell by embracing Islam. This is reflected in the first tradition translated above.[2]

1 *Vide supra*, p. 8 *sqq*. 2 P. 20.

The next question (that of the second tradition)[1] is: What is Islam? The way to escape from Hell is no longer the centre of interest, but the question is: What are the characteristics of Islam and who are the true Muslims? The course of history had made it clear that there were Muslims of many varieties, and that the observance of religious rites was not necessarily the sign of faith or conviction. The next tradition, therefore, seeks to state that there is a difference between faith and acceptance of the official religion; that faith, though expressing itself in the performance of rites and duties, lies deeper than these, just as the roots of the tree are beneath the surface. This is laid down in a brief form in a tradition that is hidden in the collection of Aḥmad ibn Ḥanbal:[2] The Apostle of Allah used to say: "Islam is external, faith belongs to the heart". Thereupon he pointed to his heart three times, saying: "The fear of God is here".

This tradition, although expressing a living conviction that will ultimately find its way to the *credo*, has not become popular. It does not occur in any of the other collections. In the stately chapter on Faith, which by Muslim is placed at the head of his work, we find the standard tradition on the subject. It is this: One day the Apostle of Allah gave audience. There came to him a man, who asked him: "O Apostle of Allah, what is faith?" He answered: "Believing in Allah, His angels, His book, His meeting, His Apostles, and the final resurrection". The man asked: "O Apostle of Allah, what is Islam?" He answered: "Islam is serving God without associating anything with Him, performing the ordered *ṣalāt*, paying over the obligatory *zakāt*, and fasting during Ramaḍān". The man asked: "O Apostle of Allah, what is righteousness?" He answered: "Serving Allah as if He were before thy eyes. For if thou seest Him not, He seeth thee". The man asked: "O Apostle of Allah, when will the Hour[3] be?" He answered: "He who is asked, knows no more of it than

1 P. 21.

2 *Musnad*, iii. 134 *sq.*

3 *I.e.* the end of all things.

the asker does. But I will tell thee something about its conditions. When the handmaid shall give birth to her lord, this is one of the conditions thereof. When the barefooted and the naked shall be the rulers, this is one of the conditions thereof. And when the shepherds[1] shall make sumptuous buildings, this is one of the conditions thereof. [The Hour belongeth] to five other things, which are known to Allah alone". Thereupon the Apostle of Allah recited: "Aye! God!—With Him is the knowledge of the Hour; and He sendeth down the rain; and He knoweth what is in the wombs—but no soul knoweth what it shall have gotten on the morrow: neither knoweth any soul in what land it shall die. Verily God is knowing and informed of all".[2] Then the man went away. Thereupon the Apostle of Allah said: "Bring that man back to me". When his companions tried to do so, they could find no trace of him. Then the Apostle of Allah said: "This was Gabriel, who came in order that men might have knowledge of religion".[3]

In this tradition it is for the first time conceded that faith is not identical with Islam. Still, no philosophical definition of faith is given; nor is its nature described here, but its contents only. The enumeration of the objects of faith is founded on the Kuran.[4] It may be asked why in this enumeration the mention of the meeting with God should come in between that of Allah's book and that of His Apostle. The commentators, who are puzzled as to the meaning of the distinction between the meeting with God and the last day, give us no answer. We can only conjecture that the term was added in later times and that it was directed against heretics who denied this point of eschatology. This conjecture is corroborated by the fact that the author of the Waṣīyat Abī Ḥanīfa has deemed it desirable to call the meeting with Allah a reality.[5]

1 The text has "keepers of brutes". There is much variety in reading and explication; cf. al-Nawawī, i. 18.

2 Sura xxxi. 34.

3 Muslim, *Īmān*, trad. 5.

4 Sura iv. 135.

5 Art. 24; cf. *infra*, pp. 130, 179.

The definition of Islam opens with the commandment to serve God alone. In the enumeration of the duties of Islam the pilgrimage has not yet received its fixed place. An entirely new element is the addition of the definition of *iḥsān*, "righteousness". It shows that the true religious attitude is something more than is contained in the definition of faith or in that of Islam. The definition of it is: serving God as though He were before your eyes; this reminds us of the New Testament phrase "seeing Him who is invisible".[1]

The passage on the Hour calls for some notice. No doubt Muhammad had not only preached the coming of the Hour, but also its near approach.[2] Although the expectation that the Hour would occur in Muhammad's lifetime had not been realized, tradition took up the idea that it could not be far off. "Verily, the connection between my prophetic mission and the Hour is as close as the relation of this finger to that" is a tradition put into the mouth of Muhammad, who pointed in illustration thereof to two of his fingers.[3]

But the Hour did not come as early as it was expected and people began to search for signs that would probably be seen immediately before it. In some cases historical events are said to be the signs of the coming Hour, especially the *fitan*.

In our tradition three signs only are mentioned: the handmaid giving birth to her lord, the lowest classes becoming the ruling ones, and the poor indulging in luxury. The limitation of the signs to three points to the relatively early date of the tradition. On the other hand it appears to reflect the change that had begun to take place in Arabian society in consequence of the expansion. Many traditions appear to owe their origin to the reaction of pious circles against this social revolution.

1 Hebrews xi. 27.
2 *E.g.* sura xlvii. 20.
3 Bukhārī, *Riḳāḳ*, b. 39; Muslim, *Fitan*, trad. 132–9.

The types of tradition we have dealt with in this chapter—of salvation, of Islam, of the difference between faith, religion and righteousness—may, all of them, be regarded, in a sense, as forerunners of the tradition of the pillars of Islam.

This tradition itself occurs in different forms. Its general type is this: Islam is built on five [pillars]. The first is faith, the second *ṣalāt*, the third *zakāt*, the fourth the fast of Ramaḍān, the fifth pilgrimage.

This means that Islam is declared to consist of a combination of faith and works. It is, consequently, the conjunction of the brief enumeration of the duties of Islam with the emphasis on faith in contradistinction to Islam; in this way faith obtains a precedence over works, while, on the other hand, Islam, the bond between the two elements, appears as the wider idea. In view of all this the tradition of the pillars of Islam must be regarded as a masterpiece of early Muhammadan theology.

The versions of the tradition are not, however, exempt from the traces of slightly divergent opinions. Various readings regarding the four duties are rare. In the version handed down by Muslim as the first of four different forms,[1] it is said that a man tried a slight correction by interchanging the place of the fast of Ramaḍān with that of the pilgrimage, whereupon Ibn 'Umar said: "No, first the fast of Ramaḍān, then the pilgrimage; so I have heard it from the mouth of Muhammad". We do not know to what tendencies such deviations were due. As a matter of fact, there is one version of the tradition in which pilgrimage precedes the fast of Ramaḍān.[2]

Another difference finds expression in two versions preserved by Aḥmad ibn Ḥanbal.[3] Both go back to Ibn 'Umar, who is said to have been asked: "And the holy war?" He answered: "The holy war is only one of the good works. The Apostle of Allah used the same wording as I did". In the second tradition the same question is asked. Here Ibn 'Umar answers: "Whoever takes part in

1 *Īmān*, trad. 19–22. 2 *Īmān*, trad. 20. 3 ii. 26, 92 *sq.*

the holy war, does so to his personal profit". This means that taking part in the holy war, although a good work, does not deserve a place in the series of the cardinal duties.

The mention of the holy war in some versions of the tradition, as well as its absence from the primary version, throws some light on its historical background. If the tradition had originated in the age of the first conquests, it would have been hard to refuse the holy war a place in the summary of the duties of Islam. That period is apparently over and holy war has lost its primary significance, so that Ibn 'Umar feels justified in refusing it a place in the series.

Distinct traces of earlier discussions concerning the sequence of works in relation to their intrinsic value are contained in traditions of the following type: "The Apostle of Allah was asked: Which is the most excellent of works? He answered: Faith in Allah.—Which next?—War in the path of Allah.—Which next?—A blameless pilgrimage".[1] Here *djihād* comes directly after faith, and the latter is characterized as a work. These two features point to a very early origin. In others, apparently somewhat later examples of the type, the sequence is: *ṣalāt*, dutifulness towards parents, holy war.[2]

This type has not had any lasting influence on the determination of the pillars of Islam.

So much for the last four pillars. More must be said of the first. Perhaps the most primitive form of the tradition is the following: "Islam is built upon five:[3] serving God and denying anything besides Him; the performance of *ṣalāt*" and so on.[4] In this version faith is not mentioned; only the service of God and the exclusion of any partner.

The second stage of the development of the first pillar may be found in those traditions which call it "the

1 Muslim, *Īmān*, trad. 135, 136. 2 Muslim, *Īmān*, trad. 137–40.

3 Neither the word "pillars" nor any synonym is mentioned in any of the redactions.

4 Muslim, *Īmān*, trad. 20.

confession of the unity of Allah".[1] The final stage is reached in the accepted form: the confession that there is no God but Allah and that Muhammad is His Apostle.[2] It may be asked whether the difference between the second and third stages is of any importance. The answer to this is not easy. Apparently the full form of the s̲h̲ahāda, the confession of Muhammad's apostleship side by side with the unity of Allah, did not at once obtain a fixed place in Islam. We may conclude this from the fact that not only in the tradition of the pillars of Islam, but also in numerous other cases, the confession of the unity of Allah alone is mentioned as the essential fact for man.[3] It is clear that for Muslims the confession of Allah included that of Muhammad's mission; and this may have made it superfluous to add anything to the confession of Allah. It may be supposed that the full confession of faith was especially used as the symbol of Islam as opposed to Judaism and Christianity, which religions confessed God's unity, but denied that Muhammad was His Apostle.

It may be remembered here, that, although Eastern Christianity saw the number of its adherents gradually diminish in favour of Islam,[4] conversions scarcely ever took place under compulsion. Though we know very little concerning the form in which they took place, it may be supposed that pronouncing the *s̲h̲ahāda* was sufficient proof of the change of religion.

In this connection we may consider anew the standard tradition for the holy war: "I am ordered to make war on people till they say: There is no God but Allah. And whoever says: There is no God but Allah, has thereby rendered inviolable his possessions and his person, apart

1 Muslim, *Īmān*, trad. 19, 22; Aḥmad ibn Ḥanbal, ii. 26; iv. 363; Nasā'ī, *Īmān*, b. 3.

2 Aḥmad ibn Ḥanbal, ii. 26, 120, 143; Buk̲h̲ārī, *Īmān*, b. 2; Muslim, *Īmān*, trad. 21. Buk̲h̲ārī, *Tafsīr*, sura 2, b. 30 has "faith in Allah and His Apostle".

3 Cf. *Handbook of Early Muhammadan Tradition*, s.v. *Unity*.

4 Cf. Arnold, *The Preaching of Islam*, p. 81 *sqq*.

from the duties he is obliged to pay; and it is for Allah to make him give account". This is the current form of the tradition.[1] Its tendency is described by one of the commentators[2] as postulating the *tawḥīd* (confession of the unity of Allah) only. It therefore covers the field of the holy war with pagan populations. In other versions the full *shahāda* is mentioned.[3]

The tradition is, however, more interesting from a different point of view. It is said by the commentator just mentioned that only the outward expression of faith is called necessary. This point requires some elucidation. Our tradition occurs in more extensive forms in which either the performance of *ṣalāt*[4] and the handing-over of *zakāt*, or the observance of the rites of prayer and of slaughtering,[5] are mentioned as a minimum which may save non-Muslims from the sword. These versions prove that a simple confession of the unity of Allah was deemed insufficient, and therefore had to be reinforced by more solid proofs of the convert's sincerity.

These elaborate versions have not, however, succeeded in overthrowing the short one, which has remained the accepted form. In the latter the sincerity of the convert is dispensed with by means of the clause: "And it is for Allah to make him give account", that is, not for man, for man must be content with the confession of *tawḥīd*. It is expressly stated by the commentators that this is the sense of the clause. There have been preserved other traditions of a similar tendency. Usāma ibn Zaid is made responsible for the following tradition:[6] "The Apostle of Allah sent us on an expedition to al-Ḥuraḳāt. The enemy, however, got news of us and took to flight. We got hold of one of the

1 Bukhārī, *Zakāt*, b. 1; *Djihād*, b. 101; *Istitāba*, b. 3; *I'tiṣām*, b. 2, 28; Muslim, *Īmān*, trad. 32, 33, 35; Tirmidhī, *Īmān*, b. 1; *Tafsīr*, sura 88.

2 al-Sindī, on Bukhārī, Cairo, 1304, i. 178.

3 Muslim, *Īmān*, trad. 34.

4 Muslim, *Īmān*, trad. 36.

5 Bukhārī, *Īmān*, b. 28; Abū Dāwūd, *Djihād*, b. 95.

6 Abū Dāwūd, *Djihād*, b. 95 *c*.

men and when we fell upon him, he said: There is no God but Allah. Yet we beat him till he was dead. I narrated this to the Prophet, who said: How will you render an account for this 'There is no God but Allah' on the day of the resurrection? I answered: O Apostle of Allah, he said it only from fear of our arms. Thereupon the Prophet said: You have of course not neglected to split open his heart in order to know whether fear was his motive. How will you account for this 'There is no God but Allah'? And he did not cease repeating these words till I wished I had not been a Muslim before".

This tradition is of special importance. Muhammad's ironical words: "You have of course not neglected to split open his heart...", allude to the theory and the practice of the Khāridjites. We shall have occasion to discuss their position later.[1] Here it is enough to state that this tradition cannot be separated from the standard tradition of the holy war, and that the tendency of the latter, especially the clause "and it is for Allah to make him give account", is directed against the Khāridjites.

So the tradition of the holy war, at least in its full form, proves to have its origin not in the attitude assumed by the tribes at Muhammad's death, but in the events following the battle of Ṣiffīn in A.D. 667: the secession of the Khāridjites and the battle of Nahrawān.

We must take leave of the Khāridjites for the present and return to al-Nawawī's commentary[2] on our tradition. According to one of the authorities cited by him, those whom Muhammad is ordered to fight are pagan peoples, not the people of the book. For the latter have no objections to the *tawḥīd*; yet they must be combated till they submit to Muslim authority and pay the tax called *djizya*. Then he goes on: "One of the conclusions to be drawn from the tradition is, that when a man embraces Islam, but remains an infidel in his heart, his conversion is accepted in the opinion of the majority of the authorities. Mālik is of opinion that the conversion of a *zindīḳ* should

1 Cf. especially *infra*, p. 41. 2 i. 105.

not be accepted, and it is said that this was also the opinion of Aḥmad ibn Ḥanbal.... The Shāfi'ī authorities are of divergent opinions in regard to the conversion of a *zindīḳ*, *i.e.* one who radically denies the obligatory force of the law. According to one, the right view is, that such a conversion must be accepted, without any restriction, on account of the genuine traditions that reject all restriction; another view is, that such a conversion must not be accepted and such a person must be killed; yet, if his conversion be sincere, this will be profitable to him in the other world and he will be one of the inhabitants of Paradise; another, that the first time such a conversion must be accepted; if he falls and is converted another time, his conversion is not then accepted; another, that if the conversion is spontaneous, it is accepted; but not if it takes place through the sword; another, that if he be a propagator of his own false ideas, his conversion is not accepted; otherwise, it is".

As may be seen from this passage, conversion is, generally speaking, accepted by Islam without further scrutiny.[1] Yet it may be stated at once, that in later definitions of faith, confession and conviction receive equal emphasis.[2]

The passage from al-Nawawī's commentary translated above contains an explanation of the fact that the confession of the unity of Allah, with the exclusion of any mention of Muhammad's apostleship, is deemed a sufficient safeguard from the sword. We have already said that such a use of the first sentence of the *shahāda* alone does not stand by itself, but may be observed in many important traditions, a phenomenon which may generally be explained in the sense that the Muslims themselves did not want a special mention of Muhammad's mission after that of the unity of Allah. Neither was this necessary where Islam combated pagan peoples, as neither Muslim nor pagan could conceive of belief in Allah without belief in

1 On the position of the Khāridjites, cf. *infra*, Chapter III. On the whole question, cf. al-Baghdādī, *Uṣūl*, p. 188 *sq*.

2 Cf. Waṣīyat Abī Ḥanīfa, art. 1; *infra*, p. 125.

the Apostle who was the intermediary between Allah and the world. This state of things was still felt by Ḳāḍī 'Iyāḍ in his commentary on the tradition of the holy war: "The fact that the saving of life and person is based upon the confession of the unity of Allah, means that it is connected here with embracing the faith, and shows that the tradition has in view the Arabs who denied it, who were pagans and rejected the belief in the one God. They were the first to be summoned to embrace Islam and were combated. As to those, however, who recognize one God, the formula of *tawḥīd* is not sufficient to save them...".[1]

We have already seen that it is wrong to suppose that Abū Bakr and 'Umar directed their armies against the tribes of Arabia on account of traditions; for the latter originated at a time when theoretical discussions were the topic of the day. It is not the so-called *ridda*, but the epoch of the conquests and of the rise of the sects that promoted these discussions and encouraged the formation of traditions which contain the formulae worked out by the schools of theologians of Madina and the centres of science.

We return now to the *shahāda*. An indication of its comparatively early origin lies in the fact that it is used in the *ṣalāt*. In the technical language of *fiḳh* the term *tashahhud*, *i.e.* the reciting of the *shahāda*, does not, however, simply denote the confession of faith, but the whole of the formulae recited at the end of every second *rak'a*, as well as at the end of the whole *ṣalāt*, followed by the benediction on Muhammad and the *taslima*.

It may be conceded that the ritual of the *ṣalāt* was not yet standardized when Muhammad died. But the period of development cannot have lasted very long, for there are no traces of deviation from the common ritual of the *ṣalāt* among the sects, and it is not probable that these would have taken over from the orthodox community the final form of the *ṣalāt* after their secession. Moreover, it cannot be supposed that a matter of so great importance

1 Citation from al-Nawawī's commentary on Muslim's *Ṣaḥīḥ*, i. 105.

as the formulae of the daily *ṣalāt* could long be left in a variable state in an empire which had been widely and rapidly extended.

A further indication of the time in which the *shahāda* originated may be found in the use which is made of it in canonical tradition. This may be illustrated by a few instances. ʿAbd Allah ibn Salām, a man of note among the Jews of Madina, is represented to have asked Muhammad three questions in order to test by his answer the truth of his mission. Muhammad having stood the test successfully, ʿAbd Allah declared his own conviction, at the same time expressing a fear lest the Jews, when hearing of his conversion, would belittle him in Muhammad's eyes. Muhammad, therefore, asked the Jews the question: "What is the position of ʿAbd Allah in your community"? They answered: "He is the most learned and the best, the son of the most learned and best". Muhammad said: "What if this man had embraced Islam"? They said: "May God preserve him from such a thing". Thereupon ʿAbd Allah came forth, saying: "I witness that there is no God but Allah, and I witness that Muhammad is the Apostle of Allah". Then the Jews said: "He is the worst son of the worst father", and they threw themselves on him.[1]

This story is devoid of historical value; its main features belong to a well-known scheme. All that can be deduced from it is the use of the *shahāda* by converts.

A second instance, also of a legendary nature, is the story of how Abū Dharr al-Ghifārī, one of the saints of early Islam, travelled to Makka in order to become acquainted with Muhammad and his preaching. At Makka he met the Prophet and, being at once convinced of the truth of his gospel, he went straightway to the mosque where he addressed the people with the words: "O ye Ḳuraishites, I witness that there is no God but Allah and I witness that Muhammad is His servant and His Apostle".[2]

Likewise it is narrated how Thumāma, one of the chiefs

1 Bukhārī, *Anbiyā'*, b. 1.
2 Bukhārī, *Manāḳib*, b. 11.

of al-Yamāma,[1] was made captive on an expedition and fastened to one of the pillars of the mosque of Madina. Muhammad came to him, saying: "What hast thou to say, O Thumāma"? He gave a proud answer after the manner of the knights of the desert. Muhammad left him alone. Coming back the next day he repeated his question and received the same answer. On the third day the same scene was enacted. Then Muhammad gave order to loosen his bonds. Thereupon Thumāma went up to a palmgrove near the mosque, bathed thrice as converts used to do, returned to the mosque and said: "I witness that there is no God but Allah and I witness that Muhammad is His servant and His Apostle".[2]

For our present purpose this story has the same value as its two predecessors; together, they prove that in the time of those who handed them down—Ibn 'Abbās, Anas ibn Mālik, Abū Huraira—and who lived in the second half of the seventh century A.D., it was customary for anyone who embraced Islam to proclaim his conversion by the recitation of the *shahāda*.

It would be superfluous to repeat what has been said above[3] of the value of the numerous conversions that took place in the seventh century A.D. and on the way in which pious circles reacted to this phenomenon. It may be sufficient to repeat here that the counter-effect was that the distinction between *islām* and *īmān* did not fail to become more rigorous. We shall hear more of this in the following chapter. One proof only may be mentioned here. It dates from the time when the community had already rejected the views of the Ḳadarites, but it may still belong to the later years of the seventh century. It is a new version of the tradition on *islām* and *īmān*. Muslim has given it the first place in his collection. It may be regarded as the outcome and conclusion of a whole series, namely the traditions of salvation, of the duties of Islam, of the distinction between faith and Islam, of the

1 A region in the north-eastern part of Arabia.

2 Muslim, *Djihād*, trad. 59.

3 *Supra*, p. 22.

pillars of Islam and the *shahāda*; it rests on the authority of 'Umar and runs thus: One day we were with the Apostle of Allah, when a man approached, clad in garments of a pure white colour, and with raven-black hair; no traces of travelling were visible on him. He sat down at the side of the Prophet, knee to knee. Placing his hands on his thighs he said: "O Muhammad, give me information on Islam". The Apostle of Allah said: "Islam is witnessing that there is no God but Allah, and that Muhammad is the Apostle of Allah; performing the *ṣalāt*, handing over the *zakāt*, fasting during Ramaḍān, and the pilgrimage if there be no hindrance". The stranger said: "Right". We wondered how he could ask for information and at the same time say: Right. Thereupon the stranger said: "Now give me information on faith". Muhammad answered: "Believing in Allah, His angels, His books, His Apostles and in the last day, and believing in the decree, the good and the evil thereof". The stranger said: "Right. Now give me information on righteousness". He answered: "Serving Allah...". This tradition has in fact already come to our notice.[1]

We now take leave of the "pillars of Islam" and the *shahāda*. They do not pass into oblivion in the course of history; they remain popular as summaries of Islam (especially the *shahāda*), each in its own way and to its own purpose, and they have never been replaced by a generally recognized short phrase. On the contrary we shall have occasion to observe[2], in the form and contents of the creed, a return to the *shahāda*.

1 *Supra*, p. 23.
2 Cf. Chapter IX, towards the end.

CHAPTER III

Faith, Works and Will

Islam under the first caliphs witnessed a marvellous expansion, such as its founder had never dreamt of. Religion was no longer the object of scorn and laughter; it had become the possession of myriads. The little flock was not, however, merged into these myriads; it formed the conscience of Islam, guiding and watching lest the pure gold should become defiled. One of its first achievements was to establish a distinction between religion as a matter of ritual only and religion as an inner experience.

It was not only in relation to islamized Beduins, Christians and pagans that this distinction became necessary. It was in the cradle of Islam itself, in Madina, that worldliness, envy and hatred began to show themselves in a way that caused protests to be made both there and in other parts of the Muslim world. The murder of 'Uthmān, the worst symptom of this illness, may have been the work of a small band of rioters, and its immediate consequences were an illustration of *corruptio optimi pessima*; for it was among the aristocracy of Islam that hatred, ambition and greed threatened to obscure the less selfish tendencies that were at the bottom of the first *fitna* or scandal. It was only in the formation of the first sect, the Khāridjites, that a nobler turn of mind appeared and that ideas came to light, of which only a glimpse can be discerned in the earlier history of Islam.

The political doctrine of the Khāridjites was that the Muslim community must be governed by a head whose claims to this office were based upon his being the best qualified Muslim. Those who were actually striving to occupy the highest places, as well as those who backed them, were to a large extent evildoers.

Although at the outset this doctrine was of an exclusively political nature, it led to results which were to become of the highest importance for the development of Muslim theology. For the Khāridjite position contains the germ of the leading idea of the Ḳadarites, and the latter were the heralds of the Mu'tazilites, who influenced primitive Islam to such an extent and placed before it problems of such an importance, that it is not too much to say that they led to a crisis of Islam. History follows the logical line of the concatenation of these ideas.

The rise of the Khāridjites[1] forced the Muslim community to define its own position. The old question of the difference between *īmān* and *islām* returned in this more pointed form: Who is a Muslim and who is an infidel? Who will be saved and who will be damned? This was a problem as difficult of solution as that of the caliphate after the murder of 'Uthmān. It appears so unexpectedly—to us at least—and the discussions which turn on it show so much theological skill, that we are inclined to ask: Was not the theological position of the Khāridjites prepared for by the discussions on the nature of faith, that have been described in the foregoing chapter?

However this may be, if the Muslim community had not been compelled by the Khāridjites to give answers to the questions they dared to ask, it would have been forced to do so by the course of its own historical development. When in 661 Mu'āwiya had become caliph and the high offices were occupied by the descendants of those who had been the bitterest opponents of Muhammad, by governors whose personal behaviour displayed little of the qualities suited to true Muslims, the problem raised by the Khāridjites became of central interest to the community.

Its solution is expressed in the sentence: "The only heirs of the Prophets are the doctors of the law". In this sentence the separation between the temporal and the spiritual power, which became and remained a fact, was proclaimed.

1 On the name cf. Levi Della Vida in the *Encyclopaedia of Islām*, s.v.

The theological problems were not so easily solved. Our most valuable source of information is again Tradition. The plain facts and names are to be found in the books on sects and parties. From the latter sources we know that the extreme opponents of the Khāridjites were the Murdjites, a sect which went far in complying with the government and in ignoring the behaviour of the temporal rulers. Their name denotes this attitude; it means those who shrink from judging the conduct of man and its consequences, leaving this exclusively to God.

This point is indeed ultimately connected with the question: Who is a Muslim. It cannot be denied that the answer given to it by the community is nearer to that of the Murdjites than to that of the Khāridjites.

The frequent descriptions of the latter in Tradition[1] are usually characterized by a bitterness which shows how much outward and inward trouble this sect had caused to the community. The following is an example: "One day we were with the Apostle of Allah, who was distributing portions, when Dhu'l-Khuwaiṣira, a man from the tribe of Tamīm,[2] came up to him, saying: O Apostle of Allah, distribute in a just way. The Apostle of Allah answered: Hold your tongue, who would be just if not I? I would be a poor thing, if I were not just. Thereupon 'Umar said: O Apostle of Allah, shall I not cut off his head? The Apostle of Allah answered: Leave him alone, he will have companions so zealous that any of you will think his own prayer and fasting trifling in comparison with theirs. They will recite the Kuran, but it will not pass beyond their throats.[3] They will pass through Islam as an arrow passes through a hunted animal; if you look at its point there are no traces of blood or excrements in any of its parts[4]...".[5]

1 Cf. *Handbook of Early Muhammadan Tradition*, under *Kharidjites*.

2 The tribe that was the focus of Khāridjism.

3 *I.e.* it will not descend to their hearts. According to a different explanation "their recitation will not be accepted".

4 Which are enumerated in the text of the tradition.

5 Muslim, *Zakāt*, trad. 148.

This tradition gives a lively impression of the fanaticism of the K͟hāridjites; their religious zeal is acknowledged, but their understanding is defective. In other traditions they are called "hell-hounds" and the killing of them is declared to be meritorious.[1]

At the basis of the theological position of the K͟hāridjites is the distinction between venial and mortal sins, which is not peculiar to them but common to the theology of Islam. It must, therefore, be supposed that this distinction had been generally acknowledged before the rise of the K͟hāridjitic schism. As a matter of fact, traces of its origin are to be found in Tradition. In the Kuran "heinous things of crimes and filthinesses" are mentioned.[2] The term kabā'ir has become the scriptural basis of the distinction of sins. Yet it may be supposed that this dogma would never have originated without influence from elsewhere.

Its first stage may be found in those traditions in which Muhammad is asked: What is the greatest sin? The answer is: Polytheism. Then it is asked: What next? The answer is: Killing one's own child, or: Inhuman treatment of parents. The third in the list is either adultery or false witness.[3]

The second stage may be found in the traditions in which seven mortal sins are enumerated. The standard tradition is the following: "The Apostle of Allah said: Avoid the seven mortal sins. It was asked: Which? He answered: Polytheism, magic, unlawful manslaying, spending the money of orphans, usury, desertion from battle, and slandering chaste but heedless women who are faithful".[4]

The variants of this tradition may be passed over. The important point is, that the distinction between light and grave sins is readily admitted;[5] beyond this point the way

1 Handbook, under K͟haridjites.
2 Sura xlii. 35: kabā'ir alit͟hm wa'l-fawāhis͟h.
3 Muslim, Imān, trad. 141 sq. 4 Muslim, Imān, trad. 144.
5 For details, cf. the art. K͟hatī'a in the Encyclopaedia of Islam.

of the Khāridjites branches off. According to the orthodox view polytheism is the only sin which is inconsistent with being a Muslim. A man who is guilty of other sins does not thereby lose this character. Allah may punish him in Hell, or He may grant him forgiveness even without previous repentance.

According to the Khāridjites, on the other hand, anyone who is guilty of a grave sin is no longer a Muslim. If he desires to return to the community, he must formally repent of his sin, else he will suffer everlasting punishment. In this train of thought, the line of demarcation between Muslims and infidels passes between blameless Muslims on one side, and infidels as well as sinners on the other. The latter are called *fāsiḳ*.

From this thesis a practical conclusion and a theoretical inference were drawn. The practical conclusion was, that Muslims who were guilty of grave sins must be combated with the sword as being infidels. The theoretical inference was, that faith is not a constant entity, but that it is impaired by sin. Both points require a short elucidation. The first was rejected by the community in the tradition[1] in which it is said that the sword must withdraw before the confession of faith and that it belongs to Allah alone to judge of the sincerity of the confessor. A further step was taken in a tradition which is one of the first indications of the Catholic tendency of Islam.

This tradition is handed down in various forms, the shortest and perhaps the oldest of which is the following: "If any of you should call his brother an infidel, this epithet would suit either him or yourself".[2] Without any doubt the intention of this tradition is to deter any Muslim from applying the epithet of unbelief to any fellow-Muslim, as the Khāridjites did; Mālik ibn Anas was still acquainted with the fact that the tradition was directed against them.[3] Yet the wording caused the theologians grave difficulties,

1 Cf. *supra*, p. 13 *sq*.

2 Aḥmad ibn Ḥanbal, *Musnad*, ii. 18; on *takfīr* cf. also Ibn Ḥazm, *Kitāb al-Fiṣal*, iii. 246 *sqq*.

3 al-Nawawī, i. 151.

for it implies that a mortal sin—declaring a fellow-Muslim to be an infidel—may deprive a Muslim of this character. This was precisely the K͟hāridjite thesis which orthodoxy wanted to combat. So the tradition misses its aim. Nevertheless a way has been found out of the difficulty, as appears in a variant reading.[1]

The extremists among the K͟hāridjites were led by their thesis to the practice of asking every Muslim the question: Do you share our views or not? This question was often asked at the point of the sword[2] and it even gave rise to the term *isti'rāḍ*, which literally means "inviting someone to speak his opinion", in practice "killing for the sake of religion".

In this connection we must remember the tradition which culminated in Muhammad's ironical reproach: "You have of course not neglected to split open his heart in order to know whether fear was his motive",[3] followed by: "How will you account for this 'there is no God but Allah'?" Historians record cases of people who were actually split open by the K͟hāridjites.[4] Another allusion to such facts is contained in a different version of the tradition in which a characteristic description of the K͟hāridjites is given.[5] When Muhammad was distributing gold-ore among his companions, "there came up to him a man with hollow eyes, sharp cheek bones, protruding forehead, profuse beard, shorn hair and tucked up tunic,[6] saying: O Apostle of Allah, fear God. He answered: Hold your tongue, am I not the nearest to fear God? Then the man turned his back, whereupon K͟hālid ibn al-Walīd[7] said: Shall I not cut off his head? Muhammad answered: No, perhaps he will perform prayer. K͟hālid replied: How many pronounce with their tongue what is not in their

1 Muslim, *Īmān*, trad. 111.
2 Houtsma, *De strijd over het dogma*, pp. 26, 29.
3 *Supra*, p. 30.
4 Ṭabarī, ed. de Goeje, I. 3375; Aḥmad ibn Ḥanbal, v. 110.
5 Cf. *supra*, p. 38.
6 The type of a fanatic.
7 "The sword of religion."

heart. Thereupon the Apostle of Allah said: I am not ordered to split open the hearts of men, nor their bellies. Then, gazing at the man who was going away, he said: From the descendants of this man there will arise people who fluently read the book of Allah, but it will not pass beyond their throats. They will pass through religion as an arrow passes through a hunted animal. Methinks, says the narrator, he added: If I find them, I shall kill them, as the Thamūd were killed".[1]

The Khāridjitic practice of combating as infidels those who did not share their views culminated in the killing of children, as was proposed by the most fanatical among them.[2] The importance of this point for our present subject is its connection with the doctrine of natural religion (*fiṭra*).[3]

In Tradition it is related that Nadjda,[4] one of the heads of the Khāridjites, wrote a letter to Ibn 'Abbās, in which he asked his opinion on some questions. Ibn 'Abbās answered him, though with reluctance, as follows: "You have asked me whether the Apostle of Allah allowed women to accompany his military expeditions. As a matter of fact they did; they nursed the wounded, they received something from the booty, but no regular share was given them. The Apostle of God did not kill children; you must not do this either...".[5]

In accordance with this tradition the killing of women and children is prohibited (*ḥarām*) in Islam.[6] This attitude is also based upon the notion that every child is born in the *fiṭra*, the natural basis of the true religion. The standard tradition is: "Every child is born in the *fiṭra*;[7] it is his parents who make of him a Jew or a Christian or a Parsi. In the same way cattle give birth to calves without defects".[8] This conception is in its turn the answer to the

1 Muslim, *Zakāt*, trad. 144.

2 al-Ash'arī, *Maḳālāt*, i. 82⁵, 104¹⁰; cf. the art. *Azraḳites* by Levi Della Vida in the *Enc. of Islām*.

3 Cf. *infra*, p. 214 *sqq*.

4 al-Ash'arī, *Maḳālāt*, i. 84 *sqq*.; cf. p. 88³.

5 Muslim, *Djihād*, trad. 137.

6 al-Nawawī, v. 260.

7 On the other characteristics of the *fiṭra* cf. *Handbook*, under *Religion* (*Natural*).

8 Muslim, *Ḳadar*, trad. 22.

question as to the fate of children who die before reaching the adult age. We cannot desire a more trustworthy authority on such points than al-Nawawī. His exposition runs:[1] "The doctors of some authority are agreed on this point, that children of Muslim parents, who die, will be of the inhabitants of Paradise, because they have not been under the obligation of the law.[2]...As to the children of the infidels there are three opinions. According to the majority of the doctors, they will go to Hell, like their fathers. Others take up an attitude of reserve. The third group—whose opinion is the right one—thinks that these children will go to Paradise. This opinion is supported by various arguments; by a reference, for instance, to the tradition according to which Muhammad saw Abraham in Paradise surrounded by children. When those who were present, exclaimed: Even by the children of the infidels? Muhammad answered: Even by the children of the infidels.[3] Another reference is to sura xvii. 16: 'And We punished not, until We had first sent an Apostle'.—And so it is agreed upon that the law imposes no obligation upon the children under age, even if they should be reached by the preaching of an Apostle".

Here we may break in upon al-Nawawī for a moment. It is clear that this view regarding the eternal fate of children may come into conflict with the dogma of predestination. Apparently this dogma had not been established at the time when the tradition on the *fiṭra* arose. As a matter of fact al-Nawawī mentions the difficulty of harmonizing the tradition with the dogma of predestination. This induced theologians to attempt new explanations. One of these is, that the child is born in the religion of its parents. Another, that it is born in accordance with the state of happiness or unhappiness for which it is destined. When God knows that a child will become a Muslim, it is born in Islam; otherwise, it is born in unbelief. A third explanation is, that there is a kind of natural knowledge

1 vi. 278 *sq.*; cf. also Ibn Ḥazm, *Kitāb al-Fiṣal*, iv. 72 *sqq.*

2 *taklīf*; cf. *infra*, p. 261 *sqq.*

3 Bukhārī, *Djanā'iz*, b. 93.

of God as the Creator. Then al-Nawawī continues: "The best explanation is the following. Every child is born with a predisposition towards Islam. If one of its parents is a Muslim, the child remains Muslim as to its state in this world and in the next. If both its parents are infidels, the child follows their state in this world.... When it reaches the adult age, it remains in the state of unbelief of its parents. If it is destined for eternal happiness, it will embrace Islam; otherwise it will die as an infidel. The question of the fate of those who die during minority is answered in three ways as has been said above. The best is that these children are in Paradise".[1]

The counterpart of this passage may be found in the report that some sections of the Khāridjites held the view that children, whether born of the Faithful or of infidels, were in a state of neutrality. In reaching the age of majority, they should be invited to embrace Islam.[2] Here it appears that the tradition of the natural religion in which every child is born, was directed against the Khāridjites.

How far the ideas of Islam are in accordance with those of Christianity, in this respect, may be seen from the following description of the limbus: "In the belief of Christianity the *limbo* was the temporary place or state of the souls of the just, who, although purified from sin, were excluded from the beatific vision until Christ's triumphant ascension"; and also: "The permanent place or state of those unbaptized children and others, who, dying without grievous personal guilt, are excluded from the beatific vision on account of original sin alone".[3]

We must now return to the theological thesis of the Khāridjites, that of faith being impaired by sin, and see how orthodoxy replied to it. Its first answer was this: "Whoso commits fornication cannot be faithful at the

1 It will be seen later, that according to the Mu'tazilites *fiṭra* was identical with Islam.

2 al-Ash'arī, *Maḳālāt*, i. 84, 95, 104 *sq*.

3 *The Catholic Encyclopaedia*, s.v. *Limbo*; cf. Asín, *La escatologia*, p. 101 *sqq*.

same time and whoso steals cannot be faithful at the same time and whoso drinks wine cannot be faithful at the same time".[1]

In this tradition it is emphasized that works are not irrelevant to faith, as was the opinion of the Murdjites, who thereby endangered the value of ethics. The community could not follow them along this path; if it had done so, it would have given up an essential element of Islam.

The Murdjites went so far as to maintain that faith is an entity of its own that cannot be impaired by sin and is not liable to increase and decrease. Hence the statement of the opposite view in some traditions.[2] In some forms of the creed, however, the Murdjitic thesis of the stability of faith is taken over.[3]

Nevertheless, traditions which go rather with the Khāridjite than with the Murdjite position are not lacking, as, for instance, the traditions which enumerate the signs of the *munāfiḳ*: "There are four features which give a man the stamp of a *munāfiḳ*: when he speaks, he lies; when he makes a contract, he deceives; when he promises, he fails to fulfil his promise and when he litigates, he is dishonest".[4]

In this and similar traditions it is acknowledged that immoral acts are characteristic of the *munāfiḳ*, that is, of one who has no faith, but sham faith only. Consequently, in this and similar cases a close connection between faith and works is taught. It is, therefore, not surprising that "a group of theologians consider this tradition as being of doubtful value, for these features may be found in the sincere Muslim who is free from doubts. As a matter of fact the doctors unanimously declare that one who is sincere in heart and word and becomes guilty of any of the sins mentioned, is neither an infidel nor a *munāfiḳ*".[5] This

1 Muslim, *Īmān*, trad. 100; cf. 101–5; cf. Ibn Ḥazm, *Kitāb al-Fiṣal*, iv. 178 *sqq.*

2 Ibn Mādja, Introduction, b. 9; cf. Bukhārī, *Īmān*, b. 1. The tradition does not go back to Muhammad and was not universally accepted.

3 Cf. *infra*, Waṣīyat Abī Ḥanīfa, art. 2; Fiḳh Akbar II, art. 18.

4 Muslim, *Īmān*, trad. 106; cf. 107–10.

5 al-Nawawī, i. 149.

is the orthodox view which is taught in traditions[1] in which the chief doctrine of the Khāridjites is combated. One of these is even said to have been communicated to Muhammad by Gabriel himself. Still more stress is laid on the orthodox view in the following tradition: "I[2] came to the Prophet and found him sleeping in a white garment. I came a second time and found him still sleeping. The third time I found him awake. When I sat down near him, he said to me: Whosoever sayeth: There is no God but Allah and dieth in this belief, will enter Paradise. I replied: Even if he should have fornicated and stolen? He answered: Even if he should have fornicated and stolen". The question and the answer thereto are repeated three times. "The fourth time Muhammad added: Even though Abū Dharr should turn up his nose."

The clue to this tradition is that Abū Dharr was one of the moral pillars of ancient Islam, who was exiled by 'Uthmān for his intransigent attitude. In the above tradition he is represented as one of the spiritual fathers of the Khāridjites, whose chief doctrine is expressly combated in it. It is quite possible that the way was prepared for the doctrines of the Khāridjites by men of the stamp of Abū Dharr.

In another tradition the orthodox view of the punishment of grave sins is expressed. 'Ubāda ibn al-Ṣāmit relates that he and his companions did allegiance to Muhammad, promising that they would not steal or commit fornication or any transgression. Then the Apostle of Allah said: "Whosoever fulfils his promise, shall receive his reward from God. Whosoever commits any of the sins mentioned and is punished for it in this world, this is his atonement. If he is not punished, he is left to the mercy of God who may forgive him if He please or punish him if He please".[3] al-Nawawī supports this tradition by a reference to sura iv. 51 (116): "Verily,

1 Muslim, *Īmān*, trad. 150–4.
2 The narrator is Abū Dharr.
3 Bukhārī, *Īmān*, b. 11; al-Nawawī, i. 147.

God will not forgive the union of other gods with Himself; but other than this He will forgive to whom He pleaseth", as well as to the common orthodox opinion that whoever commits fornication or theft or other grave sins, except *shirk*, may not be declared an infidel for this reason; he is faithful, but his faith is incomplete. If he repents, his punishment is cancelled and when he persists in his sins, he is left to the mercy of God: if He pleaseth, He will forgive him and cause him to enter Paradise at once; if He pleaseth, He will punish him and cause him to enter Paradise afterwards.

This means that according to the orthodox doctrine the Muslim remains Muslim whatsoever sin he may commit, except polytheism. According to the Khāridjites, on the other hand, those who have committed grave sins no longer belong to the community.

It may be observed here that the position of the Khāridjites shows a close affinity to that of Christianity. Catholicism divides sins into two classes, *peccatum mortale* and *peccatum veniale*. The latter does not cause eternal but only temporary punishment. Mortal sins, on the other hand, turn man away from God and from the state of grace; one sin of this category may cause eternal punishment.

It is possible that the affinity between the Khāridjite and the Catholic doctrine of sin is not fortuitous. We shall have occasion to observe that in matters of dogmatics it is now orthodox Islam, now one or more of the sects, which accord with Christianity. It may be concluded from this fact, that within Islam no line of demarcation could be drawn between the elements in harmony with, or in opposition to, Christianity.

At any rate the position taken by the orthodox Muslim community in face of the Khāridjites was of a nature to accentuate the differences between Christianity and orthodox Islam. For, since the influence exercised by Saint Augustine was decreasing, Christianity was gradually tending towards a preference for works over faith. Islam, on the other hand, by rejecting the doctrine of the Khāridjites, secured the preponderance of faith, without however complying with the views of the Murdjites. A translation of another tradition may be given in further illustration of the orthodox doctrine: "We were sitting around the Apostle of Allah; in our company were Abū Bakr, 'Umar and some others. The Apostle of Allah rose and left the company. As he did not return, we feared lest some enemy might have surprised him. So we rose in terror; I was the first to go in search of him. I reached an enclosure of the Anṣār, of the tribe of the Banu 'l-Nadjdjār, and went round it in order to find a gate, but in vain. Perceiving a rivulet entering from a fountain without, I dug the earth around the entrance away, as a fox digs. So I reached the Apostle of Allah, who said: Abū Huraira? I said: Yes, O Apostle of Allah. He said: What do you seek? I answered: You left our company without returning, so that we feared lest an enemy should have surprised you when you were alone. So we rose in terror... the other people came behind me. Thereupon he said: O Abū Huraira, here are my sandals; take them and go, and whomsoever you find behind this enclosure witnessing in full conviction that there is no God but Allah, promise him Paradise. The first whom I met was 'Umar. He asked me: What are these sandals? I answered: These are the sandals of the Apostle of Allah; he gave them to me, saying: Whomsoever you meet.... Thereupon 'Umar smote my breast with his hand, so that I fell down backwards. He said: Return, O Abū Huraira. So I returned to the Apostle of Allah, wholly disturbed and well nigh weeping, while 'Umar was close behind me. The Apostle of Allah said to me: What is the matter? I told him what had happened. Thereupon the Apostle of Allah said: O 'Umar, why did you act thus? He answered: O Apostle of Allah, you are dear to me as my father and mother; did you really send Abū Huraira with your sandals and with that order? The Apostle of Allah answered: Yes. Thereupon 'Umar said: Do not act in this way, for I fear lest people should grow neglectful; let them rather perform good works. Thereupon the Apostle of Allah said: Yes, let them do so".[1]

To the same effect is a tradition according to which Muhammad said to Mu'ādh ibn Djabal: "Whosoever witnesses that there is no God but Allah and that Muhammad is His servant and His Apostle, is safeguarded from Hell. Mu'ādh asked: Shall I not proclaim these happy tidings? He answered: No, for people would grow neglectful. So Mu'ādh told this story for the first time when he was on his deathbed, in order to relieve himself of it".[2]

This, then, is the position of orthodox Islam: faith alone is sufficient for salvation; but this should not become a reason for neglecting works.

The contradiction between these two notions was, however, sharply felt. It grew more painful when Islam was placed in the necessity of speaking its mind on the question of predestination and free will.

It may be asked whether the contradiction between Allah as the ruler of the universe and man as a morally responsible being had not caused any conflict in the Muslim mind before.

It must be remembered that Muhammad, the founder of the theocracy, had accentuated the power of Allah, the creator and governor of the universe, as well as the impotence of man as compared with this overwhelming personality. There is a strong likeness between the genesis of Israelitic and Arabian monotheism. As the Israelites at Mount Sinai entered upon the service of a deity who was a powerful personality as compared with the bounteous but impersonal *el*'s who had appeared to the patriarchs, so the people of Arabia were led by Muhammad into the presence of a terrible personality, superhuman, yet with human qualities—the God of Past, Present and Future, side by side with Whom none of the faint-hearted and powerless gods of Arabia could any longer exist. But

1 Muslim, *Īmān*, trad. 52.
2 Muslim, *Īmān*, trad. 53.

Muhammad was also a preacher and as such he had to deal with man and to influence him. He had to preach that it is man's duty to study the ways of God in nature and in history, to believe in His power to quicken the dead, and to fulfil the religious, moral and social obligations incumbent on him. Certainly, if Muhammad's countrymen remained incredulous, this could be described as Allah's work, His punishment, for "He leadeth astray whomsoever He pleaseth, and guideth unto Himself whomsoever He pleaseth".[1]

Yet this punishment could also be represented as a consequence of their own stubbornness. Muhammad did not fail to do so, as will appear, for example, from the following passage from the Kuran: "Nor did We ever send a Prophet to any city whose people We did not afflict with adversity and trouble, that haply they might humble themselves.

"Then changed We their ill for good, until they waxed wealthy and said, Of old did troubles and blessings befall our fathers: Therefore did We seize upon them when they were unaware.

"But if that the people of these cities had believed and feared us, We would surely have laid open to them blessings out of the Heaven and the Earth: but they treated our signs as lies and We took vengeance upon them for their deeds.... Is it not proved to those who inherit this land after its ancient occupants, that if We please We can smite them for their sins, and put a seal upon their hearts, that they hearken not? As to these cities, We will tell thee their story. Their Apostles came to them with clear proofs of their mission; but they could not believe in what they had before treated as imposture. Thus doth God seal up the hearts of the unbelievers".[2]

Characteristic of the dual aspect of the question is the following passage:

"This truly is a warning; and whoso willeth, taketh the way to his Lord;

1 Sura xiii. 27; xvi. 95; lxxiv. 34. 2 Sura vii. 92–4, 98 *sq*.

"But will it ye shall not, unless God will it. Verily God is knowing and wise".[1]

Side by side with utterances like the foregoing, in which the stubbornness of unbelievers is emphasized together with Allah's "sealing up their hearts", there are passages in the Kuran, in which the preacher Muhammad speaks, a preacher anxious to exercise influence on his audience:

"As to Thamūd, We vouchsafed them also guidance; but to guidance did they prefer blindness".[2]

And:

"The truth is from your Lord: let him then who will, believe; and let him who will, be an unbeliever".[3] Yet in the same sura there is also the following verse:

"Guided indeed is he whom God guideth, but for him whom He misleadeth, thou shalt by no means find a patron, a guide".[4]

These quotations show that the advocates of predestination, as well as those of free will, could claim a scriptural basis for their view. Yet, to all appearance, the main attitude of Islam was in favour of predestination. Tradition has not preserved a single *ḥadīth* in which *liberum arbitrium* is advocated. If this should be due to the extirpation of such traditions at a time when the doctrine of free will had received the stamp of heresy, we may adduce evidence from the works of John of Damascus, who flourished in the middle of the eighth century A.D. and who was well acquainted with Islam. According to him the difference regarding predestination and free will is one of the chief points of divergence between Christianity and Islam.[5]

C. H. Becker has paid special attention to the fact that this question was a point of debate between Christians and Muslims, and according to this scholar it was due to the influence of Christian theology that the debates on

1 Sura lxxvi. 29 *sq.*
2 Sura xli. 16.
3 Sura xviii. 28.
4 Verse 16.
5 Migne, vol. XCIV. col. 1589 *sqq.*

this point were introduced into Islam.[1] Professor Macdonald assents to this opinion,[2] in so far as the first opposition against predestination in Islam was, in his view, due to Christian influence. Goldziher, on the other hand,[3] ascribes the anti-predestinarian feelings to the reaction of the religious mind against the harshness of predestination.

But the first view need not, surely, exclude the second. We have already seen[4] and we shall see later, that the history of Muslim dogmatics follows a logical course —that is to say, the sequence of the ideas is not of foreign origin, but is indigenous. At the same time, however, something must be attributed to the influence of Christianity.

Similarly, the keen debates between the K͟hāridjites and the Murdjites on the relation between faith and works necessarily lie near the problem of the origin of both. Are they a product of the will of man, or a creation of Allah? On this question opinions were divided. The K͟hāridjites, or at least the majority of their subdivisions,[5] acknowledged predestination. A minority, however, preferred the other solution of the problem and declared man to be the author of his own acts. This minority was known by the name Ḳadarīya, and their views formed the basis of the movement of the Mu'tazilites. So strongly was the likeness between the two sects felt, that their names are often used without discrimination.[6]

Yet the distinction between them is historically well-founded. Tradition is well acquainted with the views and the name of the Ḳadarites. The Mu'tazilites, on the other hand, are never mentioned, and the chief subjects of their discussions, the essence of God and the theodicy, have left scarcely any trace in the canonical collections.

This negative statement is illustrated by the fact that

1 *Zeitschrift f. Assyriologie*, XXVI. 184.
2 Art. *Ḳadar* in the *Encyclopaedia of Islām*.
3 *Vorlesungen*, p. 89.
4 *Supra*, p. 37.
5 Exceptions are mentioned by al-As͟h'arī, *Maḳālāt*, i. 93 *sq*.
6 *E.g.* in al-Bag͟hdādī's *Farḳ*.

the term *i'tizāl* in Tradition exclusively conveys the idea of retirement and asceticism, an idea which is of no importance for the position of the sect.[1] That the name Ḳadarites has been misinterpreted is not a matter for surprise. In Muslim theology *ḳadar* denotes the eternal decree of Allah. Now it was precisely this conception that the Ḳadarites rejected. It was therefore supposed that their name could not be derived from this *ḳadar*, but must necessarily be connected with *ḳadar* in the meaning of *liberum arbitrium*.

Such a use of the term cannot, however, be said to be based upon Arabic literature. It is true, of course, that the expression *ḳāla bi'l-ḳadar* denotes an adherent of the doctrine of free will. But this expression has its origin in the name Ḳadarīya. The real origin of the latter must be sought in expressions like the following, which is the opening phrase of Muslim's collection of traditions: "The first who instituted discussions on the *ḳadar* at Baṣra was Ma'bad al-Djuhanī".[2] Such people were called *ḳadarī* and Ma'bad is sometimes called the father of the Ḳadarīya.[3]

Muslim's statement is not only remarkable as an explanation of the name of the sect. It points also to the place and time of its origin. Ma'bad's death is dated at 80/699 or a few years later. According to one report he was killed by order of the caliph 'Abd al-Malik († A.D. 705). At this time Baṣra was already one of the centres of Muslim thought, just as were Kūfa, Madina and Damascus. We may suppose that in the region of the Lower Euphrates it was not only Christianity but also other religions that influenced Islamic ideas. As a matter of fact it is reported that Ma'bad conversed with a Christian from Mesopotamia, named Sūsan, who embraced Islam, but later returned to Christianity.[3]

We may say, that the debates on predestination inaugurated rationalism in Islam. Like Judaism and Christi-

1 See *infra*, p. 59.

2 Cf. C. A. Nallino in *Rivista degli studi orientali*, VII. 461 *sqq.*

3 *E.g.* Ibn Ḥadjar al-'Asḳalānī, *Tahdhīb al-Tahdhīb*, x. 225 *sq.*

anity, Islam condemns the rationalistic attitude. There are many traditions according to which Muhammad emphasized his refusal to be questioned by pointing to earlier examples of communities destroyed in consequence of their disputations. Here Tradition has several things in view.[1] Theological speculations are especially referred to in the following *ḥadīth*:[2] "People will not cease scrutinizing, till they shall say: Here is Allah, the creator of all things, but who has created Him?"

The orthodox doctrine of heavenly decrees is not specifically Islamic. It has a broad Semitic basis, as is proved by Babylonian and Israelitic religious tradition, which regards not only the ways of man, but the course of the world as the *replica* of what had been recorded long before in heavenly books or on heavenly tablets. The canonical collections of traditions contain specimens of this popular theology: "When the embryo has passed two-and-forty days in the womb, Allah sends an angel, who gives it a form and creates his hearing, sight, skin, flesh and bones. This having been done, the angel asks: O Lord, shall this be male or female? Then the Lord decrees what He pleaseth, and the angel writes it down. Then he asks: O Lord, what shall be his term?[3] Then the Lord will say what He pleaseth, and the angel will write it down. Thereupon the latter will go away with the scroll in his hand and nothing will be added to or subtracted from the decree."[4]

It is clear that such popular tales could not be the last word in a dogmatical question like that of predestination. The following tradition comes nearer to a theological conception: "God wrote down the decrees regarding the created world fifty thousand years before He created the heavens and the earth, while His throne was on the water".[5] Yet this could not be the last word of the theo-

1 Cf. *infra*, p. 112.
2 Bukhārī, *I'tiṣām*, b. 4; cf. *Handbook*, in voce *Disputations*.
3 The term of his death.
4 Muslim, *Ḳadar*, trad. 3; cf. 1, 2, 4, 5.
5 Muslim, *Ḳadar*, trad. 16; Tirmidhī, *Ḳadar*, b. 17.

logians. "The tradition", says al-Nawawī, "only intends to fix the time at which the decrees were written on the preserved table[1] or elsewhere, not the origin of the decrees, for this is a thing of eternity, without a beginning."

The idea that God fixed the course of the world before the creation inevitably brought forward the question of its relation to the acts of man. This question implies two others, viz.: Is man the author of his works? and: Do man's works have any relation to his eternal fate?

The last question is answered in the affirmative, though not plainly. Muslim has attached it to the tradition on the guardian angel of the embryo, which has been translated above. This tradition goes on: "It may be that one of you performs the works of the people of Paradise, so that between him and Paradise there is only the distance of an arm's length. But then his book[2] overtakes him and he begins to perform the works of the people of Hell, the which he will enter. Likewise one of you may perform the works of the people of Hell, so that between him and Hell there is only the distance of an arm's length. Then his book will overtake him and he will begin to perform the works of the people of Paradise, the which he will enter".[3]

This tradition implies that the final works serve as the criterion. This is plainly stated in a different series of traditions. Two of them are related by Muslim in the following form: "A man may perform the works of the dwellers in Paradise for a long time, yet his work may receive finally the stamp of that of the dwellers in Hell. Likewise a man may perform the works of the dwellers in Hell for a long time, yet his work may finally receive the stamp of that of the dwellers in Paradise".[4] In other collections this doctrine is summarized in the sentence:

1 Cf. *Encyclopaedia of Islām*, under *Lawḥ maḥfūẓ*.
2 *I.e.* what has been decreed concerning his fate.
3 Muslim, *Ḳadar*, trad. 1.
4 Muslim, *Ḳadar*, trad. 11; cf. 12.

"Works must be judged from the concluding acts (*al-khawātīm*) only".[1]

The other question is answered in a series of traditions which also touch upon the relation between works and man's eternal fate. Here is the first of these traditions:[2] "We accompanied a bier on the Baḳī‘ al-Gharḳad.[3] When the Apostle of Allah joined us, he sat down and we sat down with him. He had a stick in his hand with which he began to touch the sand,[4] letting his head sink on his breast. Then he said: There is no living soul for which Allah has not appointed its place in Paradise or in Hell, and the decision of happy or unhappy has already been taken. Then a man said: O Apostle of Allah, shall we not then leave all to our book and give up works? Muhammad answered: Whosoever belongs to the people of happiness will come to the works of the people of happiness, and whosoever belongs to the people of unhappiness will come to the works of the people of unhappiness.—Then he said: Perform works, for everyone is guided, the people of happiness are guided to the works of the people of happiness, and the people of unhappiness are guided to the works of the people of unhappiness. Thereupon he recited: As then for him who giveth alms and feareth God, and yieldeth assent to the Good, to him will We make easy the path to happiness. But as to him who is covetous and bent on riches, And calleth the Good a lie, to him will We make easy the path to distress".[5]

In the tradition following on this one, the essence of the doctrine is condensed into the phrase: "Everyone is guided to that for which he was created".[6]

We shall touch upon the subject of free will and pre-

1 *Innama 'l-a‘māl bi'l-khawātīm*, Bukhārī, *Ḳadar*, b. 5; *Riḳāḳ*, b. 33; Tirmidhī, *Ḳadar*, b. 4.

2 Muslim, *Ḳadar*, trad. 6.

3 The cemetery of Madīna.

4 Cf. John viii. 6.

5 Sura xcii. 5–10.

6 كُلٌّ مُيَسَّرٌ لِمَا خُلِقَ لَهُ; also Bukhārī, *Djanā'iz*, b. 2.

destination in later chapters. Here it may be said that the main position of the community never changed. The Ḳadarites were declared in Tradition to be the Parsis of the community: "Do not visit them when they are ailing, nor accompany their biers when they are dead".[1] This means that they are excluded from the community, for visiting the sick and accompanying biers are duties of Muslims towards their fellows.[2]

1 Abū Dāwūd, *Sunna*, b. 16.
2 *E.g.* Bukhārī, *Djanā'iz*, b. 2.

CHAPTER IV

God and the World

The concatenation of ideas which has been discussed in the previous chapter appears still more clearly in the exposition of the theodicy. The movement of the Ḳadarites was followed immediately by that of the Mu'tazilites, for the discussions of predestination and free will could not fail to call forth the question of the justice of God, and the latter must necessarily lead to that of His essence and qualities.

The period in which these questions were debated covers the second and third centuries A.H. This period is that of the dogmatic crisis of Islam. There were moments, especially in the first part of the third century, when it might have seemed that Islam, from the stern, uncompromising religion which manifests itself in Kuran and Tradition, would take a turn towards the mild, ethical attitude of post-Augustine Christianity, as well as towards the rationalistic tendencies that lingered in the air as a legacy from antiquity. It was without doubt a momentous period in the life of Islam. Nor did it pass without leaving enduring traces. Though Mu'tazilism was rejected, it tinged Islam with rationalism. It is said that the triumph of al-Ash'arī was the triumph of genuine Arabic religion. To us, however, the dogmatic efforts of those who walked in the footsteps of al-Ash'arī, al-Māturīdī and their friends, are too intellectualist to be interesting in a religious sense. Had not mysticism in course of time acquired a place in official Islam, chiefly through the influence of al-Ghazālī, the Muslim religion would have become a lifeless form.

The answer given in Tradition to the question of predestination did not go beyond the emphatic statement that everything that happens, human acts inclusive, is the product of the divine decree that had settled all things before the creation of the world. This answer gave rise to an objection which could not be easily parried. If all human acts are the product of the divine decree, how is it that man is punished for them?

To all appearance this and similar questions were the subject of warm debates in the beginning of the second century A.H. Hitherto Tradition has proved a trustworthy guide in the dogmatic history of Islam. Henceforward this source of information will no longer provide us with materials of equal importance. As a matter of fact, the essence of God and the theodicy do not belong to the contents of Tradition. The main explanation of this is that the large mass of materials contained in the canonical collections, though it received its final form in the middle of the third century A.H., covers a period reaching no farther than the beginning of the second century. There are allusions, it is true, to events of the early ʿAbbāsid period, but they are rare. The Khāridjite and the Ḳadarite movements, as well as the persons who played a prominent part in them, occupy a considerable place, as also do the questions of canon law up to the formation of the earliest schools, *i.e.* till the middle of the eighth century A.D. This chronological limit explains also why the beginnings of Ṣūfism are not reflected in Tradition.

It has already been pointed out that the use of the term *iʿtizāl* in Tradition does not betray any acquaintance with the Muʿtazilites. We have therefore to seek information from other sources, the chief of which are the books dealing with religious sects and divisions. It is from these that Professor Nallino, in endeavouring to explain the name of the Muʿtazilites,[1] has collected materials which point to a connection of this name with the question of grave sins and the resultant state of the sinner. We have seen that the Khāridjites denied the qualification of "faithful" to great sinners, whereas the orthodox did not exclude the Faithful from their ranks on account of grave sins

1 *Rivista degli studi orientali*, VII. 429 *sqq.*

committed. The Mu'tazilites took a middle position: they withdrew (*i'tazalū*) from the two extreme views and declared the sinner to be in an intermediate state (*manzila bain al-manzilatain*).[1] Professor Nallino himself has warned his readers not to overrate the value of the name for the characteristics of the sect. As a matter of fact the Mu'tazilites have a much wider outlook than that of an intermediate position regarding the question of faith and works, and, as is well known, adopted for themselves the much broader designation of "partisans of justice and unity" (*ahl al-'adl wa'l-tawḥīd*). This phrase may form a convenient starting-point for the following description.[2]

The Mu'tazilites took over the view of the Ḳadarites, that man is the author of his acts, a view which originated in the tendency to safeguard the ethical nature not of man, but of God. They could certainly quote the Kuran in favour of an ethical conception of God. The frequent use of the epithets *al-raḥmān al-raḥīm*, "the Compassionate, the Merciful", is sufficient evidence. Moreover there are utterances like the following: "God will not burden any soul beyond its power. It shall enjoy the good which it hath acquired, and it shall bear the evil for the acquirement of which it laboured".[3] And: "God is not unjust towards His servants".[4] And: "God truly will not wrong anyone the weight of a mote; and if there be any good deed, He will repay it doubly".[5] Wronging (*ẓulm*) is precisely one of the actions most abhorred by Muhammad, so the Mu'tazilites were not wholly out of tune when they emphasized the justice of Allah.

In the next chapter we shall see how Islam reacted to this ethical postulate. Here we must point out its conse-

1 Cf. al-Baghdādī, *Farḳ*, pp. 94, 98.

2 For a concise description of the views and the position of the Mu'tazilites see also Nyberg's introduction to the *Kitāb al-Intiṣār* (p. 49 *sqq.*) and p. 126 *sq.* of the text. Nyberg emphasizes their activity as the apologists of Islam against Manichaeism. I have criticized their attitude from the Muslim point of view.

3 Sura ii. 286.

4 Sura xxii. 10.

5 Sura iv. 44.

quences for the Mu'tazilite position itself. The importance attached to grave sins, the denial of Allah's authorship of human acts, and the emphasis laid on man's will as the cause of sin, resulted in man being punished severely for his evil deeds. The Mu'tazilite view regarding the retribution of sin is consequently very severe as compared with that of orthodox Islam, which made an extensive use of the idea of intercession on behalf of sinners, to such an extent that it was held that everyone in whose heart an atom of faith had subsisted would be brought back from Hell.[1] With an eye to the Mu'tazilites, who denied this doctrine, it is declared that Muhammad's intercession will be valid even on behalf of those who had committed grave sins.[2] Such a notion was inconsistent with the doctrine of justice and retribution, on account of which the Mu'tazilites are often called *ahl al-wa'īd*. Adherents of the doctrine of justice protested against intercession. An echo of their protests has even been preserved in canonical tradition, where it is related that a Beduin came to Muhammad saying: "Pray to Allah for rain on our behalf, we appeal to your intercession with Allah and we appeal to Allah's intercession with you". The Apostle of Allah answered: "Shame upon you, know you what you say? This be far from Allah". He did not cease repeating the last words till the effect could be read upon the faces of his companions. Thereupon he said: "For shame, it is not allowed to appeal to the intercession of any of Allah's creatures. Allah is elevated above this. Know you what Allah is? His throne is on His heavens, in this way"—and he formed something like a cupola with his fingers—"and He makes it crack, as the rider makes the saddle crack".[3]

This is certainly a curious tradition among a number of pronouncements to the contrary, and rather of Mu'tazilite than of orthodox origin. As a matter of fact the Mu'tazi-

1 Muslim, *Īmān*, trad. 148.

2 Tirmidhī, *Ḳiyāma*, b. 11. The tradition is not in the *Ṣaḥīḥ*'s.

3 Abū Dāwūd, *Sunna*, b. 18.

lites taught that anyone who had entered Hell could not be delivered from it.[1]

The second consequence of the doctrine of justice, especially of free will, was the detriment it caused to one side of the being of Allah, which was emphasized in the Kuran and consequently belonged to the fundamental notions of Islam, viz. Allah's creating function, which made Him the only really existent being. Human action side by side with His, was to early Islam an absurd idea. The consequence of the Ḳadarite and Mu'tazilite view was, that man, being considered as the author of his acts, became thereby a second creator. For this reason the Ḳadarites are called in Tradition the "Dualists of the community". Orthodox Islam showed itself conscious of being essentially monistic. "The Mu'tazilites unanimously maintain, that man decides upon and creates his acts, both good and evil; that he deserves reward or punishment in the next world for what he does. In this way the Lord is safeguarded from association with any evil or wrong or any act of unbelief or transgression. For if He created the wrong, He would be wrong, and if He created justice, He would be just."[2]

The third consequence of the doctrine of justice was the rise of the theodicy. "The Mu'tazilites unanimously declare that the Wise can only do what is salutary (*al-ṣalāḥ*) and good, and that His wisdom keeps in view what is salutary to His servants."[3] al-Shahrastānī has observed that the attitude of the Mu'tazilites was rationalistic and that their highest norm was reason (*al-'aḳl*). According to them, things are not good or evil because God declares them to be so. No, God makes the distinction between good and evil on account of their being good or evil. "The principle of the Mu'tazilites is justice in accordance with what reason postulates from wisdom, that is, producing acts in the

1 al-Baghdādī, *Farḳ*, p. 99; *Encyclopaedia of Islām*, art. *Shafā'a*, at the end; Ibn Ḥazm, *Kitāb al-Fiṣal*, iv. 63 *sqq*.

2 al-Shahrastānī, i. 30.

3 al-Shahrastānī, *loc. cit.*; cf. also Ibn Ḥazm, *Kitāb al-Fiṣal*, iii. 164 *sqq*.

way of what is right and salutary. There is no decree from eternity; God has ordered and prohibited and promised and menaced by non-eternal speech. Accordingly, he who is saved deserves reward on account of his own acts, and whoso is damned, has caused his punishment by his own acts. This is postulated by reason as applied to Wisdom."[1] The thoroughgoing rationalism of the Mu'tazilites is thus expressed by al-Shahrastānī: "The adherents of justice say: All objects of knowledge fall under the supervision of reason and receive their obligatory power from rational insight. Consequently obligatory gratitude to the divine bounteousness precedes the orders given by the [divine] law, and beauty and ugliness are qualities belonging intrinsically to what is beautiful and ugly".[2]

We now turn to the second principle of the Mu'tazilites, the unity of Allah. The discussions of this principle include the whole doctrine of God. It may be that they started from the question whether Allah will be seen by the Faithful in Paradise. It is, at any rate, certain that this question is reflected in Tradition, as may be seen from the following passages: "Some persons asked the Apostle of Allah: Shall we see our Lord on the day of the resurrection? The Apostle of Allah answered: Would you importune anyone with such a question regarding the moon in a night of full moon, or concerning the sun on a cloudless day? They answered: No. He said: In the same way you will see your Lord...".[3] Still more realistic is the following:[4] "When the people of Paradise have entered Paradise, Allah will say to them: If you have any desire I will fulfil it. They will answer: Have You not made our faces bright, have You not made us enter Paradise, have You not saved us from Hell? Thereupon Allah will remove the veil and the vision of their Lord will be the most precious of the gifts lavished upon them. Then he recited the verse: They who do right shall

1 al-Shahrastānī, i. 30.

2 al-Shahrastānī, *loc. cit.*, and cf. J. Obermann in *Wiener Zeitschrift*, xxx. 65 *sqq*.

3 Muslim, *Īmān*, trad. 299.

4 Muslim, *Īmān*, trad. 297 *sq*.

receive a most excellent reward and a superabundant addition".[1]

al-Nawawī opens his comment upon these traditions with the following passage: "The position of all the people of the *sunna* is that seeing Allah is possible and not absurd,[2] further that this will happen in the next world and that only the Faithful, not the infidels, will see Him. Some of the schismatics, namely, the Mu'tazilites, the Khāridjites and some of the Murdjites, maintain that Allah will not be seen by any of His creatures and that this would be absurd....As to the question of seeing Allah in this world, we have already said that this is possible; yet the large majority of the ancient and later *mutakallimūn* and others maintain that the vision of Allah will not happen in this world...".

A more detailed account of the views of the Mu'tazilites is given by al-Ash'arī:[3] "The Mu'tazilites are unanimously of opinion that Allah cannot be seen by eyesight; they differ regarding the question whether He can be seen by our hearts. Abu'l-Hudhail[4] and the majority say: We think that we see Allah with our hearts, in the sense that we know Him with our hearts. But Hishām al-Fuwaṭī[5] and 'Abbād ibn Sulaimān deny this".

It may be seen from these quotations that the question had at least the double aspect of seeing God in this world and in the next. This double aspect is explained by the history of the idea, which can be traced back as far as the earliest parts of the Old Testament. As the ideas of the early Israelites about the next world were not yet developed, what they might desire was only to see God in this world. This is what Moses asked as a supreme favour;[6] and it was granted to him, but only in part.

1 Sura x. 27.

2 On the opposition "possible", "absurd", cf. *infra*, Fiḳh Akbar II, art. 16 and commentary.

3 *Maḳālāt*, i. 150; cf. also Ibn Ḥazm, *Kitāb al-Fiṣal*, iii. 2 *sqq.*

4 al-'Allāf.

5 Cf. *Kitāb al-Intiṣār*, p. 57 *sqq.*; Fakhr al-Dīn al-Rāzī, iii. 184 *sqq.*, 299 *sqq.*

6 Exodus xxxiii. 12 *sqq.*

This is in accordance with the then prevaliing opinion, that when the divine and the human spheres meet, the result is a collision fatal to man. "Thou canst not see my face: for there shall no man see me, and live."[1] Even in the New Testament it is said: "No man hath seen God at any time".[2]

Meanwhile the idea of a general resurrection had spread in the old world and the chief question now became: Shall man see God in the next world? An affirmative answer to this question could be more easily given, since the vision of God in the next world could be represented in degrees of spirituality, as was done through the medium of Hellenistic mysticism,[3] in which on the one hand God was often represented as light, whilst on the other the expression "seeing God" could be explained as "knowing God". We have already seen that some of the Mu'tazilites held the same opinion.

To official Christianity of the early Middle Ages the point of interest was the *visio beatifica*, God as seen by the blessed in Paradise. This is also the chief point for Islam, as may be seen from the traditions translated above, the last of which seems even to contain an allusion to the term, or what may correspond to it, in the words "and the vision of their Lord will be the most precious of the gifts lavished upon them".[4]

To what extent the ideas of medieval Christianity and Islam were akin to one another may be seen from the definition of the *visio beatifica* as it is given in the *Catholic Encyclopaedia*: "The immediate knowledge of God which the human mind may attain in the present life. And since in beholding God face to face the created intelligence finds perfect happiness, the vision is termed 'beatific'". With this definition may be compared a part of the text of the dogma as it has been defined by Benedict XII:[5] "quod

1 Exodus xxxiii. 20.
2 St John i. 18.
3 Cf. *Bar Hebraeus' Book of the Dove*, Leyden, 1919, p. 1 *sqq*.
4 For al-Ghazālī's views see his *Iḥyā'*, iv. 280 *sqq*.
5 1334–42. The text from H. Denzinger, *Enchiridion symbolorum et definitionum*, 12th ed., p. 216 *sq*. (No. 530).

secundum communem Dei ordinationem animae Sanctorum omnium...martyrum, confessorum, virginum et aliorum fidelium defunctorum...etiam ante resumptionem suorum corporum et iudicium generale post ascensionem Salvatoris Domini nostri Iesu Christi in coelum, fuerunt, sunt et erunt in coelo, coelorum regno et paradiso coelesti cum Christo, sanctorum Angelorum consortio aggregatae, ac post Domini Iesu Christi passionem et mortem viderunt et vident divinam essentiam visione intuitiva et etiam faciali, nulla mediante creatura in ratione obiecti visi se habente, sed divina essentia immediate se nude, clare et aperte eis ostendente, quodque sic videntes eadem divina essentia perfruuntur" etc.

It is not improbable that the discussions concerning anthropomorphism (*tadjsīm*, *tashbīh*) started from this point. However this may be, the problem in its totality was entered upon by the Mu'tazilites. They were in a difficult position, fighting as they did against the letter of the Kuran, yet they ultimately won the battle.

It has been seen above that Muhammad emphasized the greatness and power of Allah to such an extent that hardly any room seemed to be left for any other individual existence apart from Him. But just this idea of Allah as a superhuman being was described in terms borrowed from the human sphere; Allah was modelled after the image of man. The Kuran speaks of the eyes of Allah;[1] of His hand in which "is the empire of all things",[2] "in which there are plentiful gifts"[3] and which is "over the hands of those who plight fealty to Muhammad".[4] Allah says to the angel who refuses to prostrate himself before Adam: "O Iblīs, what hindereth thee from prostrating thyself before him whom I have created with Mine own hands?"[5] "Both His hands are outstretched".[6]

The face of Allah is likewise a representation familiar

1 Sura xi. 39; xx. 39; xxiii. 27; lii. 48; liv. 14.
2 Sura xxiii. 90; xxxvi. 83; lvii. 1.
3 Sura iii. 66; lvii. 29.
4 Sura xlviii. 10.
5 Sura xxxviii. 75.
6 Sura v. 69.

to the Kuran. It may be sought in any quarter of the sky.[1] Several human acts are said to be done in order to seek the face of Allah.[2] Allah alone must be served, "there is no God but He and all things shall perish except His face";[3] "all on earth passeth away, but the face of thy Lord abideth".[4]

Finally, the Kuran is full of descriptions of Heaven and Hell, which are not used in a metaphorical sense. To Heaven belongs the throne of Allah, He is the Lord of the throne,[5] the noble,[6] large,[7] exalted[8] throne, which is borne by the angels.[9] Here may follow one of these pictures: "But those who shall have feared their Lord shall be driven on in crowds to Paradise until they reach it, and its gates shall be opened, and its keepers shall say to them, Peace be on you!...And thou shalt see the angels circling around the throne, uttering the praises of their Lord: And judgment shall be pronounced between them with equity: and it shall be said, Glory be to God the Lord of the worlds".[10] Of special importance in the dogmatic literature are those verses from the Kuran in which Allah is said to have seated Himself on His throne.[11]

It is stated by the writers on heresies, that these and similar expressions and descriptions were taken in their literal sense by the anthropomorphists, nay, that they even went farther. According to al-As͟hʿarī,[12] His͟hām ibn al-Ḥakam[13] was of opinion "that Allah has a body, defined, broad, high and long, of equal dimensions, radiating with

1 Sura ii. 109.

2 Sura ii. 274; vi. 52; xiii. 22; xviii. 27; xxx. 37 *sq.*; xlii. 20; cf. lxxvi. 9.

3 Sura xxviii. 88.

4 Sura lv. 27.

5 Sura xvii. 44; xl. 15; xliii. 82; lxxxi. 20.

6 Sura xxiii. 117.

7 Sura ix. 130; xxi. 22; xxiii. 88; xxvii. 26.

8 Sura lxxxv. 15.

9 Sura xl. 7; xlix. 17.

10 Sura xxxix. 73, 75.

11 Sura vii. 52; x. 3; xiii. 2; xx. 4; xxv. 60; xxxii. 3; lvii. 4.

12 *Maḳālāt*, i. 197; cf. p. 146.

13 Cf. Arnold, *al-Muʿtazilah*, pp. 26, 31, 32.

light, of a fixed measure in its three dimensions, in a place beyond place, like a bar of pure metal, shining as a round pearl on all sides, provided with colour, taste, smell and touch, so that its colour is its taste and its smell and its touch, absolute colour which does not admit any other colour, and that it moves or is at rest, rises and sits down".

The Mu'tazilites held the opposite view and so were anxious to avoid anthropomorphic expressions. If they made an exception for some of them, like God's hand or His face, they took them in the sense of bounty and knowledge. This allegorical method (*ta'wīl*) they applied also to other anthropomorphic expressions in the Kuran, and in this respect they were also in line with Christianity in its position towards Biblical expressions of the same kind.

John of Damascus has devoted a chapter of his *De fide orthodoxa* to this subject. Here is a part of it in translation:[1] "Regarding the fact that in the holy Writ a great many anthropomorphic expressions are applied to God in a symbolical way, we have to reflect that it would be impossible for us—men as we are and clad in thick flesh—to speak and think of the divine, lofty and immaterial working of the godhead, except in images, in metaphorical and symbolical terms such as are familiar to us. As often as anything is said concerning God in a kind of anthropomorphic way, it is meant symbolically and has a loftier meaning; for the divine is simple and without ambiguity. So by God's eyes and eyelids and sight we must understand His all-embracing power and the essence of His knowledge. ...By His ears and audition His forgiveness and His hearing our prayers....By His mouth and speech the designation of His will....By His face His showing and revealing Himself through His works....By His hands His accomplished energy...".

If, as a matter of fact, the discussions on God's essence started from the question of anthropomorphism, as we have supposed, it is only natural that they should follow this course throughout. The next point may well have

1 Ed. Migne, col. 841 *sqq*.

been the idea of God's being infinite and exempt from the idea of place, just as this is the next point treated by John of Damascus.[1] It is worth while to quote a few lines from his chapter, if only because they could have been written by one of the *mutakallimūn*:[2] "Definite is what is comprised by time, place or conception; infinite what cannot be conceived by any of these. Consequently God alone is infinite, without beginning, without end, comprising all, comprised by nothing; He alone is uncomprised, infinite, known by nobody, contemplating Himself".[3]

On the question of God being or not being a place, John reasons as follows: "There is also an intelligible place, where intelligible and incorporeal nature is understood to be and is. There it is present and working, not in a corporeal but in an intelligible way. For it has no form, so that it could be comprised in a bodily way. Now God, being immaterial and infinite, is not in a place. For He is His own place, filling the Universe, being above the Universe and comprising it. It is said that He is a place and 'the place of God' is mentioned as the place where His working becomes visible. He permeates the Universe, without being merged with it. He makes all things partake of His working, in accordance with their aptitude and receptive power....Therefore by 'God's place' is meant that which especially partakes of His working and grace. So heaven is His throne...".[4]

With this may be compared al-Ash'arī's description of the views of the Mu'tazilites on this point: "Some of them say that God is every place. Others say, the Creator is in no place, but He is where He is dwelling from eternity. Others say the Creator is in every place, that is, He comprises all places and His being is found in all places."[5]

It will be seen later that orthodox Islam confessed

1 Ed. Migne, col. 849 *sqq*. The preceding pages seem to be spurious.

2 Cf. *e.g.* Fakhr al-Dīn al-Rāzī's commentary on the verse "Then He seated Himself on the Throne" (sura vii. 52), in the *Mafātīḥ*, iii. 227 *sqq*.

3 Ed. Migne, col. 853.

4 Ed. Migne, col. 852.

5 *Maḳālāt*, i. 202.

God's being to be infinite and exempt from the limitations of time and place.[1] Theological reasoning could not, however, come to a stop here. If God is conceded to have no human form, nay, to be without form and place, how can He be thought of as a being possessing power, life, hearing, sight, and so on?[2] And how can any of the epithets or names which are lavished upon Him in the Kuran be applied to Him?

It may be said again that this question was a link in the theological reasoning parallel with the development of the Islamic ideas as well as with several lines of Christian dogmatics. On the latter point it may be emphasized that neither orthodox Islam nor any of the sects merely took over the views of Christianity. There is no intellectual compulsion in any quarter, nor a special openness to foreign influence. If the Mu'tazilites were at one with Christianity in teaching free will and in rejecting anthropomorphism, they took up, on the other hand, a decidedly anti-Christian (and anti-Manichaean) attitude in their emphasis on *tawḥīd* and in rejecting the doctrine of the uncreated word of God.

The question of the relation between God's essence and His qualities, between His being and His names, had obtained a place in the theology of Christianity some centuries before. Among the writings of the Pseudo-Dionysius Areopagita there is a treatise *On the divine names*. It is clear why Dionysius, the Neoplatonic mystic, is so vividly interested in this problem. Neoplatonism emphasizes the idea of The One. Some parts of Plotinus's works are hymns on The One, and the highest aim of Neoplatonic mysticism is a close communion with It. The difficulty in this train of ideas is to find the logical link between unity and plurality, between God and the world, between being and names, between essence and qualities. Dionysius does not deny the contradiction that exists

1 *Infra*, p. 210.

2 Cf. Houtsma, *De strijd over het dogma*, p. 123 *sqq.*; Macdonald, art. *Ṣifa* in the *Encyclopaedia of Islām*.

between the series of ideas. He emphasizes the idea that the Superessential One cannot be reached by any knowledge. But, this highest being forming the centre of the spiritual universe, the divine names in their totality form a plurality that comes nearest to the central unity, just as the polygon with the greatest number of angles within a circle comes nearest in area to the area of the circle.

A different way of describing The One consists in the enumeration of negative qualities. This is attempted by Dionysius in his *Mystic Theology*,[1] where he says that The One is "neither soul nor spirit, nor representation, nor opinion, nor thought, nor equality, nor disparity,...nor night, nor light, nor living, nor life...".

The problem of unity and plurality is also touched upon by John of Damascus. "The divine light and workings," he says,[2] "though one and simple and indivisible, shine in various ways in the individual beings, according to their goodness, and, though imparting to all that exists the sustenance of their proper nature, yet remain simple... and Itself is above mind and above reason and above life and above essence."

In descriptions like these it is suggested that any utterance concerning this essence would be logically impossible. On the other hand, there are the human necessity and desire to speak of the unspeakable. Some concession must therefore be made. As John of Damascus says, "If our knowledge reaches existing things only, how can we know what is above existence? It is for this reason that the unspeakable bounty has agreed to be called by names borrowed from what is within our knowledge".[3]

Actually, John has inserted in his chief work two chapters on the divine names and attributes. The latter[4] enumerates the following thirty characteristics (ἰδιώματα): "uncreated, without beginning, immortal, infinite, eternal,

1 Ed. Migne, Chapter v, col. 1045; cf. John of Damascus, *De fide orthodoxa*, col. 845.

2 *De fide orthodoxa*, col. 860.

3 *De fide orthodoxa*, col. 845.

4 *De fide orthodoxa*, col. 860.

immaterial, good, creator of the world, just, luminous, invariable, apathetic, without emotion, not to be circumscribed, unlimited, indefinite, endless, indivisible, unthinkable, needless, autocratic, self-sufficient, all-governing, life-giving, almighty, all-powerful, sanctifying, communicating, comprising and holding the universe, providing".

In the former of the two chapters a distinction is made between negative and positive qualities:[1] "Some of the divine names are negative and explain the superessential in a negative way, for example, essenceless, timeless, without beginning, invisible....Others are positive and explain the cause of the universe in a positive way. For, as the cause of all existing things and all essences, He is called being and essence. And as the cause of all reason and wisdom, of all that is reasonable and wise, He is called reason and reasonable, wisdom and wise. Likewise He is called mind and minded, life and living, power and powerful...".

All these characteristics, *ἰδιώματα*, *ṣifāt*—mind, reason, spirit, wisdom, power—are applied to God, says John, "only in so far as He is the cause of these, and in so far as He is immaterial and the Creator of the universe and almighty"[2].

It is otherwise with "the reason, wisdom, power and will of the Father", for "the Son is the only power of the Father, that which precedeth the making of the universe. Thus, as a perfect hypostasis it was begotten by a perfect hypostasis in full consciousness—He who is and is called Son. The Holy Ghost, on the other hand, is the holy power of the Father, which renders manifest the hidden side of the godhead. He has proceeded from the Father through the Son, in full consciousness, without being begotten".[3]

These extracts from Christian scholastics are quoted as being closely akin to the Muslim doctrine of the attributes. The latter also are arranged in positive and negative

1 *De fide orthodoxa*, col. 845. 2 *De fide orthodoxa*, col. 848.
3 *De fide orthodoxa*, col. 849.

groups,[1] and the distinction drawn by John between these two groups corresponds to the line of distinction between the orthodox and the Mu'tazilites in relation to this problem. It may be remarked again that, on the whole, the position of orthodox Islam is in agreement with Christian dogmatics. We now proceed to give a more complete description of the views of the Mu'tazilites.

al-Ash'arī describes the Mu'tazilite idea of God in the following terms: "Allah is one, without equal, hearing, seeing; He is no body, nor object, nor volume, nor form, nor flesh, nor blood, nor person, nor substance, nor *accidens*, nor provided with colour, taste, smell, touch, heat, cold, moistness, dryness, length, breadth, depth, union, distinction, movement, rest or partition. Neither is He provided with parts, divisions, limbs, members, with directions, with right or left hand, before or behind, above or beneath. No place encompasses Him, no time passes by Him. The ideas of intercourse, withdrawal and incarnation cannot be applied to Him. He cannot be described by any description which can be applied to creatures, in so far as they are created, neither can it be said that He is finite. He cannot be described by measure, nor by movement in a direction. He is not definite; neither begetting nor begotten; measures do not encompass Him, nor do curtains veil Him. The senses do not reach Him, nor can man describe Him by any analogy. He does not resemble the creatures in any way. Neither accident nor detriment can touch Him. Nothing of what occurs to any mind or can be conceived by phantasy resembles Him. He has not ceased to be the first, the foremost, He who preceded created things and existed before the creation. He has not ceased to be knowing, deciding, living, nor does He cease to be so. Eyes do not see Him, sight does not reach Him, phantasy cannot conceive Him nor can He be heard by ears. He is a being,[2] but

1 Cf. al-Sanūsī's catechism as abridged, *infra*, Chapter IX.

2 Cf. Fiḳh Akbar II, art. 4 and the commentary; al-Baghdādī, *Farḳ*, p. 95.

is not as other beings; knowing, deciding, living, unlike those who measure living beings by their knowledge. He alone is eternal; there is none eternal besides Him, nor a God like unto Him. He has no partner in His kingdom, nor a vizier in His government, nor any who assists Him in producing what He produces and in creating what He creates. He has not created the creation after a foregoing pattern. The creation of one thing is neither more easy nor more difficult to Him than the creation of any other thing. There is no kind of relation between Him and what gives profit; no harm can touch Him; neither joy nor pleasure can reach Him, nor is He moved by hurt or pain. There is no limit set to Him, to make Him finite. The idea of ceasing to be cannot be applied to Him, nor is He subject to weakness or diminishing. He is exalted above touching women and above taking a companion and begetting children".[1]

This description of the godhead, like those of Dionysius Areopagita,[2] Plotinus[3] and al-Ghazālī,[4] is chiefly negative. Yet positive qualities, such as hearing, seeing, deciding, knowing and living are not lacking. What the Mu'tazilites rejected were the characteristics which, being of the essence of the godhead, were eternal (*ṣifāt dhātīya* or *aẓalīya*). This is made clear by al-Ash'arī:[5] "The Mu'tazilites, the Khawāridj and many of the Murdjites, as well as many of the Zaidites,[6] say that Allah is rich, majestic, great, lofty, grand, chief, monarch, seeing, lord, possessor, overpowering, high—but not on account of majesty, greatness, loftiness, grandness, chieftainship, lordship and power. Likewise they say that He is one, alone, existing, eternal, exalted, and that He is not described in this way on account of divinity, eternity, uniqueness or existence".

1 *Maḳālāt*, i. 148 *sq*.
2 *Supra*, p. 71.
3 *Enneades*, VI. 9. 3.
4 *Mishkāt*, p. 55 *sq*.
5 *Maḳālāt*, i. 168.
6 It must be concluded from the mention of the two latter sects that they joined the discussions on the *ṣifāt* although the subject did not originally belong to their tenets.

This is expressed by al-Shahrastānī[1] in the following way: "The common belief of the sect of the Mu'tazilites is, that Allah is eternal[2] and that eternity is the most peculiar description of His essence. They absolutely reject all other eternal qualities, saying: It is by virtue of His essence that He has knowledge, power and life; not because they are eternal qualities or ideas inherent in Him. For if the qualities should partake of His eternity, which is His most peculiar description, they would partake of His divinity. . . and they agree upon this, that will and hearing and sight are not ideas inherent in His essence".

So the Mu'tazilites appear unanimously to deny that Allah possesses any eternal quality except eternity. This negative attitude—negative also in relation to the Christian doctrine of the *hypostases*,[3] as has been seen by al-Shahrastānī[4]—gave rise to the question of the extent to which the working of the *ṣifāt* reached. Allah was the Creator; did this epithet end with the creation or not? If the epithet did not exist from eternity, did it last eternally? Here was a new difficulty. But such difficulties sharpened the wits of the *mutakallimūn*, who in this respect became the masters of later orthodoxy. One of their means of avoiding a positive statement was either a series of negations, as we have seen, or, in more difficult cases, a double negation. Some of the Mu'tazilites had recourse to the latter in giving a satisfactory doctrine of Allah's qualities. "One section of the Mu'tazilites", says al-Ash'arī,[5] "declare it is forbidden to say that the Creator has not ceased creating, or that He has not ceased not-creating. Likewise it is forbidden to say that He has not ceased sustaining, or that He has not ceased not-sustaining. They treat the other qualities in the same way. This is the position of 'Abbād ibn Sulaimān.[6]

1 i. 30; cf. also al-Baghdādī, *Fark*, p. 93 *sq*.

2 *ḳadīm*.

3 According to which the Son was begotten from eternity and is being begotten eternally (Abū Ḳurra, ed. Migne, vol. XCVII. cols. 1562 *sq*., 1567).

4 i. 34 *ult*.

5 *Maḳālāt*, i. 177 *sq*.

6 Cf. Arnold, *al-Mu'tazilah*, p. 44.

"A second section assert that the Creator has not ceased not-creating and not-sustaining. If they are asked: Did He not cease to be not-just, they say: He has not ceased to be not-just and not-wrong; He has not ceased to be not-being good and not-being bad; He has not ceased to be not-honest and not-lying.... This is the position of al-Djubbā'ī.[1]

"A third section assert that the Creator has not ceased not-creating and not-sustaining. But they do not say: He has not ceased to be not-just, not-good, not-bounteous, not-honest, not-wise. They reject any such utterance, whether relative or absolute, because they assert it to be ambiguous. This is the position of some of the Mu'tazilites of Baghdād and of some of those of Baṣra."

It is clear, however, that the Mu'tazilites, in so far as they did not wish to lose sight of orthodox Islam, could not go too far in their negative attitude towards the qualities, for fear of coming into conflict with the Kuran, which applies a variety of epithets to Allah. In this respect, also, there were among them both moderates and extremists, as may be seen from the following passage from al-Ash'arī's book:[2] "Concerning the knowledge and power of Allah the first section say: We say that the Creator has knowledge; yet we go back[3] to His being knowing. Likewise we say that He has power; yet we go back to His being powerful. We do so because Allah mentions His knowledge in a general way, *e.g.* 'He has made it to descend with His knowledge'.[4] Likewise He mentions His power: 'Saw they not that God their Creator was mightier than they in power'?[5]

"Yet the Mu'tazilites do not apply this to any of the qualities. Thus they do not recognize the life of Allah in the sense of His being living, nor His hearing in the sense of His being hearing. Of the essential qualities they apply this to knowledge and power only. This is the position of

1 al-Ash'arī's master.

2 *Makālāt*, i. 178 *sq.*

3 In the sense of "we prefer".

4 Sura iii. 165.

5 Sura xli. 14.

al-Naẓẓām[1] and of the majority of the Mu'tazilites of Baṣra and Baghdād.

"The second section of the Mu'tazilites say: Allah has knowledge in the sense of what is known to Him; and power in the sense of what is accomplished. And when Allah says: Nought of His knowledge do they comprehend,[2] He means, of what is known to Him. And the Muslims, when they see rain, say: This is the power of Allah, meaning thereby what is accomplished by His power. Yet this section of the Mu'tazilites do not extend these views to the other essential qualities.

"The third section say that Allah has knowledge which is Himself, and power which is Himself, and life which is Himself, and hearing which is Himself. They speak similarly of the other essential qualities. This is the position of Abu'l-Hudhail[3] and his adherents.

"The fourth section assert that it is forbidden to say: God has knowledge, power, hearing, sight. Likewise it is forbidden to say: God has no knowledge, no power. So they reason concerning the other qualities. This is the position of 'Abbād ibn Sulaimān and his adherents".[4]

I have translated this rather detailed exposition, chiefly because it may serve as an introduction to some articles of the orthodox creed, and also because it explains to some extent the Mu'tazilite position regarding the Kuran.

The denial of the eternity of the Kuran by the Mu'tazilites, or their thesis that the Kuran had been created, was only a logical consequence of their denying eternal qualities as well as of their denying the eternal decree.

We have seen[5] that according to old Oriental conceptions heavenly writ comprised two things, the course of the world and divine revelation. Judaism had given the

1 Cf. de Boer, *Geschichte der Philosophie*, p. 51 *sqq.*; Horten, *Systeme*, p. 189 *sqq.*

2 Sura ii. 256.

3 al-'Allāf; cf. de Boer, *op. cit.*, p. 49 *sqq.*; Horten, *op. cit.*, p. 246 *sqq.*; *Kitāb al-Intiṣār*, pp. 7 *sqq.*, 70.

4 *Maḳālāt*, i. 178.

5 *Supra*, p. 54.

Tora a place among the pre-existent entities. In Christianity the idea of pre-existence and eternity had been attributed to the *Logos*, the word of God that was God.

Orthodox Islam in general agreed with such conceptions. It took over the idea of the divine decree, it took over also the idea of the pre-existent book. The Mu'tazilites, the adherents of *tawḥīd*, reserved eternity for Allah and rejected it with regard to any other entity, decree, revelation, or quality. This is the deep sense of their *tawḥīd*.

The greatest difficulty in the application of the doctrine of the qualities to the Kuran was caused to the orthodox by those passages of the holy book[1] in which Allah is represented as having spoken with Moses. What was the relation of this speech to the uncreated Kuran? Out of this question grew the other: What is the relation of the latter to the single copies and to the scripture as recited by the tongues of mortals? The answer to these and similar questions is given in the creed;[2] as to the Mu'tazilites, they were of divergent opinions, as is attested by the detailed reproduction of their views by al-As͟h'arī.[3]

These discussions introduce us to the very centre of the scholastic method which in Arabic is called *kalām*. It was the spirit of Aristotle to which Christianity and Islam paid homage by accepting his logical method and distinctions and by raising them to the rank of their official philosophy and the foundation of their dogmatics.

Christianity led the way. The chief work of John of Damascus consists of three parts; the last, *De fide orthodoxa*, is a treatise on dogmatics; it is preceded by a book on the sects, and the introduction to these two is formed by the *Dialectica*, in which the logical foundation of the dogmatic system is developed. This part of the work could, *mutatis mutandis*, have been written by a Muslim, and forms an introduction to *kalām*.

1 vii. 141; xxviii. 30.
2 Waṣīyat Abī Ḥanīfa, art. 9; Fiḳh Akbar ii, art. 3.
3 *Maḳālāt*, i. 183–5.

Regarding the origin and literal meaning of this term several opinions have been expressed. It is not necessary to give a critical survey of them here,[1] and it will be sufficient to remind the reader of two facts.

The first is the temporal coincidence of the rise of scholasticism with the debates on the *kalām Allah*, the speech or word of God, an expression which is used or implied in the passages of the Kuran[2] in which God is represented to have spoken with Moses. This coincidence has inevitably caused some confusion in the discussions on the origin of *kalām* in the sense of scholasticism. It must therefore be borne in mind that the coincidence is merely fortuitous and of no value whatever for the question with which we are concerned at the moment.

The second is this, that *kalām* in the sense of scholasticism has nothing to do with the Greek *logos* or any of its derivations, but was prepared by the development of Arabic terminology itself. *Kalām* is, in the first place, speech, and *takallama* speaking. These terms have the cognate meaning of discussion and disputation.[3] "The first who opened discussions at Baṣra on free will was Ma'bad" is a well-known tradition,[4] in which the term *takallama* is used in this sense. The *mutakallimūn* were thus characterized, not as theologians, but as rationalists and philosophers, and the fact that *kalām* in the course of time received the meaning of dogmatic theology is an indication of the rationalistic direction which Muslim theology has gradually taken.

The Mu'tazilites, though they introduced rationalism and the system of *kalām* into Islam, were more than logical pedants; their views embraced God, man and the universe. We have already seen that the emphasis laid by them on the idea of God's justice and the salutary (*al-ṣalāḥ*, *aṣlaḥ*) arose from the desire for a theodicy, the outlines of which were as follows.

1 Cf. Macdonald, art. *Kalām* in the *Encyclopaedia of Islām*.
2 Sura, vii. 139, etc.
3 Cf. Muslim, *Aimān*, trad. 38.
4 Muslim, *Īmān*, trad. 1.

The idea of the salutary as a divine principle led to this question: Is this idea of an absolute or of a relative nature? a question which may be compared with the other: Is faith of an absolute or of a relative nature?[1] Here may follow the translation of what al-A<u>sh</u>ʿarī says on the subject:[2] "According to Abu'l-Hu<u>dh</u>ail the terms totality and completeness apply to what Allah decrees concerning the salutary and the good; likewise the term totality applies to the other decrees of Allah and there cannot be conceived anything more salutary than what Allah does. Others say: The salutary which Allah decrees is without limit and the term totality cannot be applied to it. Allah is able to decree salutary things other than those which He has done; but they would be like those which He has done. Others say: All that He does can be conceived. But it cannot be conceived that there should be any salutary thing which He would not do. This is the opinion of ʿAbbād.[3] Some say: Of the decrees of Allah regarding His servants one is more salutary than the other. And it may be that He abandons one salutary act for another that takes its place".

In spite of philosophical differences of this kind, the Muʿtazilites of various shades agreed with the doctrine which a thousand years later was to reappear in history in the form of the catchword: *tout pour le mieux dans le meilleur des mondes*. The application of this theory to reality gave rise to difficulties. What of those individuals, men and brutes, who were not under the obligation of the law and, consequently, could not be rewarded on account of obligations fulfilled? The unanimous answer of the Muʿtazilites was, that God has created His servants to their profit, not to their harm, and that all creatures who are not under the obligation of the law have been created for the benefit of, and as examples to, those who are under the

1 *Supra*, p. 45. 2 *Maḳālāt*, i. 239 *sqq.*

3 The relation between conception and reality is a much debated one in scholasticism; cf. Rougier, *La scolastique et le Thomisme*, p. 161 *sqq.* and passim; *infra*, p. 166 *sq.*

obligation of the law. Their opinions differed, however, on those things which could not serve as examples and in which there was no benefit. So it was inconceivable that God should create a thing that could not be seen or perceived by those who are under the obligation of the law.[1]

What of children and infidels of whom Allah knows that they will embrace the faith? Can it be conceived that He will let them die before they do so? According to al-Ash'arī,[2] opinions were divided on this point.

Another question was: How can the sufferings of little children be in harmony with the justice of Allah? The majority of the Mu'tazilites thought that the pains of children were intended to be an example to the adult, but that, nevertheless, they would receive an indemnity, for without it their suffering would be an act of injustice on the part of Allah. There was, however, variety of opinion regarding this question, as well as concerning the nature of indemnities.[3] Not only the pains of children but also the sufferings of animals postulated an indemnity; here also there was variety of opinion as to time, place, and person.[4] The Mu'tazilites could concede that these pains were created by Allah, as well as sickness and other natural evils;[5] they rejected, however, any connection between Allah and moral evil.

This gave rise to discussions on Allah's will and on the discrimination between will (*mashī'a*) and command (*amr*).[6] The following is the view of Wāṣil ibn 'Aṭā': "The Creator being wise and just, it is forbidden to establish a relation between Him and evil (*sharr*) or wrong (*ẓulm*). So it cannot be conceived that His will regarding His servants should be different from His command; likewise He would not punish them on account of His own decisions. So man is the author of good, evil, faith, unbelief, obedience and transgression, and is rewarded or punished for his

1 *Maḳālāt*, i. 240 *sq.*
2 *Maḳālāt*, i. 240 *sq.*
3 *Maḳālāt*, i. 242 *sq.*
4 *Maḳālāt*, i. 243 *sq.*
5 *Maḳālāt*, i. 235 *sq.*
6 *Maḳālāt*, i. 180 *sq.*; *infra*, Waṣīyat Abī Ḥanīfa, art. 7.

acts; but the Lord gives him power for all this. Human acts may be summarized as acts of movement and rest, as efforts, insight and knowledge. He says: It is absurd that God should say to man: Do, without rendering him able to do, whereas God Himself is conscious of His own power and action".[1] The Mu'tazilites in general say that "none of those human acts that are not commanded by Allah, or that are prohibited, have been willed by Him".[2]

Accordingly the Mu'tazilites in general did not recognize faith as a divine gift, which is lavished upon some, and withheld from others. "The Mu'tazilites say that there is neither actually nor potentially at Allah's disposal a power called grace (*luṭf*), by which faith may be generated in those of whom Allah knows that they will not believe, so that it could be said that He determines whether to set His power at work or not. For His actions towards all men are determined by what is most salutary for them from the religious point of view, and by what is best fitted to lead them into the ordered path; nor will He withhold from them anything which He knows they need for the performance of what is ordered and so help them towards the due rewards of obedience."[3]

The idea of divine grace was not, however, rejected altogether by all the Mu'tazilites, as may be seen from the views of Bishr ibn al-Mu'tamir and of Dja'far ibn Ḥarb, as presented by al-Ash'arī.[4] Nor was there uniformity in the opinions of the Mu'tazilites concerning the opposite idea of "abandoning" (*khadhlān*).[5]

1 al-Shahrastānī, i. 32.
2 al-Baghdādī, *Farḳ*, p. 94.
3 *Maḳālāt*, i. 237; cf. p. 237 *sq.* on the view of al-Djubbā'ī.
4 *Maḳālāt*, i. 236.
5 Cf. Fiḳh Akbar II, art. 6.

CHAPTER V

The Crisis of Islam and its Outcome

The Mu'tazilite movement was a powerful one, which succeeded for a time in gaining a hold upon the higher circles in matters temporal and spiritual. It would be superfluous to repeat here those details which have been described by others.[1] The change that took place in the personal attitude of the Caliph al-Mutawakkil was an indication of the fact that Islam had rediscovered its proper outlook. It rejected rationalism along with the dogmas that were based upon it. Yet it made concessions to its method, with the result that some of the elements that had in vain demanded entrance at the front door were introduced by the back-stairs. The second and third centuries witnessed a heroic war with rationalism, which proclaimed itself the highest principle in theology. The victory was won by orthodox Islam, which finally took possession of the dogmatic fortresses of the enemy. Yet it could not refrain from making use of the weapons which it found there. So there developed a likeness between the orthodox and their opponents, which to many seemed to be of more than a superficial kind.

Actually, it is a voice from antiquity that speaks through the logic of Islam from the fourth century onward. So long as this voice was heard in logic only, Islam could keep theology pure from foreign elements. In the long run, however, logic could not but influence philosophy and theology. It was just the discrepancy between this new element and the genuine conceptions of Islam that was to bring about a new crisis in Muslim theology in the teachings of al-Ghazālī. In ethical mysticism, that is, in exchanging his former Aristotelianism for a Platonic tendency, he found his personal salvation. But al-Ghazālī

1 Cf. Macdonald, *Development*, p. 153 *sqq.*; Patton, *Aḥmad ibn Ḥanbal and the Miḥna.*

did not radically reject *kalām*, and so Aristotelianism kept its place side by side with Platonism.

The Mu'tazilites had applied the norm of reason to theological and ethical ideas, even to Allah Himself. In many respects, however, this norm was in contradiction to His nature. His unlimited power, His ways with man and the world, were exclusively guided by His will. His will prescribed to man what he should do and what he should avoid. This did not, however, mean that these commandments and prohibitions sprang from a principle which could be applied to His own individuality. On the contrary, the prevailing feature of Allah in the Kuran is His absoluteness, His doing what He pleases without being bound by human rules. He extends His bounty,[1] His mercy[2] and His wisdom[3] to whomsoever He pleaseth; He guideth in the right way[4] and He leaveth to go astray[5] whom He pleaseth; if He had so pleased, He would have guided all men in the right way;[6] He createth what He pleaseth[7] and formeth man in the womb as He pleaseth;[8] He forgiveth unto whom He pleaseth;[9] in short, He doeth what He pleaseth.[10]

This was the point on which the debates between the orthodox and the Mu'tazilites turned. al-Shahrastānī expresses it as follows: "The adherents of justice say that Allah is one as to His essence, without division or quality; and that He is one as to His acts, without an associate. Accordingly what is eternal is His essence, and there is nothing which partakes of His acts. For it would be absurd that there should be two eternal beings and two governors to make decisions. This is the doctrine of unity and justice. According to the people of the *sunna*, the justice of Allah lies in His dealing as possessor and Lord,

1 Sura ii. 84; cf. iii. 66; v. 59; x. 107; lvii. 21, 29; lxii. 4.
2 Sura ii. 99; iii. 67; xii. 56.
3 Sura xxvii. 2.
4 Sura ii. 136, 209, 274; vi. 88; x. 26; xiv. 4.
5 Sura xxxiv. 34 *bis*.
6 Sura xiii. 30.
7 Sura v. 20.
8 Sura iii. 4.
9 Sura ii. 284; cf. iii. 124 *bis*; iv. 51 *sq.*, 116; v. 21, 44; ix. 15, 27.
10 Sura iii. 35.

and in making decisions according to His will as He pleaseth. Justice, in fact, consists in giving things their place, and this implies acting as Lord according to His own will and knowledge. The opposite is injustice and it is inconceivable that He should be wrong in His decisions and unjust in His dealings".[1]

The idea of the absoluteness of Allah served the orthodox as a guide on other points. We have already seen that in the question of free will they maintained the old Oriental idea of a god who fixed the course of the world and the fate of each individual.[2] The harshness of this view was mitigated by intercession, which made it possible to deliver from Hell even those who were guilty of mortal sins, nay, everyone in whose heart a grain of faith had subsisted.[3]

The idea of intercession formed a reply to the objections of the Mu'tazilites against predestination. In the matter of anthropomorphism the people of the *sunna* could easily support their view by reference to several passages and expressions in the Kuran. Yet it was not altogether safe to lay too much stress on the literal meaning of these expressions. We have seen to what strange views anthropomorphism could lead.[4] It was not to the taste of the orthodox that Allah should be represented as a being of three dimensions, possessed of colour, taste and so on. So they were obliged to take a middle position.

This position consisted in an honest effort to cling to Kuran and *sunna* without asking further questions, approximately in the same way as the pious ancestors had done. The champion of this type of orthodoxy was Aḥmad ibn Ḥanbal († 855), whose heroic personality dominates the middle of the ninth century A.D. It was not only in the field of dogmatics, but also in that of jurisprudence, that he preached the return to Kuran and *sunna*. The position of the latter he corroborated by composing his vast *Musnad*. Moreover he gave his doctrine a valuable recommenda-

1 i. 28.
2 *Supra*, p. 54.
3 *Supra*, p. 61.
4 *Supra*, p. 67.

tion by proving himself to possess a character of the first rank. It is in him that the spirit of ancient Islam resides during the rationalistic crisis.

Conscious of the dangers to the right as well as to the left, he taught that Kuran and *sunna* must be taken in their literal sense, without asking questions, *bilā kaifa*. This rule should be applied to the anthropomorphic expressions in the Kuran, such as the face of Allah, His eyes and hands, His sitting on His throne, and His being seen by the Faithful in Paradise.

There was a second doctrine for which Aḥmad was ready to give up his life, viz. that of the uncreated Kuran. It may be conjectured that he considered this dogma as the very heart of the question of the qualities. This question may well have been far removed from the centre of his interest; for, so far as we know, he was no philosopher, but a pure theologian. We may suppose, therefore, that his vigorous defence of the eternity of the Kuran had its root in the feeling that this dogma followed from the unique nature of the holy book, whereas the Mu‘tazilite view in his eyes tended to lower the position of the word of Allah.[1]

It may be said here in anticipation that the form of the creed which may be considered to embody his views in general is the Waṣīyat Abī Ḥanīfa, which will be translated and explained in Chapter VII.

However strong Aḥmad's influence both in his lifetime and after his death may have been, his *bilā kaifa* could not satisfy the minds of those who were interested in *kalām*, nor did it supply his followers with an answer to the reasonings of the Mu‘tazilites.

Muslim theology from the death of Aḥmad ibn Ḥanbal up to the time when the system became established is represented by the work of one individual. His inner history is indeed a mirror of the spiritual achievements of his age; moreover, by the turn it took, it determined the

1 Cf. al-Ash‘arī, *Ibāna*, p. 33 *sq.*, a passage which is strongly in favour of the view expressed in the text.

direction in which dogmatic Islam was to move for centuries. It was Abu'l-Ḥasan 'Alī b. Ismā'īl al-A<u>sh</u>'arī († 935) who was destined to deal the death-blow to Mu'tazilism, not, however, without being infected by its essence. He had sat at the feet of al-<u>D</u>jubbā'ī, the chief of the Mu'tazilites of Baṣra, and had been one of his most distinguished disciples. Several stories are current concerning his first disputations with his master,[1] the dreams which caused his conversion,[2] and the way in which he made it publicly known.[3] Here it may be said that in the various versions of the dreams, the emphasis laid on his return to Kuran and *sunna* is unquestionable. It is not clear, however, whether this means that he was also to give up *kalām*; some passages seem to imply this, in other instances, however, it seems doubtful.[4] This uncertainty is an indication of al-A<u>sh</u>'arī's ambiguous position.

It must, however, be borne in mind that al-A<u>sh</u>'arī stands only at the beginning of *kalām*, and that, to be quite fair, it would be necessary to make a distinction between al-A<u>sh</u>'arī and the A<u>sh</u>'arite school. This, however, is not always possible. For the moment we must judge the man by those of his works that are accessible. His *Maḳālāt al-Islāmīyīn* has been utilized to a large extent in the foregoing pages. It contains (*a*) a heresiology, (*b*) the orthodox creed, (*c*) different opinions on philosophical questions[5]—a division which is identical with that of the chief work of John of Damascus, though the arrangement is different in that in John's *Foundation of Knowledge* (the title of the tripartite work), the logical part forms the introduction to the other two.

1 Spitta, *Zur Geschichte Abu'l-Ḥasan al-Aš'ari's*, p. 41 *sqq.*; Macdonald, *Development*, p. 189.

2 Spitta, *op. cit.*, pp. 47 *sqq.*, 118 *sqq.*

3 Spitta, *op. cit.*, p. 50.

4 Cf. Mehren in *Travaux de la troisième session du congrès international des orientalistes St Pétersbourg 1876*, II. 255, as compared with foregoing pages.

5 Body, substance, atoms, movement, man, the senses, action, ideas, perception, the absurd, contradiction, causality, non-entity, affirmation, negation, *tawallud*, etc.

It is remarkable that al-Ash'arī's account of the sects in his *Maḳālāt* is given with perfect objectivity, without a word of retort. The arguments in favour of the traditional views and the refutation of those of the sectaries are in his *Ibāna 'an Uṣūl al-Diyāna*,[1] which opens with a creed. As an example of al-Ash'arī's way of reasoning, a survey of his section on the question whether Allah may be seen in Paradise may be quoted. His arguments in favour of a positive answer to the question are as follows:[2]

I. Sura lxxv. 22: "On that day shall faces beam with light, looking towards their Lord". In this verse "looking" might mean "considering as an example" (cf. sura lxxxviii. 17: "Do they not consider the camels, how they are created"? etc.). This would, however, be wrong, since the next world is not a place for considering examples. Or it might mean "awaiting" (cf. sura xxxvi. 49: "They await but a single blast"). But this would be wrong, since the word "faces" suggests the idea of seeing. Moreover, "awaiting" does not belong to Paradise, as it implies the idea of trouble, whereas the inhabitants of Paradise enjoy what no eye has seen and no ear has heard—perfect life and perpetual delight. Or it might mean "affection". This too would be wrong, as it is not becoming to creatures to show affection for their Creator. Lastly, it might mean sensual vision. This is the only right explanation. If anyone should ask, "Why do you not interpret the words 'looking towards their Lord' as 'looking towards the reward of their Lord'?" the answer would be that it is forbidden to take the Kuran otherwise than in its plain sense (*ẓāhiruhu*).

II. Sura vii. 139 *a*, where Moses says: "O Lord, show thyself to me". Moses, who as an Apostle was free from sin, cannot be supposed to have asked for an absurd thing.

III. Sura vii. 139 *b*, where God says to Moses: "But

1 *Supra*, p. 3.

2 *Ibāna*, p. 13 *sqq*. On this question cf. also Fakhr al-Dīn al-Rāzī, *Mafātīḥ*, i. 348; v. 17–21; al-Khaiyāṭ, *Kitāb al-Intiṣār*, p. 68; 'Abd Allāh ibn Aḥmad ibn Ḥanbal, *Kitāb al-Sunna*, pp. 47 *sqq*., 70 *sq*.

look towards the mountain, and if it shall stand firm in its place, then shalt thou see me".

IV. Sura x. 27: "They who do right shall receive a most excellent reward, and a superabundant addition". If it should be objected that in sura vi. 103 it is said, "No sight reacheth to Him", this objection would not be valid, because the verse may mean, "No sight reacheth to Him in this world", or, "The sight of the infidels does not reach to Him".

V. Several traditions going back to the Prophet, in which it is said that Allah will be seen.[1]

VI. Every existing thing may be seen; only what does not exist is not seen. Allah exists, so it is possible and not absurd[2] that He will allow us to see Him. Consequently to deny that Allah will be seen is *ta'ṭīl*.[3]

VII. Allah sees things. Whosoever sees not himself, sees not things. Now, if Allah sees Himself, it is possible that He will make us see Him.

VIII. The Muslims unanimously confess that "in Paradise there is what eye has not seen, nor ear heard, nor hath it entered into the heart of man, namely perfect life and perpetual delight". Now the highest delight in Paradise is to see God, and the majority of those who serve Him, serve Him with a view to seeing His face. If, apart from seeing Allah, there is nothing higher than seeing the Prophet, and to see the Prophet is the highest joy of Paradise, to see Allah is higher than to see the Prophet. If this be true, Allah will not withhold from the Prophets, the Apostles, the angels who are near Him, and the community of the Faithful and the true believers, the vision of His face. For seeing does not leave any trace in the object of sight, since it is limited to him who sees. If this be true, it is not necessary to explain "seeing Allah"

1 Cf. *supra*, p. 63.

2 On the terms "possible", "absurd" in a technical sense, cf. *infra*, p. 273 *sq*.

3 *I.e.* divesting God of what pertains to Him; the opposite of the terms *tas͟hbīh* and *tad͟jsīm*.

allegorically, and it is not absurd that Allah will let Himself be seen by the Faithful in Paradise.

A translation of the pages which follow this piece of dogmatic reasoning is unnecessary. Concerning the other subjects treated in the *Ibāna* a few remarks will be sufficient, as nearly all of them reappear in the individual creeds, which will be duly considered.

In his passage on Allah's having seated Himself on His throne,[1] al-Ash‘arī refers to several verses from the Kuran in which a similar idea is expressed. Then he attacks the Mu‘tazilites, Djahmites and Ḥarūrīya,[2] who make use of allegorical interpretation and assert that God is in all places. If this interpretation were right, says al-Ash‘arī, it might logically be maintained, for instance, that "Allah has seated Himself on the latrines".

Another argument against the Mu‘tazilites and their companions is the tradition according to which Allah descends every night to the lowest heaven and says: "Is there anyone who asks? I will give. Is there anyone wanting forgiveness? I will forgive, till the coming of dawn".

al-Ash‘arī's conclusion is that the literal interpretation should be maintained, since the allegorical one would lead to *ta‘ṭīl*[3] and negation, although its adherents pretend to remove *tanzīh*.[4] "May Allah preserve us", he exclaims, "from a *tanzīh* which would imply negation and *ta‘ṭīl*."[5]

The two specimens of al-Ash‘arī's reasoning given above—one on the vision of Allah in Paradise, the other on His sitting on the throne—show him as the spiritual son of Aḥmad ibn Ḥanbal. It is not without good reason that the creed of which the *Ibāna* is an explanation is immediately preceded by a passage in which al-Ash‘arī describes his position and method as "adhering to the

1 *Ibāna*, p. 42 *sqq.*

2 *I.e.* Khāridjites.

3 Cf. *supra*, p. 89.

4 The withdrawing of the human element from expressions and ideas regarding the Godhead.

5 *Ibāna*, p. 46 *sq.*; cf. also ‘Abd Allāh ibn Aḥmad ibn Ḥanbal, *Kitāb al-Sunna*, p. 40 *sqq.*; Ibn Ḥazm, *Kitāb al-Fiṣal* ii. 122–6.

book of our Lord, to the *sunna* of our Prophet, and to what is handed down on the authority of the Companions, the generation that succeeded them and the masters of *ḥadīth* (these are our binding authorities), and to the views of Abū 'Abd Allāh Aḥmad ibn Ḥanbal (may Allah make his face resplendent, raise his rank and render his reward considerable), opposing that which opposes him, for he is the excellent leader and the perfect head, through whom Allah has brought forward the truth, removed error, made clear the path, and subdued the heresies of heretics and the schisms of schismatics. Allah's mercy be upon him as a leader and chief and an honoured and venerated friend".[1]

Is this the al-Ash'arī whose spiritual descendants were cursed by the Ḥanbalites[2] and who is detested by Ibn Ḥazm?[3] Or is al-Ash'arī a man with two faces? His *Ibāna* shows him throughout as the stern adherent of Kuran and *sunna*, whose arguments consist chiefly of quotations from these two sources. If the specimens given above should need corroboration, it would be found in his chapter on anthropomorphic expressions and on the qualities.[4] This opens with some verses from the Kuran in which Allah's eyes and face are mentioned.[5] Then he goes on: "The Djahmites[6] deny that Allah has a face, though He says so Himself; likewise they deny His possessing hearing, sight and eyes. So they are in accord with the Christians,[7] for the latter admit God's hearing and seeing in the sense of knowing only.... The Djahmites say that Allah has neither power, nor knowledge, nor hearing, nor sight. Their real aim is bare unity and the denial of Allah's names.[8] They make a formula without being able to give it a sense. And if it were not that they

1 *Ibāna*, p. 8.
2 Cf. *e.g.* Macdonald, *Development*, p. 212 *sq.*
3 *Kitāb al-Fiṣal*, iii. 5 *sq.* 4 *Ibāna*, p. 47 *sqq.* 5 Cf. *supra*, p. 3.
6 The adherents of Djahm ibn Ṣafwān, who denied the divine qualities. 7 *Supra*, p. 68.
8 The Mu'tazilites rejected the qualities only, not the names.

fear the sword, they would plainly say that Allah is not hearing, seeing, knowing; but fear of the sword withholds them from publishing their heresy. One of their leaders has said:[1] Allah's knowledge is Allah and Allah is knowledge. So he denies Allah's knowledge, though he seems to acknowledge it. For if, according to him, Allah's knowledge is Allah Himself, he ought to say: O knowledge, forgive me", and so on. Then al-As̲h̲ʿarī produces arguments in favour of the view that Allah has a face and two hands, knowledge, power and speech. In all this there is scarcely a word that could not have been written by Aḥmad ibn Ḥanbal.

By way of contrast we may mention an abridged account[2] of al-As̲h̲ʿarī's position as described by Abu'l Maʿālī ibn ʿAbd al-Malik al-D̲j̲uwainī, the Imām al-Ḥaramain († 1085) and the teacher of al-G̲h̲azālī. Here al-As̲h̲ʿarī is not in the first place represented as the adherent of Aḥmad ibn Ḥanbal, but as the dogmatist who made it possible for Islam to take a position between opposite extremes. He admits the existence of the divine qualities with the qualification of *tanzīh*:[3] "Knowledge, but not like human knowledge, power, but not like human power...". He denies free will as well as compulsion, saying that man does not produce, but that he acquires his act (*kasb*). He affirms that Allah will be seen in Paradise, without personal appearance (*ḥulūl*), without limitation, without definition. Regarding Allah's sitting on the throne he says: "Allah existed ere there existed anything. Then He created the throne and what encompasses it, yet He did not need any place, and after the creation of the place He was just as He had been before". The Muʿtazilites explained Allah's hand as a hand of power and bounty, and the anthropomorphists took it as the member of a body; al-As̲h̲ʿarī said: "Hand and face are hand as a quality and face as a quality, just as hearing and sight".

1 Abu'l-Hud̲h̲ail al-ʿAllāf.

2 Spitta, *Zur Geschichte Abu'l-Ḥasan al-Ašʿari's*, pp. 140–3.

3 *Supra*, p. 90.

Concerning Allah's descending to the lowest Heaven, al-Ash'arī said that descending is a quality; likewise His sitting on the throne is a quality.

This may be sufficient evidence that al-Djuwainī shows us al-Ash'arī as a *mutakallim*, not as a Ḥanbalite theologian.

It is difficult for us to judge of al-Ash'arī's position so long as only a few of his writings are accessible to us.[1] That he adopted *kalām* as a method is certain.[2] But the question remains: Was he also the father of *tanzīh* and *kasb*, which are ascribed to him? No trace of them can be found in those passages of the *Ibāna*, where they could have served to mitigate his harsh views, and where they could have corroborated his reasoning, which in many cases simply consists in citing passages from Kuran and *sunna*. Judging by the general tenour of the reports about it, it may be inferred that his conversion arose from the feeling that Islam, in following the ways of the Mu'tazilites, was going to ruin. If this be so, we may suppose that his first reaction was so passionate that it made him reject not only the Mu'tazilite views, but also their methods. It might then be surmised that the *Ibāna*, in which a passionate tone may be discerned, is one of the earliest writings after his conversion, born of his desire to proclaim his return to the traditional faith and to defend it on scriptural and traditional grounds. It would not be surprising if this stern attitude which characterized the renegade should have been mitigated in the course of time.

The *Makālāt al-Islāmīyīn* may belong to a later period of his life. In this work not a single line betrays the fervour that glows in the *Ibāna*. Yet even in the *Makālāt* the methods of *tanzīh* and the term *kasb* do not appear as ideas of particular value to the author; in fact, they are not mentioned at all. On the contrary, the traditional explanation of Allah's sitting on His throne and of the anthropomorphic expressions ends with the words: "The people of the *sunna* and the adherents of *ḥadīth* maintain only what

1 A list of these is given in Spitta, *Zur Geschichte*, p. 63 *sqq*.
2 Cf. his *Risāla fi' stiḥsān al-Khawḍ fi'l-Kalām*.

they find in the Book or what is handed down on the authority of the Prophet".[1] It might perhaps be doubted whether al-Ash'arī includes himself in the people of the *sunna* and the adherents of *ḥadīth*. All possible doubt regarding this point, however, is removed by the sentence which closes the account of the traditional views on dogmatics: "This is the *summa* of what they prescribe, maintain and think. And we agree with all that we have reported concerning their views, which are also ours. Our only guidance is in God; He is sufficient and Him we ask for help, in Him we confide and to Him is our return".[2]

Must we then conclude from this that at a still later age al-Ash'arī proceeded to formulate his hair-splitting doctrine of *kasb* and of "knowing through knowledge", and to accept *tanzīh* as a method?

When other works by al-Ash'arī have been made accessible, it may perhaps be possible to give an answer to this question and to make a clearer distinction than we are able to make at present between the position of the master himself and that of his school. Such a distinction is the more desirable as the orthodox system in its later development has as a whole been stamped as Ash'arite. The gulf between the *Ibāna* and Fakhr al-Dīn al-Rāzī, for example, may be seen in the latter's treatment of the question of how Allah sits upon His throne.[3]

The changed attitude of orthodoxy towards *kalām* found its first expression in the creed called Fiḳh Akbar (II), which may have originated in the middle of the tenth century A.D. A special chapter will be devoted to the translation and explanation of this creed.[4] Here it may be sufficient to note the dogmatic position of a man who was the superior of al-Ash'arī, namely, al-Ghazālī.

To him is ascribed the final triumph of the Ash'arite system in the East—a triumph that was not impaired by the influence of such vigorous personalities as Ibn Ḥazm and Ibn Taimīya. We are fortunate in possessing much

1 *Maḳālāt*, i. 201.
2 *Maḳālāt*, i. 284.
3 *Mafātīḥ*, iii. 227 *sqq.*; and *infra*, p. 115 *sq.*
4 *Infra*, Chapter VIII.

authentic material regarding his position. One of the most brilliant scholars of the Islamic world in the second half of the eleventh century A.D., he had written books that were to become standard works in two fields, those of *fikh* and *kalām*, with their collateral theological and philosophical branches.

Among his works of *kalām* may be mentioned the *Iktiṣād fi'l-I'tikād*, which has been translated into Spanish by Asín Palacios together with extracts from other works such as the *Ildjām*, the *Miḥakk*, the *Mi'yār*, the *Maksad* and the *Mustaẓhirī*.

The *Iktiṣād* is a regular treatise on dogmatics, preceded by four prefaces on the use and methods of *kalām*.

The first chapter deals with the essence (*dhāt*) of Allah, His existence, His eternity, His being neither substance nor *accidens*, His being infinite, not subject to any modality; with the possibility of His being attained to by sight, as He is attained to by knowledge; with His being one.

The second chapter deals with the qualities of Allah, His living, knowing, being powerful, willing, hearing, seeing, speaking; His possessing life, knowledge, power, will, hearing, sight and speech; with the nature of these qualities and their mutual relation; with their being additional to His essence, yet eternal, essentially connected with His essence; with the false opinion of those who say that they have been originated.

The third chapter deals with the acts of Allah. In seven propositions it is shown that there does not rest on Him any obligation to give laws, to create, to give reward, to take into account what is salutary for His servants; that it is not absurd that He should command them to do what is above their power; that He is not obliged to punish sin; that it is not absurd that He should send Prophets. This chapter is preceded by a preface on the ideas of necessary good and evil. The fourth chapter deals with the Apostles and with the traditions on the last things, on the headship of the community, on heresies and their criterion.

The *Iḳtiṣād* is a work of al-Ghazālī, the intellectualist, who treated dogmatics with a skill which may have corresponded to the depth of his conviction. We have, however, reason to doubt this. At any rate, in the thirty-seventh year of his life he passed through an intellectual and religious crisis, in which the edifice of his spiritual existence crumbled down to its very foundations. They were never built up again, but replaced by a "religion of the heart" of a mystic character. When the crisis was passed he gradually recovered the faculty of estimating the relative importance of *fiḳh* and *kalām*. This appears to some extent in his *Iḥyā' 'Ulūm al-Dīn*. The second book of this work is devoted to the foundations of belief. In the third chapter is inserted a short treatise on dogmatics, written by him during the years of his retreat in Jerusalem. Perhaps this "Letter from Jerusalem" was the first public sign of his recovery. In the *Iḥyā'* it is preceded by a paraphrastic reproduction of the creed of the people of the *sunna*.[1]

What may interest us at present is the relation between al-Ghazālī the mystic and al-Ghazālī the dogmatist. The *Iḥyā'*, especially the second book, discloses to us something of this relation.

The paraphrastic reproduction of the creed just mentioned is intended, says al-Ghazālī, to be learnt by heart by young children. When they know it, they will gradually understand and at length firmly believe it. So it is with all popular belief. But such a faith may need corroboration. The way to obtain it is not by disputation and *kalām*, but by the recitation of the Kuran, by the reading of the commentaries and the traditions, as well as by the performance of the ceremonial duties and by intercourse with the pious. This simple faith is like a mountain rock; whereas the faith of the *mutakallimūn*, fenced about by artificial disputations, is like a reed shaken by the wind.

1 This *'aḳīda* was translated by Professor Macdonald in his *Development*, p. 300 *sqq*. Large parts of the second book of the *Iḥyā'* have been translated by Dr H. Bauer, *Die Dogmatik al-Ghazālī's*.

When the boy clings to this simple faith and exercises himself in continence, the gates of divine guidance will be opened to him, and will reveal to him the truth of the creed by the divine light that corroborates God's promises. This is the precious gem and the summit of faith, of the upright as well as of the angels who are admitted to the divine presence.

Regarding *kalām* opinions are divided. Some declare it a *bid'a*, and as such prohibited. This was the view of Mālik, al-Shāfi'ī and Aḥmad ibn Ḥanbal. Others point to the fact that technical terms are used in other branches of knowledge also; the early generations of Islam were not acquainted with them, but this does not imply that their use is prohibited.

It must be recognized, says al-Ghazālī, that *kalām* by itself does not belong to what is prohibited or recommended. In one respect it is harmful: it usually leads to zealotism. As to its use, it is often thought that it reveals reality and lays bare the foundations of things. This, however, is far from being the truth. "If this were said to you by an adherent of Tradition or of anthropomorphism, you might think that people usually hate what they do not understand. But I speak as one who has descended to the bottom of *kalām* and who has reached the highest rank of the *mutakallimūn* and has been inspired with a hatred of it; as one who has dived into the depth of other cognate sciences and has come to the conviction that the way to the foundations of knowledge is blocked up on this side. Certainly, in some cases *kalām* is not void of all light and guidance, but usually it is profitable only in questions that can also be understood without intricate scholastic reasoning. Nay, it may be said that its use is limited to a single case: *kalām* may serve to prevent the dogmatic belief of the masses from being disturbed by disputations with schismatics. For the masses are weak-minded and easily troubled by the disputes of schismatics, however weak they may be. So the weak may be combated by the weak. The masses may cling to the '*aḳīda* we have communicated, because the law enjoins them to do so for the sake of their religious and temporal affairs, and because the pious ancestors have unanimously adhered to it. And the learned will cling to it in order to preserve the masses from the disturbing arguments of schismatics, just as rulers cling to the preservation of their possessions from sudden attacks of criminals and robbers.

"If it should thus be clear that *kalām* may be useful or obnoxious, its application must be like the application of a dangerous medicine by a skilful doctor, who makes use of it only in the appropriate place, time and measure.

"Consequently the masses who are occupied with handiwork and crafts must be left alone with their sound dogmas, with which they were imbued ever since they were taught the true creed mentioned above. To teach them the *kalām* would be utterly harmful. For often it arouses doubts in them and shakes their faith beyond recovery.

"When a man from the common people embraces a heretical view, he has to be brought back to the truth in a gentle, not in a harsh way, by kind words which humble the soul and produce an impression on the heart. Such methods, for example, the use of proofs from Kuran and Tradition of a parenetic and admonishing nature, are successful in keeping attention. This is more useful than disputations in the manner of the *mutakallimūn*. For when the man from the common people hears this scholastic reasoning, he believes that it belongs to a kind of dialectic technique which the *mutakallim* has learnt in order to bring people round to his belief. And if he, for his part, cannot find an answer, he supposes that those members of his sect who are trained in disputations, will be able to refute the arguments of the *mutakallim*.

"These are the two kinds of people with whom dogmatic debates are prohibited. They are likewise prohibited in the case of doubt. For doubt must be removed by gentleness and advice and arguments that are likely to be listened to and accepted, being totally different from the intricacies of *kalām*.

"Thoroughgoing debates may be useful in one case only, namely, when a man from the common people has been won over to a heresy by means of dialectic reasoning. In that case such reasoning may be contrasted with reasoning of a similar nature, so that he may return to the true belief. Yet this method must be applied exclusively to a man who has become so familiar with dialectics that common admonitions would fail to make him humble. Such a man is in a state which can be cured by dialectics only; so this medicine may be administered to him.

"In countries where heresies are of no importance and there is no variety of sects, such an explanation of dogmas as we have given above, without proofs, may be sufficient ere doubts appear. When these appear, proofs must be used according to the need for them.

"When, however, heresies are spreading and it is to be feared that youths will be won over to them, there is no objection to teaching them the measure of dogmatics we have expounded in our 'Letter from Jerusalem', in order to impair thereby the influence of heretical dialectics, if they have been exposed to it. Yet this measure is limited and precisely for this reason we have included it in the pamphlet mentioned.

"If any of these youths be of sharp wits so as to ask questions, or if doubts have arisen in his mind, then you are face to face with the dreaded malady, which undoubtedly manifests itself in this way. In this case there is no objection to having recourse to the measure of dogmatics we have given in our *Iḳtiṣād fi'l-I'tiḳād*. This book consists of fifty leaves only and it treats of the foundations of dogmatics to the exclusion of other subjects of *kalām*. If this book should satisfy him, he should be left alone. If, however, it should fail to make him humble, then the disease is chronic and the malady has spread through the whole body and is serious. The doctor must therefore be as gentle with him as possible and entrust the course of things to the decision of God, whether it be that the truth may be revealed to the sufferer through a divine hint, or whether it be that doubt and want of certainty should continue as long as it is the will of God."

al-Ghazālī next expounds his views on the exoteric and the esoteric sides of religion. He describes the position of those who go so far as to subtract all literal meaning from the text of the Kuran and the description of the last things, as well as the narrow orthodoxy of Aḥmad ibn Ḥanbal, who is said to have admitted an allegorical interpretation of three traditions only. Then he goes on:[1] "One of the parties, trying to follow a middle way, opens the door of allegorical interpretation regarding all that is related to the qualities of Allah; whereas they take in the literal sense the descriptions of the last things, which they do not allow to be interpreted allegorically. These are the Ash'arites.

"The Mu'tazilites go farther. They explain away Allah's being seen, and His being possessed of hearing and sight; Muhammad's ascension, which they deny to have taken place in a bodily way; the punishment in the tomb, the balance, the bridge and other eschatological representations.[2] Yet they confess the resurrection of the body, Paradise and its sensual pleasures, Hell and its bodily torments.

"The philosophers go farther than the Mu'tazilites. They interpret all eschatological representations as allegories denoting mental and spiritual pain, and mental and spiritual delight. They deny the resurrection of the body, but say that the soul is immortal and that it will be punished or made happy by punishment and delight of a non-sensual nature. They are extremists.

"The true middle path between a complete allegorism and rigid Ḥanbalism is narrow and obscure. It is found only by those who enjoy divine help and who reach the heart of things by divine light, not by hearsay. Then when the mysteries of things are revealed to them, so that they see them as they are, they return to Scripture and Tradition and their wording; whatever accords with what they

1 i. 96.
2 Cf. *infra*, Waṣīyat Abī Ḥanīfa, art. 18 *sqq.*

have witnessed by the light of certainty they affirm and whatever does not accord with it they interpret allegorically.

"For whoso conforms his insight in these things to the bare wording of Scripture and Tradition will thereby fail to find a secure resting-place and a well-defined standpoint, unless he should, in doing so, join the view of Aḥmad ibn Ḥanbal.

"But a closer definition of the middle way in these things would belong to the vast subject of esoteric knowledge, which we must leave aside. Our aim was only to make clear that the literal and the allegorical conceptions may be in harmony with one another.... For it is our opinion that for the common people the explanation of the catechism we have given is sufficient and that nothing further is incumbent on them in the first degree where they stand. But when disturbance is feared on account of the spread of heresies, in the second degree recourse may be had to a catechism in which there are brief outlines of proofs which yet do not reach to the bottom of things".

CHAPTER VI

The Fiḳh Akbar I

We have already seen that the confession of faith, the *shahāda*, has a personal form: "I witness that there is no God but Allah, and I witness that Muhammad is the Apostle of Allah". This personal form is in accordance with the fact that the *shahāda* did not arise out of the needs of the Muslim community, but was designed as the religious summary of Islam which was to be used by individuals.

The creed, on the other hand—as will be seen from its contents—arose out of the struggle of the community with dissenting elements. When the community had determined its position, it was incumbent upon it to express its conviction. This was done in the creed, which consequently represents the faith of the community in opposition to that of the sects.

This difference in origin and use between the confession of faith and the creed accounts for the fact that the latter is in no sense an elaborate version of the former. Nay, in the earliest form of the creed, the Fiḳh Akbar I, neither the idea of the unity of Allah nor that of the mission of Muhammad receives the slightest mention.

The fact that the creed is an utterance of the community accounts for the phenomenon that it speaks in the first person plural, "we". The Fiḳh Akbar II, it is true, opens in the singular, probably because by doing so it seeks to uphold the fiction of Abū Ḥanīfa's authorship; but, later, the singular is dropped in favour of the plural.

The singular, on the other hand, is the form appropriate to a strictly personal confession, as, for example, in the case of the *'aḳīda* of Muhammad ibn 'Abd al-Wahhāb.[1]

The third person plural is used in forms of the creed which do not pretend to be confessions, but objective

1 Translation by R. Hartmann in *Z.D.M.G.* LXXVIII. 176 *sqq.*

summaries of the faith of Islam. An example of this is seen in the summary given by al-As͟h'arī in his *Maḳālāt*,[1] in a chapter bearing the title "Account of the summary of the opinions of the people of the *ḥadīt͟h* and the people of the *sunna*".

Although the creed fixes the position of the community in face of the sects, it refrains from open polemics, a feature which it has in common with different forms of the Christian creed. Nevertheless the separate forms of the Muslim creed are full of hidden polemics. It is their contents and the sequence of their articles that show which were the heresies deemed to be the most dangerous in the days when they were composed. A comparison between the Fiḳh Akbar I and the Fiḳh Akbar II is also instructive in this respect.

We shall now proceed to translate different expositions of the creed. The translation will be followed by an explanation of the single articles of faith, as well as by a discussion of the genuineness, origin and general meaning of the documents. We shall begin with the Fiḳh Akbar I, which, it will be observed, is totally different from the Fiḳh Akbar II, translated and explained in Chapter VIII. It is a strange fact that neither in Arabic literature nor in the European catalogues of Arabic manuscripts is any discrimination made between the two.

PARALLEL ARTICLES IN OTHER CREEDS	THE FIḲH AKBAR I TRANSLATION
Waṣīyat Abī Ḥanīfa, art. 4 Fiḳh Akbar II, arts. 11, 14 Aḳīdat al-Ṭaḥāwī, art. 10	Art. 1. We do not consider anyone to be an infidel on account of sin; nor do we deny his faith.
	Art. 2. We enjoin what is just and prohibit what is evil.
Waṣīya, arts. 6, 7 Fiḳh Akbar II, arts. 7, 23 Ṭaḥāwī, arts. 1, 6	Art. 3. What reaches you could not possibly have missed you; and what misses you could not possibly have reached you.

1 i. 290–97.

Waṣiya, art. 10
Fiḳh Akbar II, art. 10

Art. 4. We disavow[1] none of the Companions of the Apostle of Allah; nor do we adhere to any of them exclusively.

Waṣiya, art. 10
Fiḳh Akbar II, art. 10

Art. 5. We leave the question of 'Uthmān and 'Alī to Allah, who knoweth the secret and hidden things.

Art. 6. Insight in matters of religion is better than insight in matters of [2]knowledge and law.[2]

Art. 7. Difference of opinion in the community is a token of divine mercy.

Art. 8. Whoso believeth all that he is bound to believe, except that he says, I do not know whether Moses and Jesus (peace be upon them) do or do not belong to the Apostles, is an infidel.[3]

Art. 9. Whoso sayeth, I do not know whether Allah is in Heaven or on the earth, is an infidel.

Waṣīya, art. 18
Fiḳh Akbar II, arts. 21, 23
Ṭaḥāwī, art. 18

Art. 10. Whoso sayeth, I do not know the punishment in the tomb, belongeth to the sect of the Djahmites, which goeth to perdition.

COMMENTARY

Ad art. 1. It is significant that the first article of this creed is directed against the chief theological thesis of the Khāridjites,[4] who declared anyone guilty of a grave sin to be devoid of faith and an infidel; only by repenting could he become faithful anew, else he would be punished in Hell, abiding in it for ever. They adduced in favour of this view sura iv. 95: "Whoever shall kill a believer of set purpose, his recompense is Hell; for ever shall he abide in it". According to Ibn 'Abbās "for ever" in this verse means "for a long time"; and the common orthodox explanation of "killing" is "declaring that killing is

1 Reading تتبرأ with the MS. Berlin Wetzstein II No. 1785, instead of نبرا of the printed text.

2–2 Some MSS. read "law and *snuan*".

3 Some MSS. add "because he rejects the text" (of the Kuran).

4 Cf. *supra*, p. 40.

allowed".[1] It need not be emphasized that these explanations are wrong and that the Khāridjites were right. Nor was this verse from the Kuran the only text the Khāridjites could adduce in favour of their view. There is a well-known tradition in which Muhammad says: "Between faith and unbelief lies the neglect of prayer".[2] It belongs to the old stock of traditions, which in all probability date from the time before the rise of the Khāridjites; and it proves that early Islam attached the greatest value to religious observance. When, however, the Khāridjites had driven the community to the opposite quarter, the latter could no longer take the verse from the Kuran or the tradition in its plain sense; it therefore had recourse to preposterous explanations such as those mentioned above. According to the commentary on the Fiḳh Akbar I, Mālik, al-Shāfi'ī and the great majority of ancient and recent theologians interpret the tradition in this sense, that he who neglects prayer becomes thereby *fāsiḳ*,[3] his fault being a fault of behaviour, not of faith. Such an one must be admonished; should he refuse to repent, he should be killed. Another group of ancient theologians, however, was of opinion that he who neglects prayer must be stigmatized as an infidel; this was the view of 'Alī, Aḥmad ibn Ḥanbal (according to a report), 'Abd Allāh ibn al-Mubārak, Isḥāḳ ibn Rahūyā and some Shāfi'ī doctors. Abū Ḥanīfa and a group of theologians from Kūfa denied that he who neglects prayer is an infidel; such an one must not be killed, but imprisoned till he prays.

In this connection it may be remembered that even the law has stigmatized the *fāsiḳ* by excluding him from acting as a legal witness.

In regard to the relation between orthodoxy and the sects, we may observe that in the oldest forms of the creed

1 Cf. Fiḳh Akbar II, art. 11.

2 Muslim, *Īmān*, trad. 134; cf. al-Tirmidhī, *Īmān*, b. 9; al-Baghdādī, *Uṣūl*, p. 190.

3 *Supra*, p. 40.

there occur articles of faith which are directed against the Khāridjites and the Shī'ites, whereas those which attack the Murdjites, Djabrites, anthropomorphists and other sects are rare. This fact rests mainly on the far-reaching harmony between early orthodoxy and the Murdjites, Djabrites and anthropomorphists. It may even be supposed that at least some of these and other cognate groups came to be looked upon as sects after the rise of the Ash'arite school only. This school sought to adopt the mean between several groups of extremes, and it was precisely this attitude which promoted its influence and contributed to make it the official representative of orthodox Islam. In reality such "extremes" as Djabrites, Ṣifatites and anthropomorphists were not sects at all, but the remnants of early orthodoxy, who were branded as sects because the new orthodoxy took a direction different from theirs.

Ad art. 2. Enjoining what is just and prohibiting what is evil is recommended in the Kuran (cf. sura iii. 100, 106, 110; vii. 156; ix. 72, 113; xxii. 42; xxxi. 16). This attitude makes the Muslim community the conscience of the world (sura iii. 100, 106). It is the Apostle from the Gentiles who preaches this before the Jews and Christians (sura vii. 156); and it is the Faithful who strengthen one another by it (sura ix. 72), for it is a virtue which ranks with prayer and alms (sura xxii. 42; xxxi. 16; cf. ix. 113).

Many traditions are related to the same effect.[1] In one of these it is asked how the commandment must be carried out. The question is attached to the story, so well known in Tradition, of how Marwān on a day of festival introduced a new order of service by holding the sermon before prayer. On this someone remarked: "First prayer, then sermon". Marwān answered: "That order of service has been abandoned". Thereupon Abū Sa'īd al-Khudrī said: "As to this man, he has done what is his duty. I

1 Bukhārī, *Zakāt*, b. 23; *Maẓālim*, b. 22, etc.

heard the Apostle say: Whoso seeth what is reprehensible (*munkar*) must correct it with his hand. If this should be impossible for him, with his tongue. If this too should be impossible for him, with his mind. This is the minimum of faith".[1]

According to al-Nawawī there is unanimity of opinion as to the obligatory force of this commandment, which is founded on Kuran and *sunna*. Some of the Rāfiḍites alone fail to recognize the obligation. This can be easily understood in connection with the fact that the S͟hīʿites are adherents of the theory and practice of *taḳīya*, which is exactly the opposite of *taig͟hyīr*.

It may be remarked that the practice of opposition to unlawful things was not always prominent among the adherents of orthodoxy, who were in a large measure quietists to such an extent that the commandment became a phrase which was regarded as being peculiar to the Muʿtazilites.[2]

According to the commentary on the Fiḳh Akbar I this article is directed against the D͟jabrites who referred to sura v. 104 ("He who erreth shall not hurt you, when ye have the guidance"). But this, it continues, is erroneous, for it is only the fact of being hurt with a view to the other world which is denied here, whereas the duty of enjoining what is just is based on sura iii. 100.

Ad art. 3. This is the orthodox protest against the view of the Ḳadarites. This expression of the dogma of predestination, which is also in the *ʿaḳīda* of al-Ṭaḥāwī,[3] has found its way into canonical Tradition—a curious indication of the genesis of *ḥadīt͟h*. The text of the tradition in question is as follows: "I visited", says Ibn al-Dailamī,

1 Muslim, *Īmān*, trad. 78; Aḥmad ibn Ḥanbal, iii. 52 *sq.*, 92, etc. On the importance of the duty of *tag͟hyīr al-munkar*, see Goldziher, *Le livre de Mohammed ibn Toumert*, pp. 62, 85 *sqq.*, and *Z.D.M.G.* XLI. 56 *sqq.*

2 Masʿūdī, *Murūd͟j*, vi. 20 *sqq.*; Arnold, *al-Muʿtazilah*, p. 6.

3 al-G͟hazālī is still acquainted with it, *Kitāb al-Arbaʿīn*, p. 282[4].

"Ubaiy ibn Ka'b[1] and said to him: Doubts concerning predestination have arisen in my heart. Possibly Allah will make them vanish if you communicate to me a tradition on this subject. He answered: If Allah should punish the inhabitants of His heavens and the inhabitants of His earth, He would not thereby do injustice. And if you should spend in the path of Allah an amount larger than mount Uḥud,[2] He would not accept it from you unless you believe in the decree and acknowledge that what reaches you could not possibly have missed you, and what misses you could not possibly have reached you. And if you should die in a different conviction, you would go to Hell". Ibn al-Dailamī continues: "Then I went to 'Abd Allah ibn Mas'ūd[3] and heard the same from him, and likewise from Hudhaifa ibn al-Yamān.[4] Then I went to Zaid ibn Thābit, who communicated to me a similar tradition on the authority of the Prophet".[5]

It is hardly necessary to say that the background of this tradition is highly questionable. In al-Tirmidhī's collection, as well as in Aḥmad ibn Ḥanbal's *Musnad*, a tradition betraying the same tendency is related on the authority of Muhammad.[6] In a second tradition in Abū Dāwūd's collection[7] the sentence is put into the mouth of 'Ubāda ibn al-Ṣāmit. But in this version it has still the form of a personal saying of 'Ubāda, as will appear from its translation: "My son, thou wilt not experience the taste of essential faith, ere thou knowest that what reacheth thee could not possibly have missed thee, and what misseth thee could not possibly have reached thee. I heard the Apostle of Allah say: The first thing Allah created was the pen. He said to it: Write. It asked:

1 One of the readers of the Kuran and an authority on theological questions.

2 Near Madina.

3 Muhammad's former servant and a famous authority on traditions.

4 Who was renowned for his piety.

5 Abū Dāwūd, *Sunna*, b. 16.

6 *Ḳadar*, b. 10; *Musnad*, vi. 441.

7 Abū Dāwūd, *loc. cit.*

Lord, what shall I write? He answered: Write the destinies of all things till the advent of the Hour. My son, I heard the Prophet of Allah say: Whoso dieth with a belief differing from this, he belongeth not to me".

The commentator attaches to this article a discussion of how far evil is caused by Allah's will. As the orthodox opinion concerning this question is expressed in the Waṣīyat Abī Ḥanīfa, we shall deal with the question in our comment on art. 8 of this creed.

Ad art. 4. This article is directed against the followers of ʿAlī, who raised him to a rank above that of the other Companions. Some went so far as to consider Abū Bakr, ʿUmar and ʿUthmān as usurpers. The verb *bariʾa* which is used here, and which is known from sura ix, the *sūrat al-barāʾa*, seems to have been a favourite term with the Khāridjites, who used it to emphasize their separatism. It is said, *e.g.* of Nāfiʿ ibn al-Azraḳ al-Ḥanafī, that his special points were the *barāʾa* from the moderate party (*al-ḳaʿada*),[1] the examination of the feelings of those who wanted to join his camp (*ʿaskar*) and the *takfīr* of those who did not perform the *hidjra* to him.[2]

Ad art. 5. "By this article", says the commentator, "the author does not express his doubts concerning this question; but he chooses the safest way, that is, of restraining our tongue from this *fitna*, just as Allah has made us restrain our swords from it."

The first *fitna* caused a schism between those whose aim was vengeance for the murder of ʿUthmān and those who took the part of ʿAlī. The orthodox community did not, however, pronounce an official verdict on this question. Yet the murder of ʿUthmān became the cause of two schisms that were never to be mended—the schism of the Shīʿites and that of the Khāridjites.

The attitude of orthodox Islam as expressed in the

1 Cf. Houtsma, *De strijd over het dogma*, p. 27.
2 al-Ashʿarī, *Maḳālāt*, i. 86; cf. p. 90.

present article is a proof of its catholic tendencies, based on the instinct of self-preservation. This attitude is also expressed in the fact that some of the canonical collections of Tradition contain a chapter on the Companions in which the merits of Abū Bakr, 'Umar and 'Uthmān as well as those of 'Alī are enumerated. The only difference made between the four is that the historical sequence is said to correspond with the hierarchic one,[1] as this is expressed in the parallel articles of other creeds.[2]

Ad art. 6. The terminology of this article is archaic and produces a somewhat blunt expression. The use of *fiḳh*[3] in the original sense of "insight" became antiquated when the word acquired the technical sense of "jurisprudence". *Fiḳh* in the sense of "insight" does not occur in the Kuran, but frequently in Tradition: "It is a proof of a man's *fiḳh* that he goes straight to his purpose".[4] "It is a proof of a man's *fiḳh* that he says *Allāh a'lam* in matters of which he has no knowledge."[5]

In a well-known tradition the term is applied to religious matters: "When Allah has good intentions regarding a man, he instructs him in religious things".[6]

In another tradition *fiḳh* is mentioned side by side with faith: "Faith is from Yaman and *fiḳh* is from Yaman".[7] The latter tradition occurs also in the following form: "*Fiḳh* is from Yaman and wisdom is from Yaman".[8]

It is a remarkable fact that *fiḳh* in the technical sense of jurisprudence hardly occurs in canonical Tradition. Likewise *faḳīh* in that literature has not yet received the

1 Cf. especially Abū Dāwūd, *Sunna*, b. 6.

2 Waṣīyat Abī Ḥanīfa, art. 6.

3 Cf. Sachau, *Zur ältesten Geschichte*. 4 Bukhārī, *Adhān*, b. 42.

5 Muslim, *Ṣifāt al-Munāfiḳīn*, trad. 40.

6 Bukhārī, *'Ilm*, b. 10, 13; Muslim, *Imāra*, trad. 175. A similar combination of *fiḳh* and religion is given in Bukhārī, *Wuḍū'*, b. 10; al-Tirmidhī, *Witr*, b. 21; *'Ilm*, b. 4; *Manāḳib*, b. 19; Abū Dāwūd, *Ṭahāra*, b. 120, etc.

7 Muslim, *Īmān*, trad. 82; cf. 84.

8 Bukhārī, *Maghāzī*, b. 74.

special sense of *juris peritus*. It usually means "theologian", *e.g.* in the tradition: "One *faḳīh* is more annoying to Satan than a thousand (of the Faithful) who perform their ceremonial duties".[1]

Apparently the application of the term *fiḳh* to jurisprudence had not yet acquired general currency in the first century A.H.

A similar linguistic archaism is seen in the use of the terms *'ilm* and *ḥudūd*,[2] which in this article convey the meaning of what in later language was expressed by the single term *fiḳh*.

In the language of Tradition *'ilm* is used in the sense of religious knowledge, especially in connection with *ḥadīth* itself, whereas theological knowledge, apart from *ḥadīth*, would simply be brain-work (*ra'y*).

It must further be observed that *ḥudūd* in this article has not the special sense of penal law, which it received later, but the general sense of law or ordinances.

This is also the meaning of *ḥudūd* in the Kuran, where this term covers the ordinances of fasting,[3] of divorce,[4] of inheritances,[5] as well as the precepts of Allah in a general sense, *e.g.* "Those who turn to God in penitence, those who worship, who praise, who fast, who bow down, who prostrate themselves, who enjoin what is right and forbid what is unlawful and keep to the ordinances of God, shall have their recompense".[6]

In this general sense the term is also used in Tradition: "Those who maintain the ordinances of Allah and those who counteract them, can be compared with...".[7] On the whole, however, in this literature *ḥudūd* is used in the sense of penal law.

From the data assembled above it is clear that the terms

1 al-Tirmidhī, *'Ilm*, b. 19.

2 The *Fiḳh Absaṭ*, fol. 24 *b*, reads *aḥkām* instead of *'ilm* and *ḥudūd*.

3 Sura ii. 183

4 Sura ii. 229 *sq.*; lviii. 5; lxv. 1.

5 Sura iv. 17 *sq.*

6 Sura ix. 113.

7 Bukhārī, *Shirka*, b. 6.

fiḳh, *'ilm* and *ḥudūd* are used in the present article in their early, non-technical sense, which is an indication of the early origin of the Fiḳh Akbar I.

Finally, it may be observed that the version of the present article in the *Fiḳh Absaṭ* is the following: "*Fiḳh* in religion is more excellent than *fiḳh* in law; serving Allah is better than gathering knowledge".

Ad art. 7. This is another instance of an article of faith which has found its way into Tradition, though not to the canonical collections. The latter are not acquainted with the special sense in which *ikhtilāf*[1] is used in our *'aḳīda* as well as in later Tradition.

In canonical *ḥadīth* the term *ikhtilāf* is used in connection with theological discussions which are regarded as the beginnings of rationalism,[2] and which Muhammad is represented as abhorring. Here may follow some specimens of his alleged sayings on the subject: "Leave me alone as long as I leave you alone. Those who were before you were destroyed on account of their asking questions and their differing from their Prophets. Therefore, when I prohibit a thing, avoid it; and when I order it, perform it as much as is possible for you."[3] 'Abd Allāh ibn 'Umar related that two men were warmly discussing the meaning of a verse from the Kuran. When Muhammad heard this, he became angry and said: "Those who were before you were destroyed on account of their discussions regarding the book".[4] "One day, after morning prayer, the Apostle of Allah delivered to us a sermon so eloquent that tears fell from our eyes and our hearts trembled. Then a man said: O Apostle of Allah, this is a farewell sermon; what dost thou command us by thy last will? He said: I command you to fear God and to be obedient servants

1 On this tradition cf. also Goldziher, *Die Ẓâhiriten*, p. 94 *sqq*.

2 *Supra*, p. 54.

3 Bukhārī, *I'tiṣām*, b. 2; Muslim, *Faḍā'il*, trad. 130; al-Tirmidhī, *'Ilm*, b. 17.

4 Muslim, *'Ilm*, trad. 2.

even [if your *imām* were] an Abyssinian slave. For whoever of you liveth long, shall witness many dissensions (*ikhtilāf*); but beware ye of novel things, for they are errors. Whoever liveth to see this should cling to my *sunna* and to the *sunna* of the well-guided caliphs, who walked in the right path."[1]

A second sense of *ikhtilāf* is found, *e.g.* in the *Risāla fī Uṣūl al-Fiḳh*[2] of al-Shāfi'ī. Here it means discrepancy between traditions, such as those on the *tashahhud*, on *ṣarf* in connection with usury, on the time of the morning *ṣalāt*, on killing women and children of the enemy, and so on. al-Shāfi'ī uses the term also in the third sense, which has become the technical meaning of the word, that of *ikhtilāf al-fuḳahā'*, *i.e.* variety of opinion between the doctors of the law.[3]

It is this latter kind of *ikhtilāf* which in the Fiḳh Akbar I as well as in post-canonical Tradition is called a sign of the mercy of God towards the community. The idea of *ikhtilāf* survived chiefly in this sense. The remembrance of its ancient relation with theological dissensions did not, however, fall wholly into oblivion, as appears from an utterance of 'Alī al-Ḳārī:[4] "Divergence of opinions as to juridical matters is a mercy; as to matters of dogmatics and Islam it is error and innovation".

Ad art. 8. The scriptural basis of this article is sura ii. 285: "Each one believeth in God and His angels and His scriptures and His Apostles: We make no distinction between His Apostles", and sura iv. 151 (cf. 149): "And they who believe in God and His Apostles, and make no difference between them, on these will we bestow their reward at last".[5]

1 al-Tirmidhī, *'Ilm*, b. 16.

2 P. 38 *sqq*.

3 P. 77 *sqq*.

4 Commentary on Fiḳh Akbar II, p. 100.

5 In sura ii. 254 and xvii. 57 it is stated that Allah preferred some of the Apostles in some respects to others. This does not contradict the verses translated in the text, Allah being free to lavish His grace on whom He pleases.

The commentators say that these verses were directed against the Jews and Christians, the former rejecting the apostleship of 'Īsā and Muhammad, the latter that of Mūsā and Muhammad. This explanation would make it probable that the present article is also directed against the Jews and Christians.

Against this explanation, however, there is the objection that this would be the sole instance of polemics in relation to other religions to be found in the early forms of the creed. We have already seen that the creeds attack the views of sectarians. As regards the special heresy mentioned in our article, I know only one instance of a Muslim sect, namely that of the Ghassānīya, which denied the apostleship of Jesus.[1] It seems to me very questionable whether this sect was of such importance that its views were attacked in the present creed.

We shall therefore have to look for another explanation, without the help of the commentary, which is silent on this point. On the one hand this article may be supposed to take the place of pronouncement on apostleship in general, such as occurs *e.g.* in the Fiḳh Akbar II[2] and in the later '*aḳīda*'s. On the other hand it may correspond to a curious prohibition which also has a place in later catechisms. The growing number of Apostles and Prophets made it impossible for ordinary Muslims to become acquainted with their merits and their personal value; in fact, it was not long before they were counted by tens of thousands. Later catechisms accordingly declare it obligatory to acknowledge all of them, without being acquainted with their names or their number.[3]

Canonical Tradition contains prohibitions of a similar tendency. Abū Dāwūd's chapter *Sunna* has a section which bears the title "On preference for some of the Prophets",[4] in which Muhammad is represented as prohibiting people from making comparisons between the

1 *Khiṭaṭ*, ii. 350. 2 Art. 8.
3 *Infra*, commentary on Fiḳh Akbar II, art. 1.
4 Bab 13.

Prophets, including himself. The commentators are at a loss to explain the tendency of these traditions.[1]

A point to be remarked is the evolution of ideas regarding this subject. The commentator on the Fiḳh Akbar I discloses[2] to us that the orthodox sheikhs disputed among themselves on the question who was more excellent, Adam or Muhammad. It may be supposed that at the basis of such disputations was the growing tendency to elevate Muhammad above the rank of the Apostles.

It is not very probable that the present article contains a polemical sting in this direction. At any rate it was unable to check the tendency just mentioned. As early as the fifth century A.H. the majority of the community declared it allowable to acknowledge the superiority of some of the Apostles to others, and the superiority of Muhammad to any of them.[3]

Ad art. 9. The explanation given by the commentary is as follows: Whoso declares himself ignorant of whether Allah is in Heaven or on earth is an infidel, such a declaration being based upon the belief that Allah is in some place, be it Heaven or earth, and this is unbelief, for Allah is not in a place.

If the commentator were right, the article would be the expression of a spiritualizing tendency going so far as to stigmatize as unbelief a more conservative or orthodox view. This would contradict all we know of the Fiḳh Akbar I and its position. So we must assume that the commentator ascribes to the author of our '*aḳīda* the views of later *kalām*, which, as a matter of fact, went far in the spiritualizing direction.

Quite a different explanation of the article, and without any doubt the true one, is found in a tradition related on the authority of Abū Muṭī' al-Balkhī, one of the disciples of Abū Ḥanīfa, who relates that "he asked his master's

1 Cf. al-Nawawī, on Muslim, *Faḍā'il*, trad. 163 (v. 132 *sq.*).
2 P. 27.
3 al-Baghdādī, *Uṣūl*, i. 297 *sq.*

opinion of one who says: I do not know whether Allah is in Heaven or on earth. Abū Ḥanīfa answered: He is an infidel, for Allah says:[1] The Merciful has seated Himself on the throne, and His throne is above His Heavens. I answered: He acknowledges that Allah seated Himself on His throne, but he declares himself ignorant whether the throne is in Heaven or on earth. Abū Ḥanīfa answered: If he does not affirm that the throne is in Heaven, he is an unbeliever".[2]

I do not know any grounds against the genuineness of this tradition. But even if they existed there would remain the established fact that early Islam clung to the sitting of Allah on His throne, though with the restriction of *balkafīya*.[3] Even al-Ash'arī in his *Ibāna*[4] combats with vigour any allegorical or spiritual explanation of Allah's sitting on His throne,[5] and in his *Maḳālāt*[6] the opinion that Allah should be in no place is regarded as that of a section of the Mu'tazilites.

It is remarkable that in the fourth century A.H. the whole picture appears in a different light. The Mu'tazilite opinion, that God is in no place, was accepted among the dogmas of the Ash'arites and succeeded in receiving the stamp of orthodoxy. Evidence of this is found in 'Abd al-Ḳāhir al-Baghdādī (†429 = 1037/38), whose *Uṣūl al-Dīn* contains a section bearing the title "On the absurdity of the idea that God should be connected with one place particularly".[7] It is in this sense that the commentator of the Fikh Akbar I interprets the present article,[8] though wrongly, as we have seen.

Finally, it may be asked whether this article, in the blunt-

1 Sura vii. 52.

2 Cited by Schreiner, "Beiträge zur Geschichte der theologischen Bewegungen", in *Z.D.M.G.* LII. 529, note 5.

3 *Supra*, p. 86.

4 P. 42 *sqq.*

5 *Supra*, p. 90.

6 i. 212.

7 P. 76 *sqq.*; cf. pp. 112–14; 'Abd Allāh ibn Aḥmad ibn Ḥanbal, *Kitāb al-Sunna*, p. 216 *sqq.*; Fakhr al-Dīn al-Rāzī, iii. 8.

8 *Supra*, p. 68 *sqq.*, on the spiritualizing ideas of Christianity.

ness of its expression, does not aim at the rejection of spiritualizing tendencies in general. A similar tendency appears in the following article.

Ad art. 10. The punishment in the tomb probably stands for eschatological notions such as are mentioned in later creeds: the examination of the dead by Munkar and Nakīr, the balance, the bridge, and so on.

The commentator mentions three verses from the Kuran as the scriptural basis of the dogma of the punishment in the tomb, viz. sura ix. 102: "And of the people of Madina some are stubborn in hypocrisy...twice will We chastise them; then they shall be given over to a great chastisement". It is not universally agreed, however, that one of the three punishments mentioned in this verse is the punishment in the tomb. The second verse is sura lii. 47: "And verily besides this is there a punishment for the evil-doers". The latter punishment is that of Hell; the commentators of the Kuran mention, however, several kinds of punishment in explanation of the other one, the punishment in the tomb being only one out of many. The third verse from the Kuran is sura xxiii. 21: "And We will surely cause them to taste a punishment yet nearer to hand, besides the greater punishment". If the latter is again the punishment in the other world, it is probable that by the former the punishment in this world is meant. al-Baiḍāwī does not even mention the punishment in the tomb in connection with this verse.

It is curious that the commentator of the Fiḳh Akbar I has not mentioned other passages from the Kuran which seem to afford better evidence, viz. sura vi. 93: "But couldst thou see, when the ungodly are in the floods of death, and the angels reach forth their hands, saying, Yield up your souls: this day shall ye be recompensed with a humiliating punishment"; and sura xlvii. 29: "But how when the angels, causing them to die, shall smite them on their faces and their backs". Another passage is sura viii. 52: "And if thou wert to see when the angels take the life of the unbelievers: they smite their faces and their backs, and—Taste ye the torture of burning". Even this verse is connected by al-Baiḍāwī in the first place with the battle of Badr, in which angels with fiery maces are said to have beaten the enemy.

The punishment in the tomb is, on the other hand, a favourite topic in Tradition. One of the oft-repeated traditions on the subject is as follows: "The Apostle of Allah passed by two graves. He said: Verily these are being punished, and they are not punished on account of a grave sin. One of them was a backbiter and the other neglected purity regarding urine. Then the Apostle of Allah asked for a fresh palm-branch. This he rent into two pieces, and planted one of them on each grave, saying: Perhaps they will find relief, as long as these branches are not yet withered".[1]

It need hardly be said that this tradition gives rise to many questions. We may remark only that we are here face to face with ancient popular beliefs, dating from a time when the resurrection as well as a common abode of the dead were still unknown. Similar representations were current among the Jews.[2]

A second type of traditions which is adduced in favour, and as an illustration, of the punishment in the tomb, is the following, in which Zaid ibn T͟hābit is the narrator: "One day we were in an enclosure belonging to the Banu 'l-Nad͟jd͟jār, in the company of the Apostle of Allah, who was riding on a mule. Suddenly the beast threatened to throw him down, by making a side-leap, being terrified by five or six graves. The Apostle of Allah asked: Who of you knew the people who were buried here? A man said: I. The Apostle of Allah asked: When did they die? He answered: In the time of polytheism. Then the Apostle of Allah said: Verily, this generation is tormented in their

1 Muslim, *Ṭahāra*, trad. 111 and parallels (cf. *Handbook of Early Muhammadan Tradition*, p. 89 *b*, at the top).

2 Sale, *Preliminary Discourse*, p. 101; Bodenschatz, *Kirchliche Verfassung der heutigen Juden*, III. 95 *sq*.

tombs, and were it not that you would object to bury one another, I would pray Allah to let you hear of the punishment in the tomb what I hear of it. Then he turned to us, saying: Take refuge with Allah from the punishment in the tomb. This he said twice".[1]

This and similar traditions are based upon the popular belief that the dead are not deprived of the human faculty of perception. In accordance with this belief it is stated in the Fiḳh Akbar II that body and spirit are reunited in the tomb.[2] Apparently these notions stand apart from the idea of the *Barzakh*, the intermediate state of the soul between death and resurrection.

A third type of traditions declares the punishment in the tomb to be a consequence of the wailing of the living.[3]

It was only natural that those sects which indulged in more or less spiritualizing tendencies and laid stress on the ethical side of eschatology could not look very favourably upon such representations. In the text of the article it is the Djahmites who are blamed for their rejection of the punishment in the tomb. The commentators, al-Nawawī[4] and al-Ash'arī,[5] reckon the Khawāridj, the Ḳadarites and the Mu'tazilites among those who rejected the popular eschatology.[6] As to Djahm ibn Ṣafwān, his period is certain owing to the report that he was put to death at Marw about the end of the reign of the Umaiyads.[7] Descriptions of his dogmatic views have reached us in the form of a number of more or less heretical doctrines.[8] Their lack of coherence is due to the fact that Djahm does not entirely accord in his doctrines with any of the well-known schools. At the time when he was killed, the

1 Muslim, *Djanna*, trad. 67. The dogmatic questions are in al-Nawawī's commentary.

2 Art. 23; 'Alī al-Ḳārī, p. 90 *sq.*

3 Aḥmad ibn Ḥanbal, i. 36, 51; al-Ṭayālisī, Nos. 15, 33.

4 See note 1.

5 *Maḳālāt*, i. 127.

6 Cf. also al-Īdjī, pp. 269 *sqq.*, 633.

7 Ṭabarī, ed. de Goeje, II. 1924.

8 al-Baghdādī, *Farḳ*; al-Shahrastānī, i. 60; *Kitāb al-Intiṣār*, index, p. 232.

Khāridjites and the Ḳadarites were flourishing sects; the Mu'tazilites, on the other hand, were only in the beginnings of their development. The views of Djahm are in opposition to those of the older sects. It may be asked whether the points which he has in common with the Mu'tazilites are due to the influence of this sect, or a consequence of his own system.

In opposition to the Khāridjites Djahm held the view that faith is of an intellectual nature, being simply knowledge, whereas unbelief is simply ignorance.[1] The identification of faith and knowledge was a doctrine of the Murdjites, which was received into some forms of the orthodox creed.[2] A consequence of this doctrine was that little importance was attached to works or to the ethical and emotional sides of religion. In the case of Djahm the intellectual conception of faith went hand in hand with the rejection of the smallest degree of free will in man. To him Allah is the only active Power in the Universe and any expression which attributes action to any being besides Him is wrong. We say: The tree moves, the sphere rotates, the sun declines; actually, it is Allah who causes these movements and who creates will and choice in man.

The emphasis laid on the overwhelming individuality of Allah, which was truly Islamic,[3] led a consistent thinker, such as Djahm appears to have been, to the doctrine of absolute *tawḥīd*, which contradicted orthodoxy in two points.

The first of these points is this: Allah being the unique mover of the world, He must necessarily remain the only being in the world as soon as He ceases to preserve it. Allah will, therefore, become as lonely as He was before the creation. Paradise and Hell, belonging to the created

1 al-Ash'arī, *Maḳālāt*, i. 279. The other characteristics of Djahm's doctrine are also taken from this work. Cf. also *infra*, p. 132; *Le monde oriental*, xxv. 36, note 5; 'Abd Allāh b. Aḥmad b. Ḥanbal, *Kitāb al-Sunna*, pp. 4 *sqq.*, 30 *sqq.*, 169 *sqq.*, 183 *sq.*

2 Cf. Fiḳh Akbar II, art. 19.

3 *Supra*, p. 49 *sq.*

world, will vanish together with it. A consequence of this view was the denial of eternal reward and punishment.[1]

The second consequence of D̲j̲ahm's absolute *tawḥīd*—apart from the rejection of Allah's being a thing (*s̲h̲ai'*)—was the denial of His eternal qualities. The Kuran could not be uncreated, for an uncreated Kuran would be a second eternal being side by side with Allah. Nay, even the knowledge of Allah, being originated (*muḥdat̲h̲*), could not be admitted in the sense of prescience. In this respect D̲j̲ahm comes near to the Mu'tazilite position, from which he was in other respects, as a pure Islamic thinker, far removed.

In the present article D̲j̲ahm is mentioned by name as one who denied the punishment in the tomb. As far as I can see, the Arabic sources do not mention this special point among the views of D̲j̲ahm. This corroborates our conjecture that, in this as well as in other instances, our creed mentions special points where it has in view ideas of a general nature. In the present article it aims at the maintenance of traditional eschatology as a whole.

Now it may be that the D̲j̲ahmites are mentioned as the opponents of this doctrine because they radically denied the eternity of Paradise and Hell. It is well known, however, that the Mu'tazilites, by virtue of their spiritualizing tendencies, also rejected much of popular eschatology. The fact that the system of D̲j̲ahm coincided with that of the Mu'tazilites in two points may have brought about a confusion of which the wording of our article is possibly an indication. Such a confusion seems to have prevailed among those who in describing the system of D̲j̲ahm start from the points which it has in common with the Mu'tazilites. What I have sought to show is that its logical thread can only be found by beginning from its truly Islamic side.

Reviewing the contents of the Fiḳh Akbar I we find that this form of the creed maintains the orthodox position on the following points: (*a*) faith and works (art. 1); (*b*) pre-

1 Cf. Waṣīyat Abī Ḥanīfa, art. 27.

destination and free will (art. 3); (*c*) anthropomorphism (art. 9); (*d*) eschatology (art. 10). This means that it rejects the views of the Kh̲āridj̲ites, Ḳadarites and Dj̲ahmites; moreover arts. 4 and 5 attack the tenets of the Sh̲ī'a. Suggestions of a doctrine of faith and of prophecy may be hidden in arts. 6 and 8, but art. 7 must be considered as an acknowledgment of the importance of the community and of the consensus. Curiously enough, Allah and Muhammad are lacking.

These positive and negative features authorize us to state again that this creed did not arise out of the *sh̲ahāda*, but out of the necessity felt by the community to formulate its views in face of the sects.

What is its origin? Tradition ascribes it to Abū Ḥanīfa; yet it does so hesitatingly. The printed text claims "to be ascribed to Abū Ḥanīfa"; the same words occur in the commentary with the addition of "by sound chains of tradition". The *Fihrist*[1] mentions *al-Fiḳh al-Akbar* among the works of Abū Ḥanīfa; but it cannot be determined whether our '*aḳīda* is meant or the Fiḳh Akbar II. This evidence is not satisfactory. There is, moreover, the peculiar circumstance that the text has not come down to us separately, but as a part of the commentary. The latter is ascribed to Abū Manṣūr al-Māturīdī, the well-known dogmatist, on the title-page of the Haidarabad edition. This ascription seems to be due to the fact that in the text of the commentary this authority is cited several times. Actually this cannot be an argument in favour of the authorship of al-Māturīdī. Moreover, in the other manuscripts which I have consulted, the attribution of the work to al-Māturīdī is lacking and many of the citations in the text are given on the authority of different scholars.

The author of the commentary belongs to the school of Ḥanafī theologians which goes back chiefly to al-Māturīdī. To him the Ash̲'arites represent a different school. He mentions several times points of difference "between us and the Ash̲'arites". I doubt whether precise indications

1 Ed. Fluegel, p. 202.

of his period can be found in his work. On p. 13 he mentions one Ismāʿīl in support of the opinion that "in our time enjoining what is just and prohibiting what is evil" is no longer obligatory. He mentions the dogmatic school of Samarḳand, *i.e.* the spiritual progeny of al-Māturīdī. The vulgarisms of language which are to be found in the printed text do not occur in the Berlin MS. Further, all details of *kalām* such as are favoured by commentators on catechisms are lacking.

The commentary therefore leaves unanswered the question of the authenticity of the Fiḳh Akbar I. We possess, however, another document which contains valuable indications, namely, the *Fiḳh Absaṭ*. It rests on the answers given by Abū Ḥanīfa to questions regarding dogmatics put to him by his pupil Abū Muṭīʿ al-Balkhī. So far as I can see, this pamphlet, a unique copy of which is preserved in Cairo,[1] is genuine. Here we find, as a matter of fact, all the articles of the Fiḳh Akbar I, with the exception of art. 7. This makes it probable that the editor and commentator of the Fiḳh Akbar I has borrowed the text on which he commented from the *Fiḳh Absaṭ*. So the Fiḳh Akbar I, though not composed by Abū Ḥanīfa, is proved to be derived from genuine utterances of the master, with the possible exception of art. 7.

Regarding the general position of the Fiḳh Akbar I the following points may be considered:

The dissensions of the sects are of such importance that the editor does not think of enumerating the chief articles of faith. Characteristic in this respect is the absence of Allah and Muhammad.

Articles on the qualities of Allah and on the Kuran are lacking.

An article in which the Murdjites are attacked is lacking. Abū Ḥanīfa largely shared Murdjite views. In this connection it is perhaps significant that the creed opens with an article against the Khāridjites, who were the chief opponents of the Murdjites, and that articles on the nature

1 See References at the end of the book, *in voce* Abū Ḥanīfa.

of faith and on eternal punishment and reward are lacking.

The article on predestination (art. 2) does not enter into the question of the provenance of the actions of man, as is the case in later forms of the creed. It seems to have in view the Ḳadarites, not the Mu'tazilites.

In summarizing these facts and conclusions regarding the Fiḳh Akbar I, we may say that it represents the views of orthodoxy in the middle of the eighth century A.D. on the then prominent dogmatic questions; and that it reflects the dissensions of the K͟hārid͟jites, S͟hī'ites and Ḳadarites, not those of the Murd͟jites, nor those of the Mu'tazilites.

CHAPTER VII

The Waṣīyat Abī Ḥanīfa

S+ between Abu Hanifa & Ahmad b. Hanbal

PARALLEL ARTICLES IN OTHER CREEDS

TRANSLATION

Fiḳh Akbar ii, art. 18
Aḳīdat al-Ṭaḥāwī, art. 11
Cf. *supra*, pp. 23, 35

Art. 1. Faith consists in confessing with the tongue, believing with the mind [1]and knowing with the heart.[1] Confessing alone is not faith, for, if this were so, all the *munāfiḳūn* would be faithful. Neither is knowledge alone faith, for, if this were so, all the people of the book would be faithful. Regarding the *munāfiḳūn* Allah says:[2] "Allah beareth witness, that the *munāfiḳūn* do surely lie". And regarding the people of the book Allah says: "They to whom We have given the scriptures, know him[3] as they know their own children".

Fiḳh Akbar ii, art. 18

Art. 2. Faith is not liable to increase or decrease. For its decrease can only be conceived of in connection with increase of unbelief; and its increase can only be conceived of in connection with decrease of unbelief. This would imply that one individual should be faithful and infidel at the same time, and how is this possible?

Art. 3. The Faithful is really faithful and the infidel is really an infidel, for there can be no doubt concerning faith nor concerning unbelief, on account of the word: "They are really faithful"[4] and: "They are really infidels".[5]

Fiḳh Akbar i, art. 1
Fiḳh Akbar ii, art. 11
Ṭaḥāwī, art. 10
Supra, p. 45 *sqq.*

Art. 4. Transgressors of the law who belong to the community of Muhammad are all of them faithful; they are not infidels.

Supra, p. 47

Art. 5. Works are distinct from faith,

1–1 Lacking in some MSS.
2 Sura lxiii. 1.
3 Viz. Muhammad; sura ii. 141; vi. 20.
4 Sura viii. 75.
5 Sura iv. 150.

and faith is distinct from works, as is proved by the fact that often the Faithful is exempted from works, whereas it is not possible to say that he is exempted from faith. Thus the *menstrua* and the *puerpera* are exempted from the *ṣalāt* according to the word of Allah, whereas it is not possible to say that they are exempted from faith on account of the word of Allah, or that Allah has enjoined them to abandon faith. The lawgiver says to them: Give up fasting and make up for it afterwards. It is possible to say: The poor man is exempted from *zakāt*, whereas it is impossible to say: The poor man is exempted from faith.

Fiḳh Akbar I, art. 3
Fiḳh Akbar II, arts. 5, 22
Ṭaḥāwī, arts. 1, 6

Art. 6. We confess that the decision concerning good and evil wholly depends upon Allah. For whoever should say that the decision regarding good and evil depends upon another than Allah would thereby be guilty of unbelief regarding Allah, and his confession of the unity of Allah would become invalid.

Fiḳh Akbar II, art. 7

Art. 7. We confess that works are of three kinds, obligatory, supererogatory and sinful. The first category is in accordance with Allah's will, desire, good pleasure, decision, decree, creation, judgment, knowledge, guidance and writing on the preserved table. The second category is not in accordance with Allah's commandment, yet according to His will, desire, good pleasure, decision, decree, judgment, knowledge, guidance, creation and writing on the preserved table. The third category is not in accordance with Allah's commandment, yet in accordance with His will, not in accordance with His desire, yet in accordance with His decision; not in accordance with His good pleasure, yet in accordance with His creation; not in accordance with His guidance; in accordance with His abandoning and His knowledge; yet not in accordance with His intimate awareness[1] or with His writing on the preserved table.

Fiḳh Akbar I, art. 9
Supra, pp. 67, 115 *sq.*
Ṭaḥāwī, art. 7

Art. 8. We confess that Allah has seated Himself on His throne, without any necessity or permanence. He occupies the throne and what is outside it, without necessity. If there were any necessity on His part, He would not have been able to create the world and to govern it in the way of created beings; and if He should feel any necessity to sit down and to remain sitting, where then was He before the creation? He is elevated above such a supposition.

Fiḳh Akbar II, arts. 3, 26
Ṭaḥāwī, art. 3

Art. 9. We confess that the Kuran is the speech of Allah, uncreated, His inspiration and revelation, not He, yet not other than He, but His real quality, written in the copies, recited by the tongues, preserved in the breasts, yet not residing there. The ink, the paper, the writing are created, for they are the work of men. The speech of Allah on the other hand is uncreated, for the writing and the letters and the words and the verses are manifestations of the Kuran for the sake of human needs. The speech of Allah on the other hand is self-existing, and its meaning is understood by means of these things. Whoso sayeth that the speech of Allah is created, he is an infidel regarding Allah, the Exalted, whom men serve, who is eternally the same, His speech being recited or written and retained in the heart, yet never dissociated from Him.

Fiḳh Akbar II, art. 10
Cf. Fiḳh Akbar I, arts. 4, 5

Art. 10. We confess that the most excellent of this community, after Muhammad, our Prophet, is Abū Bakr al-Ṣiddīḳ, then 'Umar, then 'Uṯẖmān, then 'Alī—Allah's good pleasure be on all of them, according to His word: "And they were foremost on earth, the foremost still; these are they who shall be brought nigh to God, in gardens of delight".[2] And every one of

1 *ma'rifa*, a knowledge more intimate and sympathizing than *'ilm*.

2 Sura lvi. 10 *sq.*

them who has the foremost place is also the most excellent. Every God-fearing believer loves them, and every reprobate *munāfiḳ* hates them.

Fiḳh Akbar II, art. 22

Art. 11. We confess that man, his works, his confession, his knowledge, are created. If the doer is created, *a fortiori* his acts are created.

Fiḳh Akbar II, art. 6

Art. 12. We confess that Allah has created the creatures, who are devoid of power, because they are weak and impotent, whereas Allah is their Creator and their sustenance; as He says: "It is God who created you, who fed you, who, later, will cause you to die, and then will make you alive".[1]

Art. 13. Gain is allowed and acquiring money is allowed, but acquiring money by illicit actions is not allowed.[2]

Art. 14. Moreover, men are of three categories: the faithful of pure intention in his faith; the infidel who acknowledges his unbelief; and the *munāfiḳ* whose attitude is untrustworthy. Allah has ordained[3] work to the Faithful, faith to the infidel and sincerity to the *munāfiḳ*, saying: "O men, fear your Lord",[4] *i.e.* O ye faithful, be obedient; O ye infidels, believe; O ye *munāfiḳūn*, be sincere.

Art. 15. We confess that the faculty originates at the same time as the act, neither before nor after it. For if it originated before the act, man, when wanting anything, would not want Allah, and this is in opposition to what Scripture states, saying: "And Allah is He who is rich, whereas you are poor".[5] It would be absurd if the faculty should originate after

1 Sura xxx. 39.

2 In the Leyden MS. the redaction of this article is as follows: "Gain by knowledge is allowed, and acquiring what is allowed is allowed".

3 Reading فرض with the Leyden MS.; the text has عرض.

4 Sura iv. 1; xxii. 1; xxxi. 32.

5 Sura xlvii. 40.

the act, then the act would take place without the faculty, whereas no creature has the power to act, if the faculty has not been given him by Allah at the same time.

Fiḳh Akbar II, art. 12
Ṭaḥāwī, art. 16

Art. 16. We confess that the moistening of shoes is obligatory, for those who are at home during a day and a night, for travellers during three days and nights. This is founded on a tradition in this sense. Whosoever should reject it would be in danger of unbelief, this tradition being nearly equivalent to an absolutely reliable report.[1]

Shortening the *ṣalāt* and breaking fast when on a journey are declared to be allowed[2] in Scripture: "When ye are on travels, it shall be no crime in you if you shorten your prayers".[3] And regarding the breaking of fast: "But he among you who shall be sick, or on a journey, shall fast that same number of other days".[4]

Fiḳh Akbar II, art. 5
Ṭaḥāwī, art. 6
Cf. *supra*, p. 108

Art. 17. We confess that Allah ordered the pen to write. Then the pen said: What shall I write, my Lord? Allah said: Write what shall happen till the day of resurrection, as He says: "Every thing that they do is in the books kept by the guardian angel; every action, whether small or great, is written down".[5]

Fiḳh Akbar I, art. 10
Fiḳh Akbar II, art. 23

Art. 18. We confess that the punishment in the tomb shall without fail take place.

Fiḳh Akbar II, art. 23

Art. 19. We confess that in view of the traditions on the subject the interrogation by Munkar and Nakīr is a reality.

Fiḳh Akbar II, art. 21
Ṭaḥāwī, art. 19

Art. 20. We confess that Paradise and Hell are a reality and that they are created and existing at present, that neither they nor their inhabitants will vanish, since the Scripture says regarding the Faithful: "It [*i.e.* Paradise] is prepared for the God-

1 On this term cf. *infra*, Chapter IX.
2 *rukhṣa*. The Leyden MS. has *ḥaḳḳ thābit*, "an established right" or "duty".
3 Sura iv. 102.
4 Sura ii. 180, 182.
5 Sura liv. 52 *sq*.

fearing",[1] and regarding the infidels: "It [*i.e.* Hell] is prepared for the infidels".[2] They were created with a view to reward and punishment respectively.

Fiḳh Akbar II, arts. 1, 21, 27
Ṭaḥāwī, art. 18

Art. 21. We confess that the balance is a reality, since the Scripture says: "And we will appoint balances for the day of resurrection".[3]

Ṭaḥāwī, art. 18

Art. 22. We confess that the reading of the book on the day of resurrection is a reality, since the Scripture says: "Read thy book, there needeth none but thyself to make out an account against thee this day".[4]

Fiḳh Akbar II, arts. 1, 21
Ṭaḥāwī, art. 18

Art. 23. We confess that Allah will restore to life these souls after death, and cause them to rise, on a day of which the duration shall be fifty thousand years, for retribution and reward and paying of duties, as the Scripture says: "Verily, Allah will wake up to life those who are in the tombs".[5]

Supra, pp. 24, 62 *sqq.*

Art. 24. We confess that the meeting of Allah with the inhabitants of Paradise will be a reality, without description, comparison or modality.

Fiḳh Akbar II, art. 20
Supra, p. 61 *sq.*

Art. 25. The intercession of our Prophet Muhammad (may Allah give him blessing and peace) is a reality for all those who belong to the inhabitants of Paradise, even if they should be guilty of mortal sins.

Fiḳh Akbar II, art. 27

Art. 26. We confess that, after K͟hadīd͟ja the Great, 'Ā'is͟ha is the most excellent of the women of all kinds of creatures. And she is the mother of the Faithful, pure from immorality, free from what the Rawāfiḍ ascribe to her. And whoso witnesses that she is guilty of immorality, he is a child of immorality himself.

Fiḳh Akbar II, arts. 21, 14

Art. 27. We confess that the inhabitants of Paradise will dwell therein for ever, and

1 Sura iii. 127.
2 Sura ii. 22; iii. 126.
3 Sura xxi. 48.
4 Sura xvii. 15.
5 Sura xxii. 7.

that the inhabitants of Hell will dwell therein for ever, as the Scripture says regarding the Faithful: "They are the companions of Paradise, they shall dwell therein for ever",[1] and regarding the infidels: "They are the companions of the fire, they shall dwell therein for ever".[2]

COMMENTARY

Ad art. 1. We have seen above[3] that Tradition, however occupied with questions of faith, does not give a definition of it, but rather an enumeration of its objects: "Faith is believing in Allah, His books", and so on. This tradition is the *locus classicus* on faith in the literature of canonical *ḥadīth*.

To a still earlier phase of theological thought belongs, probably, the tradition in which faith is called the best of works.[4] The form of the tradition is generally this, that Muhammad, being asked what is the best of works, answers: Faith in Allah and His Apostle. The second place is taken by the holy war, the third by the pilgrimage.

The inconsistency between faith and mortal sins is conceded in a tradition in which Muhammad declares that he who drinks wine, steals, or commits adultery cannot be faithful at the time of these acts.[5]

These three traditions may be said to reflect the general attitude of *ḥadīth* regarding faith.

The Waṣīyat Abī Ḥanīfa takes us a step further, in so far as it attempts to establish a real definition. It presupposes the discussions of the sects on faith and its relation to works. As a matter of fact the sects which ascribed a decisive value to works—the Khāridjites, Ḳadarites, Mu'tazilites and Shī'ites—expressed this in their views on faith; whereas their opponents, such as the Murdjites, endeavoured to define faith as an entity by itself.

1 Sura ii. 76.
2 Sura ii. 75, 214, etc.
3 Pp. 23, 35.
4 Bukhārī, *Imān*, b. 18, and in other collections (cf. *Handbook of Early Muhammadan Tradition*, p. 70*a*, at the top).
5 *Supra*, p. 44 *sq*.

This appears clearly from a comparison between the descriptions given by al-Ash'arī in his *Maḳālāt* of the Murdjites on the one hand[1] and of the Mu'tazilites on the other.[2] It would take us too far to give a full translation of the passages; moreover, the differences between the numerous subdivisions of the sects are too trifling to deserve special mention.

It would appear that the twelve subdivisions of the Murdjites enumerated by al-Ash'arī have this in common regarding their opinion on faith, that they give the largest place in it to knowledge (*ma'rifa*). This knowledge may have as its object Allah alone, or it may include His revelation. The differences between these subdivisions chiefly consist in their admitting or not admitting other features to their definition of faith. Such features are love, fear and submission. The Murdjite attitude may be illustrated by two examples taken from the *Maḳālāt*. The first refers to Djahm ibn Ṣafwān,[3] whose doctrine of faith has been mentioned above in general terms: "The first section of the Murdjites say that faith in Allah consists in knowledge regarding Him, His Apostles and all that comes from Him; and that what lies beyond knowledge (such as confession with the tongue and submission with the heart, love of Allah and His Apostle, as well as respect and fear for both of them, and works performed with the limbs) does not belong to faith. In the same way they say that unbelief regarding Allah is ignorance about Him. These views are ascribed to Djahm ibn Ṣafwān".[4]

The other passage refers to Abū Ḥanīfa, who is said to have belonged to the Murdjites:[5] "The ninth section of the Murdjites, Abū Ḥanīfa and his friends, say that faith is knowledge about Allah, and confession of Him, and

1 i. 132 *sqq.*; cf. also 'Abd Allāh b. Aḥmād b. Ḥanbal, *Kitāb al-Sunna*, p. 72 *sqq.*; Ibn Ḥazm, *Kitāb al-Fiṣal*, ii. 112 *sqq.*; iii. 188 *sqq.*

2 i. 266 *sqq.* 3 *Supra*, p. 120 *sq.* 4 *Maḳālāt*, i. 132.

5 As appears clearly from his letter to 'Uthmān al-Battī (unedited).

confession about the Apostle and the acknowledgment of what has come down from Allah, in general, not in particulars. Abū ʿUt͟hmān al-Ādamī relates that Abū Ḥanīfa and ʿUmar ibn abī ʿUt͟hmān al-S͟himmazī met in Makka. ʿUmar asked Abū Ḥanīfa: Tell me what do you think of a man who says that Allah has prohibited pork, yet pretends not to know whether this refers to the species we call swine? He answered: He is faithful. Then ʿUmar said to Abū Ḥanīfa: There is further a man who says that Allah has ordered the pilgrimage to the Kaʿba, yet pretends to ignore whether this Kaʿba is meant. Abū Ḥanīfa said: He is faithful. Then ʿUmar asked him: And he who claims to know that Allah has sent His Apostle and that he is the Apostle of Allah, yet does not know whether or not he is this Zand̲jī?[1] Abū Ḥanīfa answered: He is faithful. This is a characteristic illustration of the fact that Abū Ḥanīfa maintained the indelible character of faith in its relation to the other departments of religion".[2]

The views concerning faith of the other group, which are given in al-As͟hʿarī's review of the opinions of the Muʿtazilites,[3] have in common the identification of faith and works, obligatory or supererogatory, or that of faith and the avoidance of mortal sins.

The orthodox definition of faith, though not absolutely constant, emphasizes neither knowledge nor works, belief and confession being generally admitted to represent the orthodox characteristics of faith, as appears from the current interpretation of the first of the five pillars of Islam.[4] Works are excluded from this definition,[5] knowledge is admitted only in some versions of the present article.

Among the later representatives of Islam there seems to have been a reaction against a too narrow limitation of faith, as appears from the following definition given by

1 The Zand̲jīs were African slaves.

2 *Maḳālāt*, i. 138 *sq.* Many other definitions of faith are ascribed to Abū Ḥanīfa.

3 *Maḳālāt*, i. 266 *sqq.*

4 *Supra*, p. 26 *sqq.*

5 Cf. art. 5 of the Waṣīya and the commentary on it.

'Abd al-Ḳāhir al-Baghdādī as that of the majority of the adherents of tradition:[1] "Faith consists of the sum total of good works (*ṭā'āt*), obligatory as well as supererogatory. It has three stages. In the first of these the Faithful emerges from unbelief and is delivered from eternal punishment, provided that he dies in this faith. It consists in knowledge concerning Allah, His books, His Apostles, the decree for good and for evil; and further in acknowledging the eternal qualities of Allah, in rejecting anthropomorphism and nihilism,[2] in admitting the possibility[3] of seeing Him, and in believing all other authoritative traditions which are entirely trustworthy.[4] The second stage renders the Faithful an irreproachable Muslim,[5] keeps away from him the qualification of *fāsiḳ*,[6] and preserves him from the fire. It consists in performing obligatory works and in avoiding mortal sins. The third stage brings the Faithful to the highest class, which contains those who will enter Paradise without being called to account.[7] It consists in performing obligatory as well as supererogatory works, and in avoiding all kinds of sins". Interesting as this definition is, it is clear that it is not a definition of faith in the proper sense, but rather a description of the three degrees which may successively be occupied by the Muslim. The lowest of these may be said to correspond to a definition of faith. We are here no longer in the narrow circle of *kalām*, but in the sphere of religion in its broad sense.

Finally, al-Ash'arī's definition of faith may be mentioned here: "Faith is believing in Allah and His Apostles, in accordance with what Tradition reports concerning them; and this belief is not sound unless it rests on knowledge of Allah".[8]

1 *Uṣūl*, p. 249.
2 *tashbīh* and *ta'ṭīl*.
3 *idjāza*; cf. *infra*, Fiḳh Akbar II, art. 16.
4 *mutawātir*, cf. *infra*, Chapter IX.
5 *'adl*.
6 *Supra*, p. 105.
7 Cf. *Handbook of Early Muhammadan Tradition*, p. 182 *a*, at the top.
8 al-Baghdādī, *Uṣūl*, p. 248.

The emphasis laid on knowledge in al-As͟hʿarī's definition does not rise from Murd̲j̲ite but rather from Muʿtazilite tendencies. This may seem strange at first sight, as the Muʿtazilites proclaimed a preference for works as opposed to knowledge; whilst it was knowledge that was held to be the chief element of faith by the Murd̲j̲ites. It is, however, to be remembered that the Muʿtazilites were rationalists; and it was as a result of this that knowledge entered into their definition of faith. Knowledge, in their view, means rational insight in religion, which excludes the idea of *tak̲līd*. We shall touch upon *fides implicita* later; for the moment it may be sufficient to translate the passage from al-Bag̲h̲dādī's *Uṣūl*[1] relating to the subject in general: "Our friends say that he who believes the foundations of religion on the authority of others, without knowledge of the arguments on which they are based, does not thereby belong to a fixed category. If he admits the possibility of doubt of the foundations, saying: I am not sure whether there may not be such doubts as will shake them, such a one is neither a believer in Allah, nor obedient to Him, nay, he is an infidel. If, however, he believes the truth without being acquainted with the arguments on which it is based, and if he believes, further, that his faith is free from doubts that could shake it, there is difference of opinion: some say that he is faithful and in conformity with the standard of Islam and obedient to Allah by virtue of his obedience and his other works, although he transgresses in so far as he neglects the intellectual methods that bring knowledge concerning the arguments on which the foundations of religion are based; if he dies in this state, we hope he may obtain intercession and forgiveness of sins through Allah's mercy; if he is punished on account of his transgression, his punishment will not last for ever and finally he will enter Paradise by the favour and to the glory of Allah. This is the view of

1 P. 254 *sq.*; Fak̲h̲r al-Dīn al-Rāzī, *Mafātīḥ*, v. 558; *Kitāb al-Intiṣār*, p. 75; Ibn Ḥazm, *Kitāb al-Fiṣal*, iv. 35 *sqq.*; *Le Monde Oriental*, xxv. 38, note 11.

al-Shāfi'ī, Mālik, al-Awzā'i, al-Thawrī, Abū Ḥanīfa, Aḥmad ibn Ḥanbal and the Ẓāhirites, as well as of the former *mutakallimūn* who followed the traditional lines, such as 'Abd Allah ibn Sa'īd, al-Ḥārith al-Muḥāsibī, 'Abd al-'Azīz al-Makkī, al-Ḥusain ibn al-Faḍl al-Badjalī, Abū 'Abd Allāh al-Karābīsī and Abu'l-'Abbās al-Kalānisī, and this is also our opinion.

"Some others say that he who believes the truth is thereby exempt from unbelief, as unbelief and belief of truth regarding the *tawḥīd* are opposites which cannot be united. Such an one does not deserve the name of 'faithful', unless he recognizes the truth regarding the creation of the world, the unity of its maker, and the truth of prophecy with some of the arguments on which it is based; it is immaterial whether he be able to illustrate his arguments with good examples or not. This is the point of view of al-Ash'arī.[1]

"According to him, he who believes the truth on the authority of others (*taḳlīdan*) is neither a polytheist nor an infidel. Yet al-Ash'arī does not in general apply the qualification 'faithful' to such an one, and his doctrine compels him to admit that the sins of such an one may be forgiven, since he is neither a polytheist nor an infidel.

"The Mu'tazilites are divided on this point. Those who consider knowledge as being of a primary nature[2] say that he who believes the truth, believing it as something axiomatic, and not marring this condition by mortal sins, is faithful. If such an one should, however, mar his condition by mortal sins, he would be *fāsiḳ*, that is, neither faithful nor infidel. Whoever believes the truth, but does not regard it as something of a primary nature, is under no obligation to believe.[3]

"Those Mu'tazilites, however, who say that knowledge regarding Allah, His books and His Apostles, is knowledge acquired by reasoning and deduction, are of different

1 *Supra*, p. 134 *sq*.

2 *ḍarūrī*; the term means literally "what does not admit any difference or deviation". See *infra*, Chapter IX.

3 *mukallaf*.

opinions concerning him who believes the truth on the authority of others. Some say that he is *fāsiḳ* on account of his neglect of reason and deduction; and a *fāsiḳ*, according to them, is neither faithful nor infidel. Others say that he is an infidel, whose repentance is invalid through his neglect of one of his legal obligations.

"Abū Hāshim[1] says: If an infidel should believe all the foundations of the religion of Islam, and should believe all the principles of Abū Hāshim, and should be acquainted with all the arguments in favour of all of them, except the argument in favour of one of them regarding the foundations of God's justice and unity, he would yet be an infidel and all those who should follow his authority would be infidels, according to Abū Hāshim. And I [al-Baghdādī] think he is consistent in this respect, although his premises are false".

We shall touch upon this question again, in connection with the Muslim doctrine of the roots of faith.[2] We will only remark here, that the rejection of belief on authority by the Mu'tazilites carried the implication that the common people who were not trained in dialectics did not deserve the qualification of "faithful". According to the author of the commentary on the Fiḳh Akbar I, this was also the view of the Ash'arites.[3] We have seen that al-Ash'arī himself did not wholly share the Mu'tazilite view on this point.

Finally, we may add that faith based upon partial knowledge as opposed to faith based upon complete knowledge corresponds to *fides implicita* as opposed to *fides explicita* in the dogmatics of medieval Christianity.

1 'Abd al-Salām b. Muḥammad b. 'Abd al-Wahhāb al-Djubbā'ī, cf. Arnold, *al-Mu'tazilah*, p. 53 *sqq.* It is said that he taught "blame without sin" (al-Maḳrīzī, *Khiṭaṭ*, ii. 348), apparently the doctrine of hereditary sin, which he may have adopted under Christian influence (see John of Damascus, *De fide orthodoxa*, IV. 10, 11).

2 *Infra*, Chapter VIII, Fiḳh Akbar II, art. 28; Chapter IX, Fiḳh Akbar III, art. 1.

3 Pp. 9, 31.

It is difficult to decide whether there are historical links between the two religions in regard to this question.

Ad art. 2. This article goes far towards accepting the Murdjite doctrine of faith as an entity by itself and independent of good works.[1] The version of the parallel article of the Fiḳh Akbar II[2] is more cautious. Theological circles which, in contradistinction to those in which the Waṣīya and the Fiḳh Akbar II originated, were free from Murdjite tradition and influence did not shrink from expressing the opposite opinion. For instance, al-Bukhārī opens his chapter on *Īmān* with an introduction in which he declares faith to be liable to increase and decrease. He bases this view upon a number of passages from the Kuran, of which the following may be mentioned here: "He it is who sent down a spirit of secure repose into the hearts of the Faithful that they might add faith to their faith".[3] And: "None but angels have We made guardians of the fire; nor have We made this to be their number but to perplex those who believe not...and in order to increase the faith of those who believe".[4]

Likewise Ibn Mādja[5] has inserted in his work some traditions in which such authorities as Ibn 'Abbās and Abu'l-Dardā' are made to declare that faith is liable to increase and decrease.

Ad art. 3. In accordance with art. 2 this article seeks to assert that there can be no doubt regarding man's state: he is either faithful or an infidel.[6] The commentator, who belongs to the school of al-Māturīdī, connects with this article the question whether a man may declare himself to be faithful. This is a point of difference between the adherents of al-Māturīdī and those of al-Ash'arī, the former answering the question in the affirmative, the latter in the negative sense, in so far as they deemed it

1 *Supra*, p. 133. 2 Arts. 18, 19. 3 Sura xlviii. 4.
4 Sura lxxiv. 31. Cf. also Sura iii. 167; xxxiii. 22; xlvii. 19.
5 Introduction, b. 9; cf. also Fakhr al-Dīn al-Rāzī, iii. 360.
6 *Infra*, p. 156.

necessary to add the clause "if it please Allah". The question is really much older than the period of al-Ash'arī and al-Māturīdī. In the *Fiḳh Absaṭ*[1] it is treated in connection with utterances of Abū Ḥanīfa, who has no objections to the formula: "I am really faithful"; the *Imām* adds, however, that it is not allowed to say: "I belong to the people of Paradise", for even the Faithful are punished on account of transgressions. Arguments in favour of the view of Abū Ḥanīfa and al-Māturīdī are to be found in the commentary on the Fiḳh Akbar I.[2] Arguments in favour of the opposite view are reduced by al-Ghazālī[3] to four points. The first is that one may hesitate to declare oneself faithful without any restriction, such a declaration being akin to self-elevation and self-sufficiency (*tazkiyat al-nafs*).[4] The second is the general predilection for the clause "if it please Allah" (the so-called *istithnā'*), the use of which is based upon Kuran[5] and Tradition.[6] This formula, says al-Ghazālī, does not express doubt, but rather a wish or desire, a fact which may justify its use in connection with faith. The third is, that the clause, when applied to faith, expresses doubts concerning its perfection, and this is obligatory, for the perfection of faith is impaired by two circumstances—a secret *nifāḳ* which cannot be done away with, and its relation with good works which deprives everyone of the consciousness of its perfection. al-Ghazālī's views are wholly opposed to the tendency which finds expression in the present article. In the fourth place, he mentions the fear of the *khātima*, *i.e.* a man's final acts and state which correspond to his eternal destiny,[7] which latter depends upon "the eternal decision and will, which can be known only by their effects and on which no human being can ever cast a glance before". al-Ghazālī then proceeds to give instances of the fear of

1 Fol. 28 *sq.*

2 P. 14 *sqq.*

3 *Iḥyā'*, i. 114–17.

4 Sura iv. 52; liii. 33.

5 Sura xviii. 23; xlviii. 27.

6 Muslim, *Aimān*, trad. 22–5, and al-Nawawī, commentary, iv. 106.

7 *Supra*, p. 56.

the last act as expressed by some of the pious, as for example: "If I should have to choose between the *shahāda* at the front door and death with the confession of the unity of Allah at the door of the inner room, I should take the latter alternative, as I am ignorant of the deviations from *tawḥīd* that might occur to my mind between the front door and the door of the inner room".

Ad art. 4. A too vigorous expression of the doctrine that nobody may be declared an infidel on account of mortal sins, as was done by the Khāridjites (Fiḳh Akbar I, art. 1). We have already seen[1] that canonical Tradition admits that faith is impaired by sins, at least at the moment when they are committed. Abū Ḥanīfa's unshaken conviction of the absoluteness of faith is illustrated in the story of how some Khāridjites approached him with unsheathed swords. They asked him whether a woman who had committed fornication and had killed the child born from the forbidden union could be called faithful. "Yes," was the answer of Abū Ḥanīfa, "for I dare not say that a certain part of her *tawḥīd* is lacking on account of her sin. Could *you* tell me whether half of it is lacking? No. Or a third? No. Or a fourth? No. So I cannot deny that this woman may be faithful." Thereupon the Khāridjites put up their swords and went away.[2]

The commentator of the Waṣīya, on the other hand, is somewhat reserved:[3] "The Faithful does not become an infidel on account of mortal sins or transgressions; for faith consists of confession and belief, and these latter subsist (in case of mortal sins), consequently faith subsists. Yet transgressions may cause unbelief and faith may vanish, for unbelief makes faith vanish." Still more in the orthodox manner is al-Ṭaḥāwī in his *'aḳīda*, art. 10: "We declare no one of those who follow the *ḳibla* to be an infidel on account of a sin, in so far as he does not declare it to be allowed.[4] We do not, however, say that sin is

1 *Supra*, p. 44 *sq.*
2 Cod. Warner, MS. 706, fol. 44.
3 P. 6.
4 *Supra*, p. 104 *sq.*

without consequences to him who commits it, even if he be one of the Faithful. We entertain hope for the righteous[1] among the Faithful, but we have no certainty and we do not testify that they will be in Paradise. We ask forgiveness for those who commit evil, but we are full of anxiety for their fate. Yet we will not discourage them. False security, as well as despair, serves to turn men away from religion. The true way for those who follow the *ḳibla* lies between these".

Of a similar tendency are arts. 11 and 14 of the Fiḳh Akbar II (see *infra*, Chapter IX).

Ad art. 5. The foregoing article, in which sinners are not excluded from faith, leads here to the conclusion that faith and works are separate entities, each standing by itself without being influenced by the other. The commentator cites the following passage from Ibn Ḥadjar al-Haitamī († 974/1567): "It is said that belief as an element of faith must necessarily be accompanied by confession with the tongue, and by works performed by the other limbs. Whoever omits any of the three, becomes thereby an infidel. This is the doctrine of the Khāridjites". In this respect the Khāridjites were in sympathy with one current of Christian theology which has its scriptural basis in the Epistle of St James ii. 17: "Faith, if it hath not works, is dead". This conception of faith is illustrated by the doctrine of John of Damascus on this point. He distinguished the objective and the subjective sides of faith. The former, he says, is based on Scripture, "by hearing,[2] but it is supplemented by the performance of all the commandments imposed on us by Christ. And whosoever does not believe according to the tradition of the church, or whosoever associates with Satan through evil[3] works, he is an infidel".[4] The mutual influence of faith and works has been expounded by al-Ghazālī;[5] cf. further

1 *al-muḥsinīna*, cf. *supra*, p. 23.

2 Romans x. 17, *sam'ī* as it is called with an Arabic term.

3 ἀτόπων. 4 *De fide orthodoxa*, IV. 10. 5 *Iḥyā'*, i. 115.

what has been said above in explanation of arts. 1 and 4.

Ad art. 6. See the explanation of art. 3 of the Fiḳh Akbar I. In the present article the dogma of predestination is contrasted with dualism, in accordance with the traditions in which the Ḳadarites are called the dualists of the community.[1]

Ad art. 7. This article, with which may be compared arts. 6 and 7 of the Fiḳh Akbar II, seeks to efface those consequences of predestination which are in too sharp a contrast with theodicy. It gives a refined specialization and classification of the relation between the acts of Allah and those of man, such as could be reached only by a considerable theological advance.

The relation between Allah and human acts, in so far as they refer to the next world, is divided under twelve heads, and human acts under three, as may be seen from the following table:

	HUMAN ACTS		
	Obligatory resulting from	Supererogatory resulting from	Sins resulting from
DIVINE	command	—	—
	will	will	will
	desire	desire	—
	pleasure	pleasure	—
	decision	decision	decision
	decree	decree	decree
	creation	creation	creation
	judgment	judgment	—
	knowledge	knowledge	knowledge
	guidance	guidance	—
	—	—	abandoning
	record	record	record

The interest of this division lies in the difference between

1 *Supra*, p. 57.

the first two categories on the one hand and the third on the other. Sins result from Allah's decision, decree, creation, knowledge, writing down, will and abandoning; not according to His command, desire, pleasure, judgment or guidance.

An echo of the theological discussions on which this refined classification is based may still be heard in the sources available to us.

The views of the Ḳadarites and the Mu'tazilites regarding the connections between Allah and evil are chiefly negative. The commentator on the Fiḳh Akbar I contents himself with the statement that these sects take Allah's will, decision, decree and judgment in the sense of knowledge, and on this basis avoid all contact between the divine will (*irāda*, *mas͟hī'a*, *ḳaḍā'*) and evil.[1]

al-Naẓẓām[2] has no objection to the term *ḥākim* as a characteristic of Allah's government of evil, which term he explains in the sense of "proclaiming".[3] According to al-Bag͟hdādī[4] this means that al-Naẓẓām (as well as al-Ka'bī)[5] does not really ascribe a will to Allah. "If He willeth any of His own acts, this means that He does it; if He willeth anything done by others, it means that He orders it." The Mu'tazilites of Baṣra say that Allah is willing with a will that happens without a *substratum*. Further, they say: "He willeth what does not happen; and He dislikes what happens (for transgressions are contrary to His pleasure) and He intends to guide all men and He does not intend that any of them should err".[6]

The general opinion of the Mu'tazilites is that Allah ceases to guide the sinner or, as al-As͟h'arī says, He abandons him to sin.[7] In As͟h'arite dogmatics the term *k͟had͟hlān* is used, which goes back to the Kuran.[8] This is

1 Fiḳh Akbar I, p. 21, at the top.
2 *Supra*, p. 77.
3 al-As͟h'arī, *Maḳālāt*, i. 190 *sq*.
4 *Uṣūl*, p. 146.
5 Abu'l-Ḳāsim 'Abd Allāh b. Aḥmad b. Maḥmūd al-Balk͟hī, † 929.
6 al-Bag͟hdādī, *Uṣūl*, p. 146 *sq*.
7 *Maḳālāt*, i. 190: *k͟hallā bainahum wa-bainahu*.
8 Sura iii. 154; *infra*, pp. 191, 195, 213

the doctrine of the Mu'tazilites in a more popular form. In so far as it falls also under the doctrine of the qualities, they give a definition which denies also the everlastingness of the quality in the following terms: "The Mu'tazilites unanimously deny that Allah has not ceased to will transgressions and they deny unanimously that Allah has not ceased to will acts of obedience".[1]

The thoroughly Islamic point of view is substantially accepted by the Ash'arites, who came to be looked upon as neo-orthodox. al-Baghdādī expounds the orthodox opinion, as it was formulated in his day, in two passages of his *Uṣūl*, the translation of one of which is as follows: "Our friends share the common opinion that the will (*mashī'a*) of Allah is diffused into the single acts of His will, corresponding to His knowledge of them. For when He knows that a thing shall happen, He wills so, be it good or evil. And when He knows that a thing shall not happen, He wills that it shall not happen. And all that He wills happens at the time He wills and in the way He wills. And all that He wills not does not happen, quite apart from His having given a commandment in this sense or not.[2] This is their general opinion.

"They differ, however, in particulars. Some say: I say, in general, that Allah wills the happening of all things that happen, be they good or evil. But I do not say, in particular, that He wills unbelief and the transgressions that happen, though they belong to the sum total of the things that happen. As we, in prayer, say in general: O Creator of the bodies, and: O Sustainer of the beasts and of all animals. But we do not say: O Sustainer of the bugs and the beetles, though these belong to the totality of the created things to which we refer in general. This is the view of our master Abū Muḥammad 'Abd Allah ibn Sa'īd[3] and of many of our friends.

1 *Makālāt*, i. 185.

2 Here again the distinction between Allah's command and His will.

3 al-Kilābī, one of the early *mutakallimūn*.

"Many of them, however, connect Allah's will with the single acts of His will, not only in general but also in particular, yet with a restriction in the latter case. They say in general: Allah wills the happening of all of that which He knows will happen, be it good or evil. And they say in particular: He wills the happening of unbelief on the part of the infidel, in so far as this will be *kasb*[1] of evil on his part. And they have objections, as we have said, to saying in a general way that He wills unbelief and sin without restriction. This is the view of our master Abu'l-Ḥasan (al-As͟h'arī).

"Others say: When we say of sin and unbelief that they happen, we say that Allah wills that they happen, but we do not say that He wills unbelief and sin when we say that He has willed the happening of this thing which is unbelief or sin".[2]

As regards the doctrine of the Mu'tazilites, it may be added that they did not reject the connection between Allah and evil in the sense of accidents, sickness, and so on. 'Abbād[3] however rejected even this connection.[4]

Eastern Christianity also was interested in this question. It rejected the connection between God and sin; yet it maintained the government of God by taking it in the sense of permission.[5] In case of evil there is permission (συγχώρησις), and in case of good there is good pleasure (εὐδοκία), on the part of God. Free will was given to men and angels. It is in will that the nature of evil must be sought, not in a being that is evil by nature in opposition to God who is good by nature. So Christianity takes a middle position between Islam and Manichaeism. The chapter in which John of Damascus proves that God cannot be the cause of evil is followed by a chapter against Manichaeism and dualism. It may be remembered in this

1 Fiḳh Akbar II, art. 6.
2 *Uṣūl*, p. 145 *sq.*; cf. p. 104.
3 Cf. Arnold, *al-Mu'tazilah*, p. 44, and *supra*, p. 80.
4 al-As͟h'arī, *Maḳālāt*, i. 245.
5 John of Damascus, *De fide orthodoxa*, IV. 19.

connection that in Islam the Manichaean view was imputed to those who advocated the *liberum arbitrium*.[1]

John has also illustrated the Christian view in two separate works, a dialogue between a Christian and a Saracen,[2] and a similar dialogue between a Christian and a Manichee.[3] We may leave aside the latter here; the former may claim attention, as it contains some illustration of the present problem, the attitude of the two religions regarding it, and their mutual relation.

The *Disputatio Christiani et Saraçeni*, as it is reproduced in vol. XCIV of Migne's collection, differs from the *Disputatio Saraceni et Christiani* (as it is called in the different version of vol. XCVI) chiefly in that the two subjects touched upon in the former are Christ, His pre-existence and incarnation, and also the question of evil and predestination, whereas in the latter these subjects are arranged in the opposite order.

In this dialogue the Saracen requests the Christian to explain to him the cause of evil. The Christian rejects the view that this should be sought in God. No, it is to be sought in the co-operation between the devil's influence and human weakness. Man's choice of evil was possible on account of his free will, which allowed him to do good as well as evil. Here the Saracen replies: "Are not the sun and the stars good? Yet you cannot make any of them". The Christian answers that he speaks of human works only, and proceeds in his turn to ask questions. If good and evil are caused by God's willing them, how should God punish evil? This would be unjust.

The Saracen gives no answer to this question, but attacks the problem from a different side. "You concede", he says to the Christian, "that God creates the embryo in the womb. So God co-operates with adulterers and fornicators. Apply now your foregoing argument to yourself".

1 *Supra*, p. 57.

2 Migne, *Patrologia*, vol. XCIV. col. 1585 *sqq.*; a different redaction is given in vol. XCVI. col. 1338 *sqq.*

3 Migne, *Patrologia*, vol. XCIV. col. 1503 *sqq.*; cf. vol. XCVI. col. 1319 *sqq.*

The Christian answers: "No, God consummated the creation in a week. Ever since then the generation of men, animals and plants goes on in an uninterrupted chain. Adam begat Seth, Seth begat Enoch, and so on. Scripture does not say: God created Seth, God created Enoch". Then the Christian returns to the starting-point, asking: "Now, if God says: Thou shalt not, does He will it or not"? "No", answers the Saracen, "else He would not have prohibited it". Thereupon the Christian closes the discussion, saying: "I am happy to perceive that we agree on this point, that God willeth not that we do evil".

The last point touches the question of will and command, and we have already seen[1] that the orthodox Muslim solution is totally different from the opinion ascribed by John to the Saracen.

Attention may be paid to the resemblance between the idea of perpetual generation as brought forward by the Christian—in order to avoid all connections between God the Creator and this sinful world—and the idea of *tawallud* as taught by some Muʿtazilite thinkers.[2]

On the general question reference may be made to art. 6 of the Fiḳh Akbar II, and the commentary.

Ad art. 8. The question of how Allah seated Himself on His throne (cf. sura vii. 52) has been mentioned several times,[3] and it has been seen that the orthodox position gradually turned half-way round. Here this tendency appears again. The Fiḳh Akbar I (art. 9) declares him a *kāfir* who says that he knows not whether Allah is in Heaven or on earth, *i.e.* who doubts His sitting on the throne. The present article attacks the anthropomorphic consequences of this representation. al-Ṭaḥāwī has the following article on this subject: "The throne and the chair are real in accordance with the description of them in the book of Allah. Yet He does not need the throne, nor what is less

1 *Supra*, p. 126.

2 *Kitāb al-Intiṣār*, p. 76 *sq.*; al-Baghdādī, *Uṣūl*, pp. 137–9; Ibn Ḥazm, *Kitāb al-Fiṣal*, v. 59 *sq.*

3 *Supra*, pp. 67, 115 *sqq.*, 127.

than the throne; He encompasses all that is above it and has made the knowledge of it inaccessible to His creatures". Here there is no description of, but merely allusion to, the sitting of Allah on His throne. The commentator on the Fiḳh Akbar I even goes so far as to distort the sense of art. 9 of that creed by declaring him who associates with Allah the idea of a place to be a *kāfir*.

We may here take leave of the question, which is highly illustrative of Muslim theology. The commentator of the present article emphasizes Allah's being elevated above any need. Strangely enough, he then proceeds to give a lengthy description of throne and chair (*kursī*) which belongs wholly to popular theology and is based on early Semitic ideas: "Opinions regarding the throne differ. According to some it is a seat of light, according to others, *e.g.* the author of the *Baḥr al-Kalām*,[1] it is a red hyacinth. The author of the *Daḳā'iḳ al-Akhbār*[2] says: Allah created the preserved table from a white pearl which is seven times longer than the distance between Heaven and earth, and He attached it to the throne. On it is written what shall happen till the day of resurrection. Ibn Abī Ḥātim in his commentary and Abu'l-Shaikh in his *Kitāb al-'Iẓma* have a tradition which goes back to Wahb ibn Munabbih, who says: Allah created the throne from His light, and the chair is attached to the throne, and all water is within the chair, and the water is on the back of the wind. Round the throne are four rivers, a river consisting of shining pearls, a river of flaming fire, a river consisting of snow so white that sight is dazzled by it, and a river of water. Angels stand at these rivers, praising God. The throne has tongues equal in number to the tongues of all creatures and all these praise God. Ibn Abī Ḥātim has a tradition which goes back to Ka'b al-Aḥbār: The heavens are, as compared with the throne, like a lamp hanging between Heaven and earth. Ibn Djarīr,[3] Ibn Mardawaih and Abu'l-

1 *I.e.* al-Nasafī (Abu'l-Mu'īn Maimūn b. Muḥammad).
2 A work of which nothing more is known to me.
3 *I.e.* al-Ṭabarī.

Shaikh have a tradition which goes back to Abū Dharr:[1] The Apostle of Allah said: O Abū Dharr, the seven Heavens are, as compared with the chair, as a ring thrown away in the desert. And the relation between the throne and the chair is as the relation between this desert and the ring. The same tradition is found also in al-Suyūṭī's *al-Hai'a al-Sanīya*".[2]

Ad art. 9. The Mu'tazilites[3] did not make a real distinction between Allah's speaking, His speech and the Kuran. Allah's speaking to Moses was a single act. Neither His speech, nor the Kuran, had a deeper significance than this.[4]

Neither did the orthodox make any real distinction between the speaking of Allah, His speech and the Kuran.[5] But here the ways of the parties separated, as the orthodox considered the three as an eternal quality.

The attitude of the Mu'tazilites was inspired by their fear of admitting eternal qualities and of endangering thereby the absolute unity of Allah. A glance at the consequences of the orthodox position is sufficient to show that their fear was not wholly imaginary. In the Fiḳh Akbar II, art. 3, it is said that Moses heard Allah speaking, that this speech was uncreated, but that the reply of Moses was created. Yet the report of the discourse as reproduced in the Kuran is the eternal *kalām* of Allah. Perhaps the whole situation was not very satisfactory to the orthodox themselves. But neither of the parties could drop the connection between the Kuran and the speaking of Allah, nor that between His speaking and His speech.

It is well known that some champions of orthodoxy

1 al-Ghifārī, the renowned saint.

2 Cf. with this description "The Ideas of the Western Semites concerning the Navel of the Earth" in *Verhandelingen der Kon. Akademie van Wetenschappen*, new series, vol. XVIII. No. 1, p. 54 *sqq*.

3 Cf. *supra*, p. 77 *sqq*.

4 This was probably also the view of the Khāridjites; cf. al-Ash'arī, *Maḳālāt*, i. 124, and Fakhr al-Dīn al-Rāzī, *Mafātīḥ*, v. 427, 494; *Kitāb al-Intiṣār*, p. 57.

5 Cf. however, the subtle exposition of Taftāzānī, p. 79 *sqq*.

have even drawn the consequence which is rejected in the present article, namely, the identification of the recited Kuran with the eternal word of God;[1] and it must be admitted that this seems hardly different in nature from the identification of Allah's speaking to Moses with the uncreated account of it in the Kuran.

Apparently the attitude of Christianity regarding the nature of the word of God has exercised an influence on the Muslim position.

The problem Christianity had to solve was closely akin to that which troubled Islam. For both religions the question was whether the highest revelations of the Godhead—the incarnation of Christ and the communication of the Kuran—were signs of divine action only, or manifestations of its own essence.

Eastern Christianity, by the mouth of John of Damascus,[2] had proclaimed that the Son was not created but that He had proceeded from the Father, being ὁμοούσιος with Him. There was never a time when the Son was not; for the Son has come forth from the nature of the Father.[3] This coming forth (γέννησις) must, however, be kept apart from the idea of time; otherwise it would necessitate a change in the hypostasis of the Father. So "the eternal God creates His own word, perfect, without beginning,[4] without end,[5] γεννητός,[6] but ἀγένητος".[7]

Christianity did not, however, identify the eternal word of God with the single "words", nor with Scripture as a whole. It distinguished λόγος from ῥήματα (θεοῦ). In this way[8] Christianity avoided the difficulty which faced

1 The Ḥanbalites went far in this direction, cf. Taftazānī, p. 82.

2 Migne, vol. XCIV. col. 809 *sqq.* (*De fide orthodoxa*, I. viii).

3 ἐξ αὐτοῦ γὰρ, ἤγουν τῆς τοῦ πατρὸς φύσεως, φαμὲν τὴν τοῦ Υἱοῦ γέννησιν. This corresponds to the *ṣifa dhātīya* of Muslim *kalām*.

4 ἀνάρχως = أَزَلِى. 5 ἀτελευτήτως = أَبَدِى.

6 Ṭaḥāwī, art. 3: وان القران كلام الله منه بَدَأ.

7 غير مُحْدَث

8 Theodore Abū Ḳurra, Migne, vol. XCVII. col. 1592.

orthodox Islam in consequence of its identifying the *kalām* of Allah with His speaking and with the Kuran.

The Ash'arites did what they could to establish a distinction between the speech of Allah and the Kuran. According to them[1] (1) the speech of Allah was different from His self; (2) Allah had one *kalām* only; (3) what was revealed to Muhammad was a reflex (*'ibāra*) only of the *kalām* of Allah. What was in the copies of the Kuran was still farther from the *ṣifa* of the Godhead, for otherwise, they argued, burning a copy of the Kuran would mean burning the speech of Allah; to which the orthodox replied that if the contents of the copies of the Kuran should not be identical with the speech of Allah, the latter would be lacking among mankind.[2]

Later orthodoxy tried to avoid the difficulty by assuming a mental speech (*kalām nafsī*) of Allah.[3]

The subject is mentioned again in connection with the divine qualities (art. 2 of the Fiḳh Akbar II). Probably the idea of the pre-existence of the Kuran was supported by the popular representation of the preserved table.[4]

Ad art. 10. Something has been said on this subject in connection with our discussion of arts. 4 and 5 of the Fiḳh Akbar I.[5] In the present article there is some development of thought, in so far as the hierarchy,[6] corresponding to the historical sequence, is fixed. In art. 10 of the Fiḳh Akbar II an honorific epithet is added to each name. It might be surmised that the origin of these titles is to be sought in those idealizing tendencies to which also the hierarchic sequence is related. A comparison between arts. 4 and 5 of the Fiḳh Akbar I and the present article as well as arts. 8–10 of the Fiḳh Akbar II and Ṭaḥāwī's *'aḳīda*

1 Ibn Ḥazm, *Kitāb al-Fiṣal*, iii. 5.

2 Commentary on Fiḳh Akbar I, p. 23.

3 Taftazānī, p. 82.

4 *Supra*, p. 55; *Encyclopaedia of Islām*, under *Lawḥ maḥfūẓ*.

5 *Supra*, p. 109 *sq*.; cf. also Fakhr al-Dīn al-Rāzī, *Mafātīḥ*, vi. 563; *Kitāb al-Intiṣār*, p. 99.

6 *Supra*, p. 110, note 1.

shows that, as a matter of fact, the original background, namely, the dissensions which gave rise to the Shī'ite and Khāridjite movements, vanishes in the course of time and that the hierarchic idea, which takes its place, tends to cover not only the Muslim community, but also other classes of beings. On this subject more will be said later.[1] Here it may be sufficient to note that the hierarchic sequence was worked out in detail, as may be seen from 'Abd al-Ḳāhir al-Baghdādī,[2] who enumerates seventeen classes of Companions and distinguishes between several ranks of the Followers.

As to the historical sequence, al-Baghdādī says that his friends are of different opinions regarding the mutual precedence of 'Alī and 'Uthmān. He adds that al-Ash'arī put 'Uthmān in the third place and 'Alī in the fourth, because he did not deem it allowable to deviate from the historical sequence.[3] This means apparently that he considered the latter as being the expression of divine preference. The obligation of the Faithful to love the Companions is reflected in canonical Tradition.[4]

Ad arts. 11, 12. Even after a reference to predestination, the author of the Waṣīya thinks it not superfluous to say that the personal acts and convictions of man are created by Allah. The emphasis laid on this point is due to the fact that this was one of the much debated theological questions.[5] Cf. further, *infra*, art. 15.

In art. 12 emphasis is laid on Allah as the Creator. This idea also implied dogmatic difficulties as may be seen from art. 6 of the Fiḳh Akbar II and the commentary.

Ad art. 13. In explanation of the practical importance of this article it may be borne in mind that Muslim commercial law is partially based upon the tendency to avoid

1 Chapter VIII, Fiḳh Akbar II, art. 10.
2 *Uṣūl al-Dīn*, p. 289 *sq*.
3 *Uṣūl al-Dīn*, p. 304; cf. also *Kitāb al-Intiṣār*, p. 97 *sq*.
4 al-Tirmidhī, *Manāḳib*, b. 58.
5 al-Ash'arī, *Maḳālāt*, i. 40 *sq*., 43 *sq*., 72, 93, 96, 108, 259 *sqq*.

two faults—usury and anything which resembles gambling. This law therefore reduces gain to narrow limits; the objects of commercial transactions must be present in the state in which they pass to the purchaser, chance being thus reduced to a minimum. The collections of canonical Tradition also contain numerous instances of this tendency.[1]

Thus it is natural that all gain arising from unlawful transactions is severely condemned in Tradition. It is stated in this literature that one characteristic of future generations, which will reach the verge of depravation, is that they will be unscrupulous regarding the sources of gain.[2] In opposition to this moral laxity it is emphatically asserted that Allah accepts alms only if they are given out of honest gain.[3] "The tradition to this effect", says al-Nawawī, "belongs to those traditions which are the foundations of Islam and the groundwork of the law. I have collected forty of these traditions into a volume, in which it is urged that expenses should be met from honest gain, other expenses being prohibited; that food, drink and clothes should be plainly in accord with the law, and that whoever desires to pray to Allah should pay more attention to this than other persons."[4]

The accumulation of wealth which is mentioned in the second place and declared to be lawful was as delicate a question in early Islam as it was in early Christianity. In so far as these two religions breathe the spirit of Hellenism, they are as unworldly as any religion ever can be; they turn their backs on worldly ambition and wealth; they feel themselves in opposition to the lords of the world, to temporal power, and to all who enjoy authority and wealth. "It is easier for a camel to go through the eye of a needle, than for a rich man to enter into the kingdom of God."[5] The Muslim Hell is full of "tyrants, haughty

1 Cf. *Handbook of Early Muhammadan Tradition*, s.v. *Barter*.
2 Bukhārī, *Buyū'*, b. 7.
3 Bukhārī, *Zakāt*, b. 7; Muslim, *Zakāt*, trad. 63 *sqq*.
4 iii. 29.
5 Matthew xix. 24; cf. *Kitāb al-Intiṣār*, p. 102.

persons, kings and nobles".[1] Characteristic in many respects is the following tradition: "Zaid b. Wahb relates that he passed al-Rabaḏha, where he met Abū Ḏharr,[2] who lived there in exile. He said to him: How is it that you are dwelling here? Abū Ḏharr answered: I was in Syria with Muʿāwiya, when dissension arose between us regarding the verse of the Kuran: 'As for those who gather gold and silver without spending it in the way of Allah, proclaim to them a painful punishment'.[3] According to Muʿāwiya this was said of the people of the book,[4] whereas I maintained that it referred to us as well as to them. On account of this dissension he wrote to ʿUthmān complaining of me. Thereupon the latter summoned me to Madina. When I arrived there people gathered around me in crowds, as if they had never seen me before. When I protested before ʿUthmān he said to me: You had better go away and live close by. This is the reason why I am staying here; for even if an Abyssinian were in authority over me, I would obey".[5]

On the authority of the same Abū Ḏharr rests the tradition according to which the Apostle of Allah said: "Everyone who leaves gold or money at his death will be branded on account of it".[6]

There are, however, other traditions, which rather doubtfully admit extenuating circumstances: "The Apostle of Allah said: Forlorn are the wealthy. People said: Except....He repeated: Forlorn are the wealthy. People said: Except....He repeated: Forlorn are the wealthy. People said: Except..., till we feared that no restriction would be admitted. At last, however, he said: Except those who act thus and thus".[7]

---

1 Aḥmad ibn Ḥanbal, iii. 13.   2 *Supra*, pp. 33, 46.
3 Sura ix. 34.
4 Who are mentioned indeed in the first half of the verse.
5 Bukhārī, *Zakāt*, b. 4.
6 Aḥmad ibn Ḥanbal, v. 168.
7 Aḥmad ibn Ḥanbal, iii. 331. The last words must be imagined to have been accompanied by the gesture of throwing away.

This and similar traditions are indications of the different turn which the appreciation of wealth was about to take in Islam.

In the present article nothing of the old attitude has been preserved.

It has been seen above[1] that the Leyden MS. of the Waṣīya has a different version of art. 13: "Gain by knowledge is allowed and acquiring of what is lawful is allowed". The second sentence requires no further comment, but the first conveys a new idea. It may be said at once that this idea does not accord with the general opinion on this subject. Yet it does not stand wholly by itself. Bukhārī has the following *tardjama* at the head of a well-known tradition in his *Kitāb al-Idjāra*:[2] "According to Ibn 'Abbās the Apostle of Allah said: The worthiest remuneration is on account of the Book of Allah. al-Sha'bī[3] said: The only condition the teacher may make is that something shall be given him and this he may accept. al-Ḥakam[4] said: I never heard of the remuneration of the teacher being resented. al-Ḥasan[5] accepted ten *dirham*. Ibn Sīrīn[6] had no objection to executors being remunerated and said: People used to say that the objectionable practice was to bribe an arbiter; and it was customary to accept payment for valuing".

It is evident from this heading that respectable authorities of early Islam made no objections to teaching the Kuran for payment. According to al-Ḳasṭallānī, this opinion was the prevalent one. But with regard to teaching in general the opposite tendency prevailed as may appear from the following data. There is a tradition on the authority of 'Ubāda ibn al-Ṣāmit[7] which runs: "I had taught some of the *ahl al-ṣuffa*[8] to write and to read the Kuran. One of them presented me with a bow. I thought:

1 P. 128, note 2.
2 Bab 16.
3 The traditionist († 728).
4 Ibn 'Utaiba.
5 al-Baṣrī.
6 † 110/728.
7 One of the earliest Companions.
8 The poorest of the Muhādjirs.

It is not money and I can use it in the holy war; I shall go and consult the Apostle of Allah. I did so and told him what I thought about it. He answered: Accept it, if you like to wear a collar of fire".[1]

In his description of the duties of the teacher al-Ghazālī says: "His second duty is to imitate the example of the lawgiver (may Allah bless him and give him peace), so he shall not ask wages in exchange for his knowledge, nor aim at remuneration or gratitude; but he must teach gratuitously and with a view to spiritual profit".[2]

In the same way professors in the universities of Mecca and Cairo do not receive a fee from their pupils, nor are they appointed at a fixed stipend. They may, however, receive presents from their pupils, as well as subventions from the funds intended for this purpose.[3]

Ad art. 14. This article starts from the same conception as arts. 2 and 3, and is similarly directed against the Khāridjites, who effaced the sharp distinction which, according to the orthodox view, exists between faith and unbelief, between the Faithful and the infidel. The present article is a mitigation of the orthodox view, in so far as it emphasizes the duty of the Faithful to perform good works. On the orthodox views regarding this subject *vide supra*, p. 44 *sqq*.

Ad art. 15. This article returns to the subject of predestination which was touched upon in arts. 6, 11, 12; it cannot be said that the Waṣīya is a good composition, any more than the Fiḳh Akbar I.

Yet this article is not merely a repetition; it treats of the psychological side of predestination, that is, the question

1 Abū Dāwūd, *Buyū'*, b. 36; Ibn Mādja, *Tidjārāt*, b. 8.

2 *Iḥyā'*, i. 52.

3 Snouck Hurgronje, *Een rector der Mekkaansche universiteit*, p. 390 (*Verspreide Geschriften*, III. 110 *sq.*). Lane, *Manners and Customs*, p. 221, erroneously connects the fact that the students of the Azhar do not pay for the instruction they receive with their belonging to the poorer classes.

of how far this doctrine is consistent with any real action on the part of man; at the same time it combats several divergent views. Those who attributed to man the faculty of acting before the time of the act were the Ḳadarites and the Mu'tazilites as well as some of the Shī'ites (Rawāfiḍ).[1] How far some of the Ḳadarites went in this direction may be seen from the statement that the faculty to act was identified with "health and soundness of the limbs".[2] Further, there were differences of opinion in all shades of doctrine from this conception to that of the rigid predestinarians who attributed scarcely any activity to man.[3] A very ample discussion of all these views is to be found in the *Kitāb al-Fiṣal* of Ibn Ḥazm;[4] and the treatment of the question of free will by al-Ghazālī in the *Kitāb al-Tawḥīd* of his *Iḥyā'*[5] is unrivalled in Muslim literature.

The commentary on the Fiḳh Akbar I[6] first combats the views of the Ḳadarites, then those of the Djabrites, who say that the activity of man is not real, but only a metaphorical expression. The writer then says that Abū Ḥanīfa formulated the view that the creation of every act belongs to Allah, and that this consists in bringing forth the faculty in man.[7] Thereupon the commentator touches upon the differences of opinion between his friends, the Māturīdites, and the Ash'arites, regarding *istiṭā'a*. According to the Ash'arites the measure of *istiṭā'a* which is sufficient for evil deeds is not sufficient for good ones. This, says the commentator, comes near to *djabr*, and, in consequence of this, the Ash'arites admit that man is overburdened by the divine law (*al-taklīf fawḳa al-ṭāḳa*). The latter doctrine was naturally rejected by the Mu'tazilites. al-Ghazālī combats them in his *Risāla Ḳudsīya*,[8]

1 al-Ash'arī, *Maḳālāt*, i. 43, 72 *sq.*, 105, 281.

2 al-Ash'arī, *op. cit.*, i. 43; al-Maḳrīzī, *Khiṭaṭ*, ii. 247, ascribes this view to Thumāmā ibn al-Ashras.

3 *Maḳālāt*, i. 43, 72 *sq.*, 96, 283.

4 iii. 22 *sqq.*

5 iv. 220 *sqq.*

6 P. 10 *sqq.*

7 *Infra*, p. 191.

8 *Iḥyā'*, i. 105; cf. also Fakhr al-Dīn al-Rāzī's commentary on the Kuran, i. 185–96, and Ibn Ḥazm, *Kitāb al-Fiṣal*, iii. 26 *sq.*

and maintains that Allah is free to demand from His creatures the performance of works which are beyond their power.

Finally, it may be remarked that in the present article the idea of *kasb* does not appear.[1]

Ad art. 16. This article is directed against the Shī'a and the Khawāridj, who rejected the wiping of sandals as a substitute for the washing of the feet, since sura v. 8 ordered that feet should be washed, no mention being made of sandals. Ḥusain ibn 'Alī is represented to have said that he never saw the Prophet practising the minor rite after the revelation of sura v. 8;[2] hence arose the proud claim that the children of Fāṭima do not wipe their sandals or their headgear.[3]

In opposition to this, canonical Tradition affords evidence for the Prophet's practising the wiping of sandals even after the revelation of sura v. 8;[4] on this evidence is based the orthodox opinion that the wiping of sandals when on travel and at home is allowed in any case; women who choose to stay at home, as well as the lame who cannot travel, are excused from washing their feet for twenty-four hours.[5]

The time during which the minor rite may be continued, as indicated in the present article, is that which is allowed by all the *madhhab*'s, except that of Mālik, which rejects any limit of time.[6]

It will have been remarked that the present article goes farther than the four *madhhab*'s, which declare the minor rite to be allowed, whereas the article makes it obligatory. This may seem extravagant at first sight. Even the commentator has recourse to an exegetical licence in order

1 Cf. *infra*, Chapter VIII, Fiḳh Akbar II, art. 6.
2 *Corpus Iuris...*, ed. Griffini, No. 60.
3 *Corpus Iuris...*, No. 61.
4 *Handbook of Early Muhammadan Tradition*, p. 262 *a*.
5 al-Nawawī, i. 337.
6 al-Nawawī, i. 344; al-Tirmidhī, *Ṭahāra*, b. 71.

to bring the author's opinion into conformity with his own. "Obligatory", he says,[1] "has here the meaning of 'believed to be allowed'; the wiping of sandals is allowed, but it is obligatory to believe that it is allowed." We have seen above that, in contradistinction to early Islam and to the K͟hāridjites, later orthodoxy interpreted some traditions in a similar way.[2] We have no reason to follow this interpretation, especially as the article admits of a literal explanation.

In the Fiḳh Akbar II, art. 12, the wiping of sandals is called *sunna*; this term is explained in the commentary by the words: "This means that the permission to practise the wiping of sandals is based upon common usage". This interpretation is wrong; it takes *sunna* in the sense of the practice of Muhammad and the community, whereas the term is used here in the sense of "recommended", the second of the so-called five categories of actions. al-Nawawī, who died in A.D. 1278, discloses to us[3] that the *idjmāʿ* declared the wiping of sandals to be allowed.

So the interpretation of this action appears to have passed through three stages in the course of centuries, being declared obligatory at the time when it was in sharp opposition to the opinions of the S͟hīʿites and K͟hāridjites; recommended at the time when the violent debates were over; allowed at the time when the data of the sacred texts were interpreted with cool heads. According to al-Nawawī the schools did not agree on the question of whether wiping or washing was to be preferred. The S͟hāfiʿites held washing in higher esteem because this was the original form of the rite, and so did many of the Companions, such as ʿUmar, his son ʿAbdallāh, and Abū Aiyūb al-Anṣārī. Many of the Followers, on the other hand, preferred wiping; as did al-S͟haʿbī, al-Ḥakam and Ḥammād. To Aḥmad ibn Ḥanbal two opinions are ascribed. According to the one he preferred wiping, according to the other he had no predilection for either.

1 P. 19. 2 *Supra*, p. 104.
3 Commentary on Muslim, i. 337.

al-Ṭaḥāwī in his *'aḳīda*[1] avoids giving a definite opinion and adheres to the wiping of sandals when on travel and at home, in accordance with Tradition.

The materials accessible to us in the collections of canonical traditions do not appear to contain any oral utterance by Muhammad regarding the practice itself; they simply mention that Muhammad wiped his sandals.[2] As to the time of twenty-four hours for those at home and three days and nights for travellers, it is ascribed to Muhammad as a rule laid down by him on his travels.[3]

The author of the present article bases the obligatory force of the tradition on the fact that in this case it is nearly *mutawātir*. By this term are denoted reports which bear the clear stamp of veracity upon them, so that they are generally recognized and cannot be doubted.[4]

Further, the shortening of the *ṣalāt* and the breaking of the fast while travelling are called a *ruk͟hṣa*, as mentioned in the Kuran. As has been seen from the note on art. 16, the Leyden MS. of the Waṣīya reads *ḥaḳḳ t͟hābit*. This is not a simple variant, for *ruk͟hṣa* means a softening of the law by divine favour, whereas *ḥaḳḳ t͟hābit* means an established right. Even if this variant reading had not been preserved, we should know from Tradition that opinions on the shortening of the *ṣalāt*[5] and the breaking of the fast when on a journey were divided, especially on the latter point. Traditions state that on the journeys of Muhammad and his Companions some fasted, and others gave up fasting, without animosity on either side.[6] In a well-known tradition, however, Muhammad says: "It is not a token of piety to fast on journeys".[7] Another tradition is in line with the present article, recommending

1 Art. 16.

2 Muslim, *Ṭahāra*, trad. 72–85.

3 Muslim, *Ṭahāra*, trad. 85 *sq*. Curiously enough these traditions go back to 'Alī.

4 Details are omitted here; they will be found in Chapter IX.

5 *Handbook of Early Muhammadan Tradition*, under *Travels*.

6 Muslim, *Ṣiyām*, trad. 89, 90.

7 Muslim, *Ṣiyām*, trad. 93.

that use should be made of the permission (*rukhṣa*) granted to men by Allah.[1]

There was, however, a group that went much farther. In one tradition it is said that Muhammad on hearing that some people fasted when travelling called them sinners (*'uṣāt*), repeating this word twice.[2] And in a tradition preserved by Aḥmad ibn Ḥanbal[3] fasting on journeys is called a sin as great as Mount 'Arafāt.

al-Nawawī[4] states that the majority of the doctors think it allowed to fast on journeys and that this fasting is valid, but that some of the Ẓāhirites held the opposite opinion. There is a further difference of opinion on the question whether fasting or breaking the fast is to be preferred. According to Abū Ḥanīfa, Mālik and al-Shāfi'ī fasting is to be preferred, unless it should be harmful or accompanied by apparent difficulties. Aḥmad ibn Ḥanbal and other respectable authorities, on the other hand, say that breaking the fast is to be preferred in any case.

All this shows that on the question of the breaking of the fast when on travel there was nearly as much variety of opinion as on the question of the wiping of sandals. We may conclude from the materials available to us that the relaxations granted by the law were considered by some as concessions to human weakness, which it was better not to make use of. According to others, however, they were positive commands, which had to be taken in their literal sense. It is not surprising that this was the opinion of some of the Ẓāhirites and of Aḥmad ibn Ḥanbal.

Possibly the opinion of the latter was also based upon the general idea that the yoke of Islam is light, a principle that finds expression in several traditions in which Muhammad warns his Companions not to overburden the Faithful;[5] this has its scriptural basis in sura iv. 33: "Ye who believe...kill not yourselves".

1 Muslim, *Ṣiyām*, trad. 94. 2 Muslim, *Ṣiyām*, trad. 91.
3 *Musnad*, ii. 71. 4 Commentary on Muslim, iii. 93.
5 Bukhārī, *Maghāzī*, b. 60; *Aḥkām*, b. 22; Muslim, *Ashriba*, trad. 71.

It may further be observed that the common orthodox views on the wiping of sandals and on the breaking of the fast when on travel run parallel also in this respect, that in the course of time the preference for the relaxations passed through the stages of obligation, recommendation and permission, and ended in being considered less meritorious than the severer practice.

Ad art. 17. Here again we find that an article of faith has passed into the collections of Tradition. Aḥmad ibn Ḥanbal[1] has a tradition on the authority of 'Ubāda ibn al-Ṣāmit, in which the latter says to his son: "I heard the Apostle of Allah say: The first thing Allah created was the pen. Then He said: Write, and it wrote at that moment all that was to happen till the day of resurrection. O my son, if thou diest without believing this, thou goest to Hell". In al-Tirmidhī's collection[2] the same tradition occurs in a slightly different form.

In this tradition it is supposed that the pen is pre-existent, as is also the case in the wording of the present article. Pre-existence is a feature which the pen has in common with other entities.[3] Of later traditions on the pen it may be sufficient to translate one item from the commentary on the present article. al-Baihaḳī hands down a tradition on the authority of Ibn 'Abbās, according to which the Prophet said: "The first thing Allah created was the pen. Then He created the throne and the chair, then a preserved table from a white pearl; its upper and nether surfaces were of white hyacinth, its pen was light and its writing was light. Allah looks towards it every day two hundred and sixty times; at every look He creates and causes life and death, He elevates and humbles, He raises some and brings others low". This may be called a specimen of post-canonical Tradition.

The subject of predestination, to which the present

1 v. 317.
2 *Tafsīr*, sura lxviii.
3 Cf. "The Navel of the Earth", p. 16 *sq.*

article is akin, has also been touched upon in arts. 6, 7, 11, 15.[1]

Ad art. 18. See *supra*, p. 117 *sqq.* To what has been said there it may be added that in Tradition the punishment in the tomb is never mentioned expressly in connection with the Faithful. It occurs either in a general way, *e.g.* in the traditions in which it is enumerated amongst the things against which an *isti'ādha* must be spoken,[2] or it is represented as a punishment for special sins.[3] In the Fiḳh Akbar II, art. 23, there is mentioned in addition the pressure (*daghṭa*) of the tomb, and this, together with the punishment, is there called real for all infidels and for some sinners among the Faithful. The commentator on the present article cites the following passage from the *Baḥr al-Kalām*:[4] "Regarding the Faithful two things are possible; if he has been obedient, he will be exempt from the punishment of the tomb; he will have to suffer the pressure only. If he has been a sinner (*'āṣī*), he will suffer the punishment of the tomb as well as the pressure; but the punishment will cease on the next Friday and it will not return before the day of resurrection. If he dies on a Friday or in the night before a Friday, the punishment and the pressure will last one hour only and the punishment will not return before the day of resurrection". Then the author goes on to cite the *Khizānat al-Riwāyāt*:[5] "If the dead man be an infidel, his punishment will last till the day of resurrection, and will be suspended only on Fridays and during Ramaḍān".

In canonical Tradition it is stated that whosoever dies on a Friday will be exempted from the punishment of the tomb.[6]

1 Cf. Fiḳh Akbar II, art. 5, where it is said that God's writing on the preserved table is of a descriptive nature only.

2 Numerous instances; cf. *Handbook of Early Muhammadan Tradition*, p. 115 *b*, at the top.

3 Cf. *supra*, p. 118.

4 P. 22. See also *supra*, p. 148.

5 A work of which nothing more is known to me.

6 Tirmidhī, *Djanā'iz*, b. 72.

Ad art. 19. For the purpose of interrogation and punishment the *rūḥ* of the dead is reunited to his body.[1]

In the present article the interrogation of the dead by Munkar and Nakīr is said to be based on Tradition. Regarding this statement it may be remarked that, so far as I see, Munkar and Nakīr—the source of the names is obscure—are mentioned only once in the collections of canonical Tradition, namely, in al-Tirmidhī, *Kitāb al-Djanā'iz*, b. 70. The interrogation of the dead by two anonymous angels, on the other hand, is a conception familiar to that literature.[2] Obviously the names do not belong to the early stock of canonical Tradition; they begin to appear only towards the close of its formation.

A further point is, that in some of the traditions only one angel is mentioned, not two;[3] there is even a tradition in which no interrogator is mentioned at all.[4] Apparently the original form from which the conception was developed was that the interrogation in the tomb took place by one angel. Among the traditions belonging to this early stage is the following:[5] "The Apostle of Allah said: When man has been laid in his tomb, if he be faithful, his work (that is, his prayer and his fasting) is at his side. Then the angel approaches from the side where his prayer is, but this will push him back. Then the angel approaches from the side of his fasting, but this will likewise push him back. Then the angel will call him, saying: Sit upright. When he is sitting upright, the angel will ask him: What do you say about this man? The dead: Whom do you mean? The angel: Muhammad. The dead: I witness that he is the Apostle of Allah. The angel: How do you know that you have understood this? The dead:

1 Cf. Fiḳh Akbar II, art. 23.

2 Cf. *Handbook of Early Muhammadan Tradition*, p. 89 *a*, in voce *Grave*.

3 Muslim, *Īmān*, trad. 163; Aḥmad ibn Ḥanbal, iv. 150.

4 Aḥmad ibn Ḥanbal, vi. 354 *sq*.

5 Aḥmad ibn Ḥanbal, vi. 352. Other traditions of this type are Abū Dāwūd, *Sunna*, b. 39 *b*; Aḥmad ibn Ḥanbal, iii. 233, 346; al-Ṭayālisī, No. 753.

I witness that he is the Apostle of Allah. The angel: In this confession you have lived, in this you have died, in this you will be raised from the dead. If the dead be an infidel or a sinner, the angel approaches him without hindrance. Then he makes him sit upright and interrogates him in the same way. On the question regarding Muhammad the dead will answer: I do not know, I have heard people say something concerning him and this I have repeated. The angel: In this you have lived, in this you have died, in this you will be raised from the dead. Then a beast in the tomb bearing a whip, the knot of which is a coal like a camel's eye, will be allowed to beat him as long as it please Allah, without any pity, this beast being deaf". The traditions in which two angels are mentioned apparently represent the second stage.[1] Possibly the development from one into two angels is due to the idea of the two guardian angels who accompany every man. This surmise is supported by the fact that the Karrāmites taught the identity of Munkar and Nakīr with the guardian angels.[2]

It is only in the third stage that the names of the angels appear. According to al-Īdjī,[3] the Mu'tazilites denied the interrogation of the dead by Munkar and Nakīr.

Ad art. 20. Some traditions concerning the creation of Paradise and Hell are to be found in Abū Dāwūd, *Sunna*, b. 22; they are, however, of no value for the understanding of the question which is treated in the present article, namely, the present and the everlasting existence of Paradise and Hell. We have seen above[4] that the view combated here is that of Djahm ibn Ṣafwān, who maintained that Paradise and Hell would vanish, so that Allah would be as lonely in the end as He had been in the

1 Bukhārī, *Djanā'iz*, b. 68, 87; Muslim, *Djanna*, trad. 70; Nasā'ī, *Djanā'iz*, b. 110; Aḥmad ibn Ḥanbal, iii. 3 *sq.*, 126.

2 al-Baghdādī, *Uṣūl al-Dīn*, p. 246.

3 P. 269 *sq.*

4 P. 121; cf. also *Kitāb al-Intiṣār*, p. 168.

beginning.[1] It is also stated that the Hishāmites, the Ḍirārites, the Djahmites and a section of the Ḳadarites denied the existence of Paradise and Hell in the orthodox sense; according to them, Adam's abode was a garden somewhere on the earth, whereas orthodox Muslim theology knows a heavenly Paradise only.[2] Yet these sects[3] did not deny the reality of reward and punishment in Paradise and Hell; these abodes would be created by Allah at the time "of the separation of the two groups",[4] but for a time only. According to the orthodox view, on the other hand, the throne and the chair, the table and the pen, Paradise and Hell with their inhabitants, the spiritual beings, will not vanish; according to al-Ṭaḥāwī,[5] they also are pre-existent.

Those who combated the orthodox view referred to a verse from the Kuran:[6] "Everything will vanish, except the face of Allah". al-Ḳasṭallānī[7] explains this verse in the following way: The face of Allah means His essence. All things besides His essence are contingent; all that is contingent vanishes, and, as compared with His essence, is non-existent.

In this way al-Ḳasṭallānī suggests the complementary idea, that Paradise and Hell will preserve the kind of reality that is proper to the whole creation.[8] Similarly, one of the commentators cited by Molla Ḥusain[9] says that the term "non-being" (*ma'dūm*), which must be applied to created things, refers to their essence (*dhāt*), without impairing their existence (*wudjūd*).

It appears from this that orthodox Islam seeks to make

1 al-Ash'arī, *Maḳālāt*, i. 148 *sq.*, 164, 279; cf. Fakhr al-Dīn al-Rāzī, v. 8 *sq.*; vi. 244; Ibn Ḥazm, *Kitāb al-Fiṣal*, iv. 81 *sq.*

2 al-Baghdādī, *Uṣūl*, p. 237; al-Maḳrīzī, *Khiṭaṭ*, ii. 347; cf. also Fakhr al-Dīn al-Rāzī, v. 335.

3 Cf. also al-Īdjī, p. 254 *sqq.*

4 Commentary on Fiḳh Akbar I, p. 28; Fakhr al-Dīn, iv. 94; Ibn Ḥazm, *Kitāb al-Fiṣal*, v. 42 *sqq.*

5 Art. 19.

6 Sura xxviii. 88.

7 As cited in the commentary, p. 24.

8 Cf. also Abu'l-Muntahā on Fiḳh Akbar II, p. 42.

9 P. 24.

a real distinction between essence and existence, just as was done by the angelic doctor on behalf of Christian dogmatics.[1] On this point the Mu'tazilites held the opposite view.[2] According to them the non-being was a thing (*al-ma'dūm s̲h̲ai'*). Their scriptural argument was sura xxii. 1: "O ye men, fear your Lord, for the quake of the Hour will be a tremendous thing". Here, the Mu'-tazilites said, the Hour, though not actually existing, is called a thing. Consequently the non-being is a thing and it is not necessary that Paradise and Hell should actually exist in order to be called things. The absence of discrimination between essence and existence on the part of the Mu'tazilites is apparently connected with the process of evaporation that left little of the Islamic eschatology unimpaired, so that al-Māturīdī is said to have exclaimed: "How trifling is resurrection in the opinion of the Mu'tazilites who say that it is found among us, though its terrors do not appear".[3]

On eternal reward and punishment cf. *infra*, pp. 184, 268.

Ad art. 21. The idea of weighing in connection with eschatology occurs in the Kuran in several passages, of which the following may be mentioned. Sura xxi. 48: "And just balances will We set up for the day of the resurrection, so that no soul will be wronged in any way; and if a work were but the weight of a grain of mustard-seed, We would bring it forth to be weighed: and our reckoning will suffice". Sura ci. 5: "Then as to him whose balances are heavy—his shall be a life that shall please him well; and as to him whose balances are light, his dwelling-place shall be the lowest pit of Hell". Closely parallel to this verse is sura xxiii. 104 *sq.* Further, sura xviii. 105: "They are those who believed not in the signs of their Lord, or that they should even meet Him. Vain,

1 Rougier, *La scolastique*, pp. 124 *sqq.*, 459 *sqq.*

2 Commentary on Fiḳh Akbar I, p. 28 *sq.*

3 Commentary on Fiḳh Akbar I, p. 30.

therefore, are their works; and no weight will We allow them[1] on the day of resurrection". And sura vii. 7: "The weighing on that day shall be just; and they whose balances are heavy, these are they who shall be happy; but they whose balances are light, these are they who have lost their souls".

Apart from sura xxi. 48, in none of these verses is it said that man's acts or scrolls will be weighed on the day of resurrection. Probably the persons themselves are meant, and as a matter of fact the verses mentioned have been taken in this sense. al-Ṭabarī in his commentary on sura vii. 7 cites a tradition which asserts that on that day even the tallest person, when placed on the balance, will not equal a fly's wing in weight. This explanation is also mentioned by al-Baiḍāwī. The idea of the weighing of the dead was familiar to Egyptian religion.

The prevalent idea in connection with the balance has, however, become this, that the books in which the acts of man have been written are thrown in the balances.[2] "The common belief is that the scrolls on which the acts are written will be weighed in a balance which is provided with a needle and two platforms. All creatures will gaze on it, as it proceeds with equity and dismisses excuses; when it interrogates them concerning their acts, they will confess them with their tongues and bear witness to them in their limbs. This conception is corroborated by the tradition according to which man will be conducted to the balance; then nine and ninety seals[3] to his debit will be opened, each of them as long as sight reaches. Thereupon a note to his credit will be brought forth, containing the two phrases of the confession of faith. Then the seals will be laid on one platform, and the note on the other; the seals will rise and the note will outweigh them."[4]

1 *I.e.* their persons.

2 Fiḳh Akbar II, art. 21; Tirmidhī, as cited in the commentary on the Waṣīya, p. 25.

3 Cf. *infra*, p. 174.

4 Baiḍāwī on sura vii. 7; cf. Aḥmad ibn Ḥanbal, *Musnad*, ii. 213.

The terror of the moment of weighing is described in the following tradition: "One day 'Ā'isha wept at the thought of Hell. When Muhammad asked her the cause of her weeping, she answered: I was thinking of Hell. Will you remember your wives on the day of resurrection? The Apostle of Allah answered: In three places man will think of himself only: at the balance, when he is longing to know whether his weight will be light or heavy; at the reading of his book, when it will be said: Read his two books, as he will be anxious to know whether his book will be given into his right hand or into his left one, or behind his back; and at the bridge, when Hell is on both sides of him".[1]

In this tradition Muhammad is not yet represented as a powerful protector on the day of resurrection. In another tradition[2] the balance is expressly mentioned as a place where Muhammad will make use of his intercession: "Anas said: I besought the Prophet of Allah to intercede on my behalf on the day of resurrection. He said: I shall be busy with mankind. I asked: Where shall I meet you on that day? He answered: Look for me in the first place at the bridge.[3] I said: And if I do not meet you at the bridge? He answered: Then I shall be at the balance. I asked: And if I do not meet you at the balance? He answered: Then I shall be at the basin. I shall not miss these three stations on the day of resurrection".

It is well known that Oriental eschatology is the reflex of primeval events.[4] Even the eschatology of Islam, which comes last among the Semitic religions, has preserved traces of this pattern. One of the instances is the balance. Bukhārī and Muslim have preserved a tradition which states that Allah's hand is full and liberal, that nothing can exhaust it, day or night: "Knowest thou

1 Abū Dāwūd, *Sunna*, b. 24.
2 Aḥmad ibn Ḥanbal, iii. 178.
3 On the bridge, cf. IV Esdras vii. 6–8; R. Bell in *The Moslem World*, Jan. 1932, p. 43 *sqq.*; Sale, *Preliminary Discourse*, p. 125 *sq.*
4 Cf. Gunkel, *Schöpfung und Chaos in Urzeit und Endzeit.*

what He has spent since He created the heavens and the earth? Yet what was in His hand was not exhausted. His throne was on the water and with His other hand He held the balance, raising and lowering".[1]

This tradition, as al-Nawawī remarks, contains the symbol of the divine decrees. I am not acquainted with other traditions regarding this pre-existent balance. Probably it was of cosmic dimensions, like the throne and the eschatological balance. The balance is described in the *Kitāb Aḥwāl al-Ḳiyāma*[2] as follows: "It is said on the authority of Ibn 'Abbās, that the Apostle of Allah said: On the day of resurrection the balance will be set up. Each of its arms will have the length of the distance between East and West. The platform will be as large as the earth in its length and breadth. One of its platforms will be to the right of the throne, and this is the platform of good works; the other will be to the left of the throne, and this is the platform of evil works. The tops of the balances (?) are like the tops of mountains, being filled with the good and evil works of men and *djinn*, on a day of which the length will be fifty thousand years". According to the description given by al-Ghazālī,[3] the platform to the right of the throne is all light, the other all darkness. In this connection it may be remembered that in Egyptian religion also the balance was an entity representative of cosmic order.

From the tradition just translated it appears that side by side with the ideas of the weighing of persons and of books there was a third interpretation, namely, that acts will be weighed. In art. 21 of the Fiḳh Akbar II it is the acts of man that are weighed. This is also stated in the tradition mentioned by al-Tirmidhī:[4] "Works will be weighed,

1 Bukhārī, *Tawḥīd*, b. 19; cf. *Tafsīr*, sura xi, b. 2; Muslim, *Zakāt*, trad. 37.

2 P. 81; cf. the commentary on the Waṣīya, p. 26.

3 *al-Durra al-fākhira*, p. 25.

4 As cited in the commentary on the Waṣīya, p. 25; cf. also Fakhr al-Dīn, iii. 188 *sqq*.

not man himself; his work, not his person, will be weighed, and the work of the Muslim will shine as light, as the light of the sun and the moon; the work of the infidel will be like the darkness of night".

There is, however, a view that a balance will not be set up for the infidels, and that their works will not be weighed at all;[1] according to al-Ghazālī, two classes of people are exempt from the weighing of works, namely, those whose works are merely evil, and those who are guiltless. The first of these classes will be thrown straightway into the fire; the second class will straightway enter Paradise. The balance is set up only for those whose works are partly good and partly evil.[2]

A third class which is exempt from the trial of the balance is the class of sufferers. This exemption is not mentioned by al-Ghazālī, but by al-Baiḍāwī in his commentary on sura xxxix. 13: "According to Tradition the balances will be set up on the day of resurrection for the people of prayer, alms, and pilgrimage; by the balances their wages will be fixed and paid to them. But no balances will be set up for the sufferers (*ahl al-balā'*), their wages will be paid out to them at once, and this will make people who were prosperous in the world wish that their bodies had been cut by scissors". Possibly the Mu'tazilites and other philosophers may have raised objections to such conceptions. Both al-Ghazālī and the commentator of the present creed bring forward an argument to meet the objection that works, being *accidentia* (*'araḍ*), cannot be weighed. The commentator confines himself to the remark that it is possible for Allah to give works such a form of existence that they can be perceived by the senses. al-Ghazālī's argument is as follows: works, being *accidentia*, cannot be weighed in the sensual way; consequently the balance must belong to the spiritual world or *malakūt*. He rejects the allegorical interpretation.[3] The Karrāmites avoided the

1 *al-Durra al-fākhira*, p. 25.
2 *Iḥyā'*, iv. 471.
3 *Durra*, p. 70.

difficulty in a different way: works, being *accidentia*, would be transformed by Allah into substances (*adjsām*) and as such be capable of being weighed.[1]

The idea of works being weighed on the last day occurs also in Persian religion:[2] "Arta Virāf, 5, a vu que Rašnû tient une balance d'or à la main dans laquelle il pèse les actions des hommes pieux et celles des impies".[3]

Another interpretation is the allegorical one. al-Baiḍāwī explains the term "the weighing" (sura vii. 7) by "judgment". And al-Ṭabarī, in his commentary, reproduces a tradition on the authority of Mudjāhid in which the balance mentioned in sura xxi. 48 is called an allegory (*mathal*); this explanation is justified by a reference to the fact that the terms "weighing" and "reality" are also explained in a sense other than the literal.

Ad art. 22. The sequence of the different eschatological scenes differs in the descriptions. In the present creed the sequence is: the balance—the reading of the book—resurrection and retribution—the meeting with Allah—intercession. In the Fiḳh Akbar II it is: intercession—the balance—the basin—redress of griefs. In al-Ṭaḥāwī's *'aḳīda* it is: resurrection—retribution—account of sins—reading of the book—the bridge—the balance.

In the systematic treatises on eschatology in later literature there is, in some measure, a more uniform sequence.

Besides sura xvii. 15, which is cited in the present article, there are other passages in the Kuran referring to the books in which the acts of man are recorded. Sura lxxxiv. 7 runs as follows: "He in whose right hand his book shall be given shall be reckoned with in an easy reckoning, and shall turn back, rejoicing, to his kindred. But he whose book shall be given him behind his back, shall invoke destruction, but at the fire shall he burn".

1 al-Baghdādī, *Uṣūl*, p. 245.
2 Sale, *Preliminary Discourse*, p. 118 *sq.*
3 N. Söderblom, *La vie future*, p. 96.

According to al-Baiḍāwī the words "behind his back" have the meaning of "into his left hand", as the left hand of the wicked will be tied behind his back. In the parallel passage, sura lxix. 19–26, the righteous receive their book in the right hand, the wicked in the left. The two views are harmonized in a tradition, according to which the sinner's hand will be passed through his breast, which will be pierced for this purpose by an angel.[1] Later eschatology distinguishes, however, three classes of people who are made to give account on the last day: those who receive their book in their right hand; these are they who shall be reckoned with in an easy reckoning; the second class consists of the sinners who receive their book into their left hand; these are they who shall be severely reckoned with; the third class consists of those who receive their book behind their back; they are the infidels, who go to Hell.[2]

This final stage is due not only to the tendency to take the expressions of the Kuran on this subject literally, it also represents an aspect peculiar to Muslim theology, as compared with the Kuran. The latter describes two absolutely opposite groups on the day of resurrection—the blessed and the damned. Muslim theology, as we have seen above,[3] tends to mitigate the punishment in Hell for those who, though sinners, have not lost their faith. This tendency corresponds to the introduction of the idea of Purgatory, which brought about some changes in eschatology. Apart from the one just mentioned we have found another in connection with the balance;[4] the third and most important will be discussed later, in connection with art. 27.

Particulars of the books mentioned in the present article will be found in the *Kitāb Aḥwāl al-Ḳiyāma*.[5] al-Ghazālī is remarkably silent on the subject. In his *Durra*[6]

1 *Aḥwāl al-Ḳiyāma*, p. 81.

2 *Aḥwāl al-Ḳiyāma*, p. 78 *sq.*, and the commentary on the Waṣīya, p. 26.

3 P. 61.

4 *Supra*, p. 171.

5 P. 77 *sqq.*

6 P. 79.

he mentions one book only in which the acts of all men are written, in accordance with sura xxxix. 69.

The conception of books in which the acts of man are recorded is found also in Jewish literature.[1] A few examples may be given here: Daniel vii. 9, 10: "I beheld till the thrones were cast down, and the Ancient of days did sit... the judgment was set, and the books were opened". Book of Enoch, lxxxi. 4: "Blessed is the man who dies in righteousness and goodness, concerning whom there is no book of unrighteousness written, and against whom no day of judgment shall be found". In Enoch lxxxix. 71 it is said that these books were sealed: "And the book was read before the Lord of the sheep, and He took the book from his hand and read it and sealed it and laid it down". Similarly, the idea that these sealed books will be opened on the day of resurrection is found in Jewish literature. Enoch xc. 20: "And I saw till a throne was erected in the pleasant land, and the Lord of the sheep sat himself thereon, and the other took the sealed books and opened these books before the Lord of the sheep".

As to the reading of the books, according to sura xvii. 15 this is done by man, whereas according to sura lxix. 19 it is the angels who read.

In sura xvii. 15 the reading of the books is combined with the computation of sins.

It has been observed that for the formation of his religious terminology Muhammad had recourse chiefly to two sources: the religious terms of the Jews and the Christians, which he partly translated and partly took over as borrowed words; and the commercial terms of his native town. The idea of the computation of sins certainly belongs to the latter class. Yet it must not be forgotten that it was not foreign to older religions, as may be seen from the references given above. It will also be remembered that in some of the parables of the New Testament the events of the Last Day are described by means of the

1 Cf. E. Schrader, *Die Keilinschriften und das Alte Testament*, 3rd ed. by Winckler and Zimmern, p. 405.

parable of a master who makes his servants give account.

The idea that man will be made to give account of his acts is found more than once in the Kuran (sura xxiii. 117; cf. xxvi. 113; lxxxviii. 26). Preaching is called the task of Muhammad; Allah will take account (sura xiii. 40). Allah is He who taketh account of all things (sura iv. 88) and He taketh a sufficient account (sura xxxix. 39). The day of resurrection is called the day of reckoning (sura xxxviii. 15, 25, 53; xl. 28); on this day Allah will proceed without delay or slowness (*sarīʿ al-ḥisāb*, sura xl. 17; xxiv. 39; xiv. 51; xiii. 41; v. 6; iii. 17, 199; ii. 198).

In Tradition a few details regarding the computation of sins are added. They refer in the first place to sura lxxxiv. 7 *sq.*:[1] "He into whose right hand his book shall be given, shall be reckoned with in an easy reckoning". The tendency of these traditions is to emphasize that a severe reckoning would be fatal to man: "The Apostle of Allah said: Anyone who is made to give account will perish. I[2] said: O Apostle of Allah (may Allah make me your ransom), does not Allah say, He into whose right hand his book shall be given, shall be reckoned with in an easy reckoning? He answered: This refers to the general review. Whoso is called to give a detailed account shall perish".[3]

A tradition on the authority of Abū Dharr gives an explanation of this easy reckoning, which is characteristic of the mildness of popular Islam: "On the day of resurrection man will be brought forward and the command will be given: Review his venial sins before him. This will be done and his mortal sins will be passed over in silence. Then he will be asked: Do you remember on such a day and on such a day? and so on. He will confess all these sins without any attempt at denial, being filled with fear of the

1 Cf. ad art. 21.

2 The tradition is related on the authority of ʿĀʾisha.

3 Bukhārī, *Tafsīr*, sura 84; Tirmidhī, *Ḳiyāma*, b. 5; *Tafsīr*, sura 84, b. 1; cf. Bukhārī, *ʿIlm*, b. 35; *Riḳāḳ*, b. 49; Muslim, *Djanna*, trad. 79.

mortal ones. Then it will be said: Give him instead of every evil act a good one. Then he will say: I have committed other sins which I do not see here. Then", continues Abū Dharr, "I saw the Apostle of Allah laugh so that his molar teeth appeared".[1]

An indication of the mildness of later Muslim theology, as compared with that of its early period, is given by the fact that according to later eschatology the severe examination need not prove fatal to the sinner; this is in opposition to the tradition cited above.[2]

The first subject of the computation of sins is prayer: "The first of man's works which will be reviewed is his prayer. If this is as it ought to be, he will be saved and happy. If it is not as it ought to be, he will be lost and unhappy. If his other obligatory works are defective, the Lord will say: See whether my servant has performed supererogatory prayers and so made good the defects of his obligatory works; his other works shall be examined in like manner."[3]

Apart from the personal computation of sins we find also the idea that several communities and their leaders, the Apostles, will be obliged to give account. The idea is perhaps connected with the Kuranic doctrine of the Apostles and their communities who are represented as witnesses on the day of resurrection, *e.g.* "Thus have we made you an intermediate community, that ye may be witnesses in regard to mankind, and that the Apostle may be a witness in regard to you".[4] Similarly: "That the Apostle may be a witness against you and you may be witnesses against mankind".[5] And: "The earth shall shine by the light of her Lord, and the book shall be set, and the Prophets and the witnesses shall be brought".[6] Cf. also sura v. 108 and sura vii. 5, where the assembling of the Apostles and their interrogation are mentioned.

1 Aḥmad ibn Ḥanbal, v. 157; cf. p. 170.
2 Cf. *Kitāb Aḥwāl al-Ḳiyāma*, p. 79.
3 Tirmidhī, *Ṣalāt*, b. 188.
4 Sura ii. 137.
5 Sura xxii. 78.
6 Sura xxxix. 69.

A description of the interrogation of the Apostles and the reciting of their scriptures, as well as of the confrontation of their people with them, is given by al-Ghazālī in his *Durra.*[1] The explanation given by al-Baiḍāwī in his comment on sura ii. 137, especially of Muhammad's community as intermediate, is as follows: "According to a tradition, the communities will deny on the day of resurrection that the Prophets have preached to them. Then Allah will demand from the Prophets the proof that they have preached, for He knows best how to prove that such a denial is false. Thereupon the community of Muhammad will be summoned and it will bear witness. Then the other communities will say: How do ye know this? They will answer: We know this through the reports in the book of Allah who has spoken through the tongue of His Prophet, the veracious. Then Muhammad will be brought and interrogated concerning the state of his community and he will witness that they are right".

Further, a tradition from the collection of Ibn Mādja may be translated here as an illustration of the idea of computation: "The Apostle of Allah said: We are the last of the communities, but the first which will be made to give account. It will be asked on the day of resurrection: Where is the community from the gentiles (*al-ummīya*) and their Prophet? So we, the last, shall be the first".[2] In another tradition it is related how Muhammad will be summoned on the day of resurrection to appear with his community.[3] Seventy members of the community will enter Paradise without computation. On being asked who they are, Muhammad answers: "Those who made use neither of cauterization nor of sorcery, but trusted in their Lord".[4]

Ad art. 23. A wonderful description of how life will

1 P. 71 *sqq.*

2 Ibn Mādja, *Zuhd*, b. 34.

3 Commentary on the Waṣīya, p. 26.

4 Muslim, *Īmān*, trad. 371 *sq.*; cf. Bukhārī, *Ṭibb*, b. 17, 42; *Riḳāḳ*, b. 21, 50; Ibn Mādja, *Zuhd*, b. 34.

be restored to mankind between the first and the second blast of the trumpet is given in al-Ghazālī's *Durra.*[1] Its main features go back to canonical Tradition.[2] Fifty thousand years as the duration of the day of resurrection is the measure mentioned in the Kuran, sura lxx. 4. To al-Ghazālī it has become the canvas of a vivid eschatological description.[3] A special form of the computation of sins is the redress of griefs, which in this article is called the paying of duties (*adā' al-ḥuḳūḳ*), but in the corresponding article (21) of the Fiḳh Akbar II is called retaliation (*ḳiṣāṣ*). The idea is also found in canonical Tradition: "When the Faithful have been saved from Hell, they will be detained on a bridge between Paradise and Hell. Then they will adjust the wrongs they have done to one another in the world. When they have been purified and cleansed, they will be allowed to enter Paradise".[4]

A different scene is depicted in the following tradition:[5] "The Apostle of Allah said: Do you know who is the bankrupt? His companions answered: He who has neither money nor possessions. He said: The bankrupt of my community is he who on the day of resurrection shall bring his prayer, his fasting and his alms; as against this it shall be remembered that he has scorned such an one, slandered another, taken the possessions of another, killed or beaten others. Then he shall sit down and all these shall take retribution from his good works. And if his good works are exhausted before all his sins have been requited, the sins of those persons shall be added to his debit account and he shall be thrown into Hell".

In another tradition[6] it is said that such redress of wrongs shall be carried out in the case of two sheep which

1 P. 40 *sqq.*; cf. also the commentary on the Waṣīya, and *Kitāb Aḥwāl al-Ḳiyāma*, p. 58 *sq.*

2 Muslim, *Fitan*, trad. 110, 116, 141–3.

3 *Iḥyā'*, iv. 466 *sq.*

4 Bukhārī, *Maẓālim*, b. 1.

5 Tirmidhī, *Ḳiyāma*, b. 2; cf. Fiḳh Akbar II, art. 21, which goes back to this tradition.

6 Aḥmad ibn Ḥanbal, iii. 29.

have fought each other with their horns. A lengthy description of the redress of wrongs is to be found in al-Ghazālī's *Iḥyā*.[1] The idea belongs to some extent to the orthodox theodicy.

Ad art. 24. The well-known controversial question,[2] whether Allah will be seen by the inhabitants of Paradise, is here answered in the affirmative and appears as an article of faith. This need not cause surprise, as we have seen that in canonical Tradition also this point is settled. Nor does it cause surprise that a restriction is added, in order to prevent anthropomorphic explanations, such as "without description, comparison or modality".

The term *liḳāʾ Allah*, "meeting Allah", and its synonyms often occur in the Kuran, but never in the sense which it acquired in later dogmatics and in the present article. In the Kuran it is used chiefly to emphasize the idea of resurrection and of the day of resurrection with all its events, in face of the incredulity of the Makkans, *e.g.* sura vi. 31: "They are lost who deny a meeting with God, until the Hour comes suddenly upon them". In a similar sense the term is used in sura vi. 155; x. 46; xviii. 105, 110; xxix. 22; xxx. 7; xxxii. 10. In other passages these people are called "those who do not dread a meeting with Us" (sura x. 7, 16; xxv. 23). The general meaning which was attached to the term is illustrated by the fact that *liḳāʾ Allah* in the Kuran is interchanged with *liḳāʾ al-ākhira* (sura xxii. 34; xxx. 15).

This general sense may receive a still darker colouring when it is used in connection with retribution, *e.g.* in sura xxxii. 14: "Taste then the recompense of your having forgotten the meeting with this your day; we have also forgotten you; taste then an eternal punishment, for that which ye have wrought". In a similar sense the term *liḳāʾ yawmikum* is used in sura vii. 49; xxxix. 71; xlv. 33.

---

1 iv. 472–4.
2 *Supra*, pp. 24, 63 *sqq.*, 130. On *liḳāʾ Allah* cf. Faḫhr al-Dīn al-Rāzī, i. 348.

In Tradition *liḳā' Allah* has the same general meaning as in many passages of the Kuran. "Till he met Allah" in this connection means "till his death".[1] We may possibly have in canonical Tradition one instance in which the dogmatic controversies are reflected. This is the tradition containing the formulae of Muhammad's night-prayer. It runs thus: "When the Apostle of Allah rose to perform his night-prayer, he used to say: O Allah, to Thee belongs the glory, Thou art the light of the heavens and of the earth and of those who dwell therein. Thou art reality, Thy promise is reality, Thy word is reality, Thy meeting is reality, Paradise is reality, the fire is reality and the Hour is reality...".[2] al-Nawawī in his commentary mentions two explanations of the term *liḳā'* in this tradition, namely, death and resurrection, of which in his view the latter only is right. Considering, however, the fact that the term "reality" (*ḥaḳḳ*) as well as the ideas to which it is applied are also used in the creed,[3] we may regard it as probable that they have the same meaning in the *ḥadīth* and in the creed, namely, that of the *visio beatifica*.

Ad art. 25. We have seen[4] that the Mu'tazilites rejected the idea of intercession and why they did so. It is precisely because of their negative attitude on this point that the dogma is explicitly stated in the orthodox creed.

The cause of its adoption by the orthodox community may be due to the need for something to counterbalance predestination, as well as the influence of Christian ideas. In early Christian literature we find the angels, the patriarchs, the Prophets, the Apostles and the martyrs as those who will intercede on behalf of sinners. The same classes of men are the holders of the privilege of intercession in Islam. The fact is the more curious, since the Kuran on

1 Bukhārī, *Mawāḳīt al-Ṣalāt*, b. 33; Tirmidhī, *Ṣalāt*, b. 113; *Zuhd*, b. 38.

2 Muslim, *Ṣalāt al-Musāfirīn*, trad. 199; cf. Bukhārī, *Tahadjdjud*, b. 1; cf. *Tawḥīd*, b. 8, 24, 35; Tirmidhī, *Da'awāt*, b. 29.

3 Art. 20, see *supra*, p. 130.

4 *Supra*, p. 61 *sq*.

the whole is not favourable to the idea of intercession. On the one hand we find passages such as the following: "Those who bear the Throne and they who encircle it, celebrate the praise of their Lord and believe in Him and implore forgiveness for the believers, saying: O Lord, Thou embracest all things in mercy and knowledge; do Thou forgive therefore those who turn to Thee and follow Thy path, and keep them from the pains of Hell" (sura xl. 7; cf. xlii. 3). And sura xxi. 26: "They say: The Merciful hath begotten issue. Nay, they are but His honoured servants...and no plea shall they offer, save on behalf of those whom He pleaseth".

In these passages it is the angels who are represented as possessing the privilege of intercession. Likewise in sura xix. 90 and sura xliii. 86 intercession is restricted to those who have a covenant with Allah and to those who bear witness to the truth; in sura ii. 256 (cf. x. 3) to those who have received permission to intercede.

From other passages in the Kuran it may be gathered that in Muhammad's circle intercession with Allah was expected from the lower gods: "They worship beside Allah that which cannot hurt or help them, and say: These are our advocates with Allah" (sura x. 19). This may explain Muhammad's unwillingness to admit intercession at all, as appears, for instance, from sura ii. 45: "Fear a day in which a soul shall not avail for a soul at all, nor shall any intercession be accepted from them, nor shall any ransom be taken, nor any help be given them".

Hardly less negative is sura xxxix. 45, where intercession is restricted to Allah Himself. Muhammad's intercession is never mentioned in the Kuran in plain words; Muhammadan theology finds an allusion to it in sura xvii. 81: "Peradventure thy Lord will raise thee to an honourable station", and in sura xciii. 5: "And thy Lord shall give thee wherewith thou shalt be well pleased".

Yet it is precisely Muhammad's intercession which is emphasized in some branches of theology such as the present article of the Waṣīya and the chief tradition on intercession in the canonical collections. In this tradition a description is given of how the Faithful on the day of intercession will implore the intercession of several Prophets. All of them will, however, excuse themselves, till they come to Muhammad; he will consent at once and receive from his Lord permission to rescue from Hell all those in whose heart a grain of faith has persisted.[1]

Muhammad's intercession on behalf of those who have committed grave sins is an idea which is also familiar to canonical Tradition:[2] "My intercession shall be on behalf of those of my community who have committed grave sins".

In other traditions the privilege of intercession is not only granted to Muhammad, but to the whole hierarchy such as is found in early Christian literature—angels, Apostles, Prophets, martyrs and saints.[3] Finally comes the intercession of Allah Himself.[4]

The intercession of the Prophets has a place in the Fiḳh Akbar II, art. 20. This is one of the points of difference between the Fiḳh Akbar II and the Waṣīya.

The second half of the present article defines the characteristics of those who will be saved through Muhammad's intercession—"all those who belong to the inhabitants of Paradise, even if they should be guilty of grave sins". The former of the two characteristics is a restriction intended to meet the latitudinarianism of the Murdjites; the latter is an extension directed against the narrowness of the Khāridjites, who excluded from Paradise those who were guilty of grave sins and had not passed through a rigid process of repentance afterwards, and that of the Mu'tazilites who rejected all intercession.[5]

1 Bukhārī, *Tawḥīd*, b. 19; Muslim, *Īmān*, trad. 322, 326–9; Aḥmad ibn Ḥanbal, *Musnad*, i. 4.

2 Abū Dāwūd, *Sunna*, b. 20; cf. Tirmidhī, *Ḳiyāma*, b. 11.

3 Bukhārī, *Tawḥīd*, b. 24; Aḥmad ibn Ḥanbal, iii. 94 *sq.*, 325 *sq.*; Ṭabarī, *Tafsīr*, iii. 6; xvi. 85; xxix. 91.

4 Bukhārī, *Tawḥīd*, b. 24; cf. sura xxxix. 44 *sq.*

5 *Supra*, p. 61 *sq.*

The Mu'tazilites were not at a loss to adduce valid scriptural evidence for their view. Sura ii. 45 (cf. above) seems to be wholly in favour of it: "And fear ye a day on which a soul shall not avail for a soul at all, nor shall any intercession be accepted from them, nor shall any ransom be taken, nor shall they be helped". The arguments of the Mu'tazilites as well as those of the orthodox are reproduced at length by Fakhr al-Dīn al-Rāzī in his commentary on the Kuran, i. 351 *sqq.*; vi. 404. al-Baiḍāwī simply says: "This verse is adduced by the Mu'tazilites in support of their negative attitude regarding intercession. It must be said, however, that it refers especially to the infidels, as appears from other passages and from the traditions regarding intercession".

It may be added here that the Wahhābites do not reject the idea of intercession; they are only anxious to limit its working to those who are pure monotheists.[1]

Ad art. 26. In this article the hierarchic sequence of holy women is settled. Like the male hierarchy (art. 10), it owes its origin to the exaggerations of the Shī'a who extolled Fāṭima above all other women, and on the other hand did not shrink from slandering 'Ā'isha.[2] Canonical Tradition has also preserved sayings of Muhammad in which Khadīdja is called the best of women[3] and Fāṭima the mistress of the women of Muhammad's community,[4] or the mistress of the women of Paradise.[5] Yet it is 'Ā'isha who ranks among the women who reached perfection.[6] It may be worth while to translate the passage from al-Baghdādī's *Uṣūl al-Dīn* referring to this subject:[7] "In Tradition it is said that the mistresses of the female creatures are four in number and that they are the

1 Cf. R. W. van Diffelen, *De leer der Wahhabieten*, p. 41 *sq.*
2 An example adduced by Lammens, *Le Triumvirat*, p. 123.
3 Bukhārī, *Manāḳib al-Anṣār*, b. 20.
4 Bukhārī, *Isti'dhān*, b. 43.
5 Tirmidhī, *Manāḳib*, b. 30.
6 Bukhārī, *Anbiyā'*, b. 32.
7 P. 306.

most excellent and the best among them, namely, Āsiya the wife of Pharaoh,[1] Maryam the daughter of 'Imrān,[2] Khadīdja the daughter of Khuwailid, and Fāṭima the daughter of the Apostle of Allah. There is a difference of opinion regarding the pre-eminence of 'Ā'isha and Fāṭima. Our shaikh Abū Sahl Muhammad b. Sulaimān al-Ṣu'lūkī[3] and his son Sahl b. Muhammad prefer Fāṭima to 'Ā'isha. This opinion seems also to agree with the position of our shaikh Abu'l-Ḥasan al-Ash'arī, as it is also shared by al-Shāfi'ī. Ḥusain b. al-Faḍl has written a pamphlet on the subject. The Bakrites[4] are convinced of 'Ā'isha's pre-eminence over Fāṭima. We think, however, that the former view is correct, on account of the tradition saying that four are the most excellent and the best of women after Fāṭima and Khadīdja, namely, 'Ā'isha, then Umm Salima, then Ḥafṣa the daughter of 'Umar, and Allah knows best who follows. According to some the daughters of a Prophet are always more excellent than his wives".

Ad art. 27. This article contains a restriction upon art. 25, where it is said that even those who are guilty of mortal sins may be delivered from Hell through Muhammad's intercession. The present article is meant to counteract the opinion that the delivery from Hell will eventually be complete,[5] and seeks to emphasize the fact that the inhabitants of Paradise and those of Hell are in two definite categories. According to the commentary on the Waṣīya[6] it was necessary to emphasize this point of view as it seemed theoretically (*'aklan*) possible to some dogmatists that the Faithful should dwell in Hell for ever on account of their sins, and that the infidels should dwell in Paradise for ever on account of divine forgiveness. This is said to have been the point of view of al-Ash'arī.

1 Sura xxviii. 8; lxvi. 11.
2 *I.e.* Mary, the mother of Jesus. 3 † 329 A.H.
4 The followers of Bakr ibn Akhshab 'Abd al-Wāḥid ibn Zaid.
5 *Infra*, p. 274; Ibn Ḥazm, *Kitāb al-Fiṣal*, iv. 83 *sqq*.
6 P. 31.

The article is at the same time a reinforcement of art. 20, where it is said that neither Paradise nor Hell nor their inhabitants shall vanish.

The authenticity of the Waṣīyat Abī Ḥanīfa can hardly be seriously defended. Nothing is known to us of the means by which such a literary work should have come down to us from Abū Ḥanīfa. In some MSS., it is true, there is an introduction in which it is stated that the great *imām* during his (last) illness said to his companions: "The orthodox creed rests on twelve articles. Whosoever clings to these will be neither an innovator nor a sectarian. Cling to them, therefore, my companions, that ye may enjoy the intercession of our Prophet on the day of resurrection".

But this introduction bears no further relation to the text and the text has not the slightest connection with Abū Ḥanīfa. The number of articles of faith—twelve—may be an imitation of the Christian creed, for it does not appear in the text itself. The theology of the Waṣīya seems to represent a later stage than that of the Fiḳh Akbar I. This point may however be treated in connection with a general characterization of the document itself.

The Waṣīya is not an attempt to formulate the chief elements of the faith of Islam, but rather a protest against heretical or sectarian deviations, presented in the form of a creed. Articles on Allah and Muhammad are lacking. The Waṣīya is therefore in no sense an extension of the "confession of faith" (*shahāda*). The most noteworthy points of difference between the Waṣīya and the Fiḳh Akbar I are the following:

The article on enjoining what is just and forbidding what is evil is not found in the Waṣīya, a sign of the widening gulf between temporal power and the community. Nor is there any trace of the article on the question between ʿUthmān and ʿAlī; of the article on the greater *fiḳh*, of the article on the dissensions of the community, or of the article on the rejection of the prophetship of Mūsā and ʿĪsā.

A comparison between the articles on Allah's sitting on His throne in the two documents is instructive. We have seen above[1] that art. 9 of the Fiḳh Akbar I was directed against allegorical explanation, whereas art. 8 of the Waṣīya appeared to show traces of this method.[2] Of equal importance for a comparison between the two documents are a number of articles on different subjects, which do not occur in the former.

Arts. 1 and 2 (cf. arts. 3 and 14) of the Waṣīya contain a definition and a description of faith, which go far beyond the utterances on faith found in canonical Tradition, and show, in their various readings, traces of the disputes between the Murdjites and the Muʿtazilites. Arts. 4 and 5 draw the logical conclusions from arts. 1–3 in regard to good and evil works; they, too, reflect the same disputes. Arts. 6, 7, 11, 12, 15 and 17, on the *ḳadar*, show a remarkable development of thought as compared with art. 3 of the Fiḳh Akbar I, in so far as they reflect the very difficult question of how Allah can be represented to will evil, yet to prohibit and to punish it. The sharp distinctions made between the commandment, desire, good pleasure, decision, decree, creation, judgment, knowledge and guidance of Allah are particularly interesting from the theological point of view. On the other hand, these articles do not yet contain the term *kasb*, which occurs in the Fiḳh Akbar II.

Considerable progress of theological thought is also shown in the article on the Kuran, which in its terminology suggests the beginning of scholastic theology and at the same time indicates the influence of Christian dogmatics. It may be remembered here that canonical Tradition does not contain any trace of the debates on the Kuran and the speech of Allah.

1 P. 116 *sq.* 2 P. 147 *sq.*

Arts. 19–27 contain an elaborate eschatology as compared with the single art. 10 of the Fiḳh Akbar I, which mentions the punishment of the tomb only.

This survey of the contents of the Waṣīya enables us tentatively to fix the origin of this creed. On the one hand it goes far beyond the Fiḳh Akbar I, which appeared to belong in the main to Abū Ḥanīfa († A.D. 767). On the other hand it does not yet show any trace of the debates on Allah's being and qualities, which occupy an important place in the Fiḳh Akbar II. Yet the preliminaries of these debates are reflected in the article on the uncreated Kuran. Similarly, the use of the terms *kaifīya*, *tas͟hbīh* and *d̲jiha* in connection with the meeting of Allah points to a time when the community still adhered to anthropomorphic expressions, yet no longer took them in their literal sense; of this attitude Aḥmad ibn Ḥanbal († A.D. 855) is the most characteristic representative.

So the Waṣīya seems to have originated in a period between Abū Ḥanīfa and Aḥmad ibn Ḥanbal, and probably belongs to the latter part of that period.

CHAPTER VIII

The Fiḳh Akbar II

PARALLEL ARTICLES IN OTHER CREEDS

Waṣīyat Abī Ḥanīfa, art. 20 *sqq.*
Akīdat al-Ṭaḥāwī, arts. 18, 19
Cf. *supra*, p. 35

Ṭaḥāwī, art. 1
Supra, p. 66 *sqq.*

TRANSLATION

Art. 1. The heart of the confession of the unity of Allah and the true foundation of faith consist in this obligatory creed: I believe in Allah, His angels, His books, His Apostles, the resurrection after death, the decree of Allah the good and the evil thereof, computation of sins, the balance, Paradise and Hell; and that all these are real.

Art. 2. Allah the exalted is one, not in the sense of number, but in the sense that He has no partner; He begetteth not and He is not begotten and there is none like unto Him.[1] He resembles none of the created things, nor do any created things resemble Him. He has been from eternity and will be to eternity with His names and qualities, those which belong to His essence as well as those which belong to His action.

Those which belong to His essence are: life, power, knowledge, speech, hearing, sight and will. Those which belong to His action are: creating, sustaining, producing, renewing, making, and so on.

He has been from eternity and will be to eternity with His qualities and His names. None of His qualities or names has come into being; from eternity He knows by virtue of His knowledge, knowledge being an eternal quality; He is almighty by virtue of His power, His power being an eternal quality; He speaks by virtue of His speech, His speech being an eternal quality; He creates by virtue of His creative power, His

1 Sura cxii.

creative power being an eternal quality; He acts by virtue of His power of action, His power of action being an eternal quality.

The agent is Allah and the product of His action is created, but the power of action of Allah is not created and His qualities are eternal; they have not come into being, nor have they been created. Whoso sayeth that they are created or have come into being, or hesitates or doubts regarding these two points, is an infidel in regard to Allah.

Waṣīya, art. 9
Ṭaḥāwī, art. 3

Art. 3. The Kuran is the speech of Allah, written in the copies, preserved in the memories, recited by the tongues, revealed to the Prophet. Our pronouncing, writing and reciting the Kuran is created, whereas the Kuran itself is uncreated.

Whatever Allah quotes in the Kuran[1] from Moses or other Prophets, from Pharaoh or from Satan, is the speech of Allah in relation to theirs. The speech of Allah is uncreated, but the speech of Moses and other creatures is created. The Kuran is the speech of Allah and as such from eternity, not theirs. Moses heard the speech of Allah, as the Kuran saith: And Allah spoke with Moses[2]—Allah was speaking indeed before He spoke to Moses. For Allah was creating from eternity ere He had created the creatures; and when He spoke to Moses, He spoke to Him with His speech which is one of His eternal qualities.

All His qualities are different from those of the creatures. He knoweth, but not in the way of our knowledge; He is mighty, but not in the way of our power; He seeth, but not in the way of our seeing; He speaketh, but not in the way of our speaking; He heareth, but not in the way of our hearing. We speak by means of organs and letters, Allah speaks without instruments and letters. Letters are created, but the speech of Allah is uncreated.

1 *E.g.* sura vii. 10 *sqq.*, 120; xxviii passim.
2 Sura iv. 162.

Supra, pp. 65 *sqq*., 121.

Art. 4. Allah is thing, not as other things but in the sense of positive existence;[1] without body, without substance, without *accidens*. He has no limit, neither has He a counterpart, nor a partner, nor an equal. He has hand, face and soul, for He refers to these in the Kuran; and what He saith in the Kuran regarding face, hand and soul, this belongs to His qualities, without how.[2] It must not be said that His hand is His power or His bounty, for this would lead to the annihilation of the quality. This is the view of the Ḳadarites and the Mu'tazilites. No, His hand is His quality, without how. Likewise His wrath and His good pleasure are two of His qualities, without how.

Fiḳh Akbar I, art. 3
Waṣīya, art. 6
Ṭaḥāwī, art. 6

Art. 5. Allah has not created things from a pre-existent thing. Allah had knowledge concerning things before they existed, from eternity; He had so decreed and ordained them that nothing could happen either in this world or in the next except through His will, knowledge, decision, decree and writing on the preserved table. Yet His writing is of a descriptive, not of a decisive nature. Decision, decree and will are His eternal qualities, without how. Allah knoweth the non-existent things in the state of non-existence, as not existing; and He knoweth how they will be. And He knoweth the existing things in the state of existence, as existing; and He knoweth how their vanishing will be. Allah knoweth the rising in the state of His rising, as rising. And when He sitteth down, He knoweth Himself as sitting down, in the state of His sitting down, without a change in His knowing and without His getting knowledge. But change and difference come into being in creatures.

Ṭaḥāwī, art. 6
Waṣīya, art. 6

Art. 6. Allah created the creatures free from unbelief and from belief. Then He

1 الثابت. Several MSS. read اثباته, *i.e.* ان تثبته.

2 *I.e.* without any explanation being demanded or given (*bilā kaifa*).

addressed them and gave them commandments and prohibitions. Thereupon some turned to unbelief. And their denial and disavowal of the truth was caused by Allah's abandoning[1] them. And some of them believed—as appeared in their acting, consenting and declaring—through the guidance and help of Allah.

Allah took the posterity of Adam from his loins and endowed them with intellect. Thereupon He addressed them and commanded them to believe and to abstain from unbelief. Thereupon they recognized His lordship, and this was belief on their part. And in this religion[2] they are born. And whosoever became an unbeliever afterwards, deviated from this and changed, and whosoever believed and professed his belief, clung to it and adhered to this belief.

Allah did not compel any of His creatures to be infidels or faithful. And He did not create them either as faithful or infidels, but He created them as individuals, and faith and unbelief are the acts of men. Allah knoweth the man who turneth to belief as an infidel in the state of his unbelief; and if he turneth to belief afterwards, Allah knoweth him as faithful, in the state of his belief; and He loveth him, without change in His knowledge or His quality. All the acts of man—his moving as well as his resting—are truly his own acquisition,[3] but Allah creates them and they are caused by His will, His knowledge, His decision, and His decree.

Doesn't kasb refer more to individual, momentary acts whose performance God grants man, although God originally created the power for the performance of these acts.

Waṣiya, art. 7
Supra, p. 142 *sqq.*

Art. 7. All acts of obedience are obligatory on account of Allah's command, wish, good pleasure, knowledge, will, decision and decree. All acts of disobedience happen through His knowledge, decision, decree, and will; not according to His wish, good pleasure, or command.

1 *khadhlān*. 2 *fiṭra*. 3 *kasb*.

Art. 8. All the Prophets are exempt from sins, both light and grave, from unbelief and sordid deeds. Yet stumbling and mistakes may happen on their part.

Ṭaḥāwī, art. 2

Art. 9. Muhammad is His beloved, His servant, His Apostle, His Prophet, His chosen and elect. He did not serve idols, nor was he at any time a polytheist, even for a single moment. And he never committed a light or a grave sin.

Waṣīya, art. 10
Cf. Fiḳh Akbar I, arts. 4, 5
Ṭaḥāwī, arts. 21, 20

Art. 10. The most excellent of men after [1]the Apostle of Allah[1] is Abū Bakr al-Ṣiddīḳ; after him, ʿUmar ibn al-Khaṭṭāb al-Fārūḳ; after him, ʿUthmān ibn ʿAffān, [2]he of the two lights;[2] after him, ʿAlī [3]al-Murtaḍā,[3] may Allah encompass all of them with His good pleasure, being His servants who persevere in truth and with truth. We cling to all of them and we name all the companions of Allah's Apostle in the way of praise only.

Fiḳh Akbar I, art. 1
Waṣīya, art. 4
Ṭaḥāwī, art. 10
Supra, pp. 45 *sqq.*, 138 *sqq.*

Art. 11. We declare no Muslim an infidel on account of any sin—even though a mortal one—if he does not declare it allowed. Neither do we banish him from the field of faith, nay, we call him really faithful; he may be faithful of bad behaviour, not an infidel.

Waṣīya, art. 16
Supra, p. 158 *sq.*

Art. 12. The moistening of the shoes is commendable. The supererogatory prayers in the month of Ramaḍān are commendable.

Ṭaḥāwī, art. 14

Art. 13. Prayer behind every faithful man, be he of good or of bad behaviour, is valid.

Ṭaḥāwī, art. 13
Cf. Waṣīya, arts. 20, 27

Art. 14. We do not say that sins will do no harm to the Faithful; nor do we say that he will not enter the fire; nor do we say that he will remain therein for ever, although he should be of bad behaviour,

1–1 Reading of MSS. Cairo 2372, 2400. The other texts read "the Prophets".

2–2 Lacking in MSS. Cairo 2400, 2402.

3–3 Lacking in MSS. Cairo 2372, 2402.

after having departed this world as one of the Faithful. And we do not say—as the Murdjites do[1]—that our good deeds are accepted and our sins forgiven. But we say, that when a man performs a good deed, fulfilling all its conditions so that it is free from any blame that might spoil it, without nullifying it by unbelief, apostasy or bad morals, until he departs this world as one of the Faithful—then Allah shall not overlook it but accept it from him and reward him on account of it. As to evil deeds—apart from polytheism and unbelief—if he who commits them does not repent ere he dies as one of the Faithful, he will be dependent on Allah's will: if He willeth He punisheth him in the fire, and if He willeth He forgiveth him without punishing him in any way in the fire.

Art. 15. If any work be mixed with ostentation, its reward is forfeited thereby, and likewise if it be mixed with vainglory.

Fiḳh Akbar I, art. 8
Ṭaḥāwī, art. 23

Art. 16. The signs[2] of the Prophets and the miracles of the saints are a reality. As to those which were performed by His[3] enemies, such as Iblīs, Fir'awn and the Anti-Christ, and which, according to historical tradition, have taken place or will take place, we do not call them signs or miracles, but we call them the fulfilling of their wants. Allah fulfils the wants of His enemies, eluding them in this world and punishing them in the next. So they are betrayed and increase in error and unbelief.

All this is contingent and possible.

Arts. 2, 5, 6

Allah was creator before He created, and sustainer before He sustained.

Waṣīya, art. 24
Ṭaḥāwī, art. 4
Supra, pp. 63 *sqq.*, 88 *sq.*

Art. 17. Allah will be seen in the world to come. The Faithful will see Him, being in Paradise, [4]with their bodily eyes,[4] with-

1 The clause is lacking in MS. Cairo 2372.

2 The text has "The signs are indubitable regarding the saints". My translation covers MSS. Cairo 2372, 2400, 2402.

3 *I.e.* Allah's.

4–4 Lacking in MS. Cairo 2400.

out comparison or modality. And there will be no distance between Him and His creatures.

Waṣīya, arts. 1–5
Ṭaḥāwī, art. 11
Cf. Fiḳh Akbar I, art. 6
Supra, pp. 45, 125, 138

Art. 18. Faith consists in confessing and believing.

The faith of the inhabitants of Heaven and earth does not increase or decrease.[1]

The Faithful are equal in faith and in the confession of the unity of Allah; they are different in degree of superiority regarding works.

Islam is absolute agreement and compliance with the commands of Allah. Language distinguishes between faith and Islam. Yet there is no faith without Islam and Islam without faith cannot be found. The two are as back and belly. Religion[2] is a noun covering faith and Islam and all the commandments of the law.

Ṭaḥāwī, art. 1

Art. 19. We know Allah with adequate knowledge, as He describes Himself in His book, with all His qualities. Nobody, on the other hand, is able to serve Allah with adequate service, such as He may truly lay claim to. But man serves Him at His command, as He has ordered him in His book and in the *sunna* of His Apostle.

All the Faithful are equal as to knowledge, subjective certainty, trust, love, inner quiet, fear, hope and faith.[3] They differ in all these, except in faith.

Allah lavishes His bounty on His servants and acts according to justice as well. He giveth them a reward twice as large as they have deserved, by grace, and He punisheth on account of sin, by justice. He forgiveth by grace.

Waṣīya, art. 25
Ṭaḥāwī, art. 5
Supra, pp. 169, 180

Art. 20. The intercession of the Prophets is a reality.

The intercession of the Prophet on

1 The printed text and some MSS. add "regarding the object of faith. It increases and decreases, however, regarding subjective certainty and belief".

2 *Dīn*.

3 The text and some MSS. add "therein".

behalf of the Faithful who have committed sins, even grave sins, and who have deserved punishment, is an established reality.

Waṣīya, arts. 20, 21, 23
Ṭaḥāwī, arts. 18, 5, 19

Art. 21. The weighing of works in the balance on the day of resurrection is a reality.[1]

The basin of the Prophet is a reality. Retaliation between litigants by means of good works on the day of resurrection is a reality. And if they do not possess good works, the wrongs, done by them to others, are thrown upon them; this is a reality.[1]

Paradise and Hell are created, and are in existence at the present time; they will never cease to exist.

[2]The black-eyed ones will never die.[2] Punishment and reward by Allah will never end.

Waṣīya, art. 6

Art. 22. Allah guideth whomsoever He pleaseth, by grace, and He leadeth astray whomsoever He pleaseth, by justice. His leading astray means His abandoning, and the explanation of "abandoning" is that He does not help a man by guiding him towards deeds that please Him. This is justice on His part, and so is His punishment of those who are abandoned on account of sin. We are not allowed to say that Satan deprives the Faithful of his faith by constraint and compulsion. But we say that man gives up his faith, whereupon Satan deprives him of it.

Fiḳh Akbar I, art. 10
Waṣīya, arts. 18, 19
Ṭaḥāwī, art. 18

Art. 23. The interrogation of the dead in the tomb by Munkar and Nakīr is a reality[3] and the reunion of the body with the spirit in the tomb is a reality. The pressure and the punishment in the tomb are a reality that will take place in the case of all the

1 Some MSS. add "which is possible". For the explanation of this term cf. the commentary on art. 16.

2–2 Lacking in MS. Cairo 2400 and in the commentary of 'Alī al-Ḳārī. MS. Cairo 2400 adds "The street is a reality".

3 Text of 'Alī al-Ḳārī; the other texts and MSS. add "that will take place".

infidels, and a reality [1]that may take place[1] in the case of some sinners belonging to the Faithful.

Art. 24. It is allowable to follow scholars in expressing the qualities of Allah in Persian, in all instances except in the case of Allah's hand. It is allowable to say *rūyi khudāy*,[2] without comparison or modality.

Art. 25. Allah's being near or far is not to be understood in the sense of a shorter or longer distance, but[3] in the sense of man's being honoured or slighted.[4] The[5] obedient is near to Him, without how, and the disobedient is far from Him, without how. Nearness, distance and approach are applied to man in his intimate relation with Allah, and so it is with Allah's neighbourhood in Paradise, and with man's standing before Him, without modality.

Above, art. 3
Waṣīya, art. 9
Ṭaḥāwī, art. 3

Art. 26. The Kuran is revealed to the Apostle of Allah and it is written in the copies. The verses of the Kuran, being Allah's speech, are all equal in excellence and greatness. Some, however, have a pre-eminence in regard to recitation or to their contents, *e.g.* the verse of the Throne,[6] because it deals with Allah's majesty, His greatness and His description.[7] So in it are united excellence in regard to recitation and excellence in regard to its contents. Others possess excellence only in regard to recitation, such as the descriptions of the infidels, whereas those who are mentioned in them, that is, the infidels, have no excellence.

Likewise all of Allah's names and qualities are equal in greatness and excellence, without difference.

1–1 Not in the text of 'Alī al-Ḳārī.
2 *I.e.* the face of God.
3 'Alī al-Ḳārī's text and MS. Cairo 2400 have "nor".
4 In a religious sense.
5 'Alī al-Ḳārī and MS. Cairo 2400 have "but".
6 Sura ii. 256.
7 Some MSS. read "qualities".

Art. 27.[1] Ḳāsim, Ṭāhir and Ibrāhīm were the sons of the Apostle of Allah.

Fāṭima, Ruḳaiya, Zainab and Umm Kulthūm were all of them daughters of the Apostle of Allah.

Art. 28. When a man is uncertain concerning any of the subtleties of theology,[2] it is his duty to cling for the time being to the orthodox faith. When he finds a scholar, he must consult him; he is not allowed to postpone inquiry and there is no excuse for him if he should persevere in his attitude of hesitation, nay, he would incur the blame of unbelief thereby.

Art. 29. The report of the ascension is a reality, and whosoever rejects it is an erring schismatic. The appearance of the Anti-Christ, Yādjūdj and Mādjūdj,[3] the rising of the sun from the place where it sets, the descent of ʿĪsā from Heaven, as well as the other eschatological signs according to the description thereof in authentic Tradition, are a reality that will take place.

Allah guideth to the straight way whomsoever He willeth.

COMMENTARY

Ad art. 1. This is the summary of faith in the form of the well-known tradition, on which see *supra*, pp. 23 *sq.* and 35, where its origin and general meaning have been discussed. Here a detailed explanation may follow, in so far as its contents have not been treated in the preceding forms of the creed, such as art. 23 of the Waṣīya[4] (the resurrection of the dead), art. 3 of the Fiḳh Akbar I, art. 6 of the Waṣīya[5] (predestination), art. 22 of the Waṣīya[6] (computation of sins), art. 21 of the Waṣīya[7] (the

1 Some texts open this article with the phrase "The parents of the Apostle of Allah died as infidels, and so did Abū Ṭālib, his uncle".

2 Lit. the knowledge of the confession of the unity of Allah.

3 Gog and Magog.

4 *Supra*, p. 130.

5 *Supra*, pp. 126, 142.

6 *Supra*, pp. 130, 172 *sqq.*

7 *Supra*, pp. 130, 167 *sqq.*

balance), art. 10 of the Fiḳh Akbar I, art. 20 of the Waṣīya[1] (Paradise and Hell).

The subjects mentioned in the present article in addition to these are belief in Allah, His angels, His books and His Apostles.

On the angels in the Kuran and in Muhammadan literature, cf. D. B. Macdonald, art. *Malā'ika* in the *Encyclopaedia of Islām*; Sale, *Preliminary Discourse*, p. 94 *sq.*; W. Eickmann, *Die Angelologie und Dämonologie des Korans*, New York and Leipzig, 1908; P. A. Eichler, *Die Dschinn, Teufel und Engel im Koran*, Leipzig, 1928.

On this subject the following remarks may be sufficient here. In the Kuran the angels are mentioned as the heavenly host side by side with Allah Himself.[2] They are His obedient servants who encircle His throne, praising Him and prostrating themselves.[3] They are His intermediaries with man,[4] and more especially the bearers of His revelation and command.[5] They console the Faithful[6] and implore Allah's forgiveness on their behalf.[7] They also accomplish the separation between body and soul when the children of man die; sometimes they combine this function with that of punishing the infidels.[8] Especially in connection with the resurrection of the dead they are often mentioned:[9] they will bear the throne on that day,[10] they will be ranged in a row with the *rūḥ*;[11] but the intercession of many of them will be of no avail.[12]

1 *Supra*, pp. 129 *sq.*, 165 *sqq.*

2 Sura iii. 16; iv. 164; xxvii. 150; lxxxix. 23.

3 Sura ii. 28; xiii. 14; xvi. 51; xxi. 19 *sq.*; xxxiv. 39; xxxix. 75; xlii. 3; xliii. 18.

4 Sura ii. 206; iii. 33, 37, 40 (Zakārīyā', Maryam), 120 *sq.*; cf. viii. 9, 13; xxxiii. 42, 56; lvi. 4 (Muhammad).

5 Sura xvi. 2; xcvii. 4; cf. lxx. 4.

6 Sura xii. 30.

7 Sura xlii. 3.

8 Sura iii. 99; vi. 93; viii. 52; xvi. 30; xxv. 24; xxxiv. 35; xlvii. 29. Cf. *supra*, pp. 117 *sq.*, 163 *sq.*

9 Sura xxi. 103.

10 Sura lxix. 1.

11 Sura lxxviii. 38; cf. lxxxix. 23.

12 Sura liii. 26.

Of special importance also, in regard to dogmatic questions,[1] is the story of how Allah ordered the angels to prostrate themselves before Adam,[2] who had given names to the creatures, whereas the angels were not acquainted with these names.[3]

In the hierarchic sequences that occur in the Kuran, the angels are usually mentioned between Allah and man.[4]

Side by side with the offices which are ascribed to the angels in general, there are others which fall to the charge of individual angels, in the first place of Djibrīl, the angel of revelation.[5] His partner is Mīkā'īl.[6] The angel of death is not mentioned by name in the Kuran;[7] Tradition calls him 'Izrā'īl. These three form, together with Isrāfīl, the angel of the resurrection, who is mentioned in later literature only, the group of the archangels.

In the Kuran are further mentioned Hārūt and Mārūt,[8] Mālik the angel of the fire[9] and his companions the *zabāniya*;[10] "Those who are near to Allah";[11] also writing and recording angels,[12] messengers[13] and guardians of the fire.[14]

Apart from some features belonging to popular theology, canonical Tradition adds to the dogmatic features of the angels only the statement that they were created from light.[15]

1 *Infra*, commentary on art. 16.

2 Sura vii. 10; xv. 28, 30; xvii. 63; xviii. 48; xx. 115; xxxviii. 71.

3 Sura ii. 29 *sq*.

4 Sura ii. 92, 156, 172, 285; iii. 81; iv. 135.

5 Djibrīl is mentioned by name in sura ii. 91 *sq*.; lxvi. 4. According to Tradition he is meant also in sura ii. 254; v. 109; xvi. 104; xix. 17; xxvi. 193–5; liii. 5–18.

6 Sura ii. 92.

7 Sura xxxiii. 11.

8 Sura ii. 96; see *Encyclopaedia of Islām*, s.v.; Littmann, in *Festschrift F. C. Andreas...dargebracht*, Leipzig, 1916, p. 70 *sqq*.

9 Sura xliii. 17.

10 Sura lxxiv. 30 *sq*.; xcvi. 18.

11 Sura iv. 170; xxi. 20. To them are added the 'Ulwīyūn (Baiḍāwī, on sura ii. 28) and the Karrūbīyūn (Baiḍāwī, on sura iv. 170).

12 Sura lxxx. 15; lxxxii. 10–12.

13 Sura xxv. 1.

14 Sura lxvi. 6.

15 Muslim, *Zuhd*, trad. 60.

In later theology[1] four points are given special prominence: their being created from light; their possessing no sex, though some authorities do not consider this point as being settled;[2] their impeccability; and the relative excellency of the angels, Apostles, and man.

We may cite here what the commentary by Abu'l-Muntahā and that by 'Alī al-Ḳārī say on the subject. The angels—says the former—are, according to the majority of the Muslims, subtle bodies, capable of assuming different forms. They are of two classes. The occupation of the first class has its centre in the knowledge of God and His transcendency. These are "the highest"[3] and "those who are near to Allah". The second class brings from Heaven to earth[4] the divine command[5] to carry out the foregoing decrees and what has been written by the divine pen.[6] These angels belong partly to Heaven, partly to the earth.

From 'Alī al-Ḳārī's commentary the following passage may be translated:[7] "They are preserved from sin; they never transgress the commands of Allah; they are free from sex. In the *Djawāhir al-Uṣūl*[8] it is said that the angels have no share in the delights of Paradise, nor in the *visio beatifica*".

The relative excellence of angels, Prophets and man may be illustrated by a passage from al-Baghdādī:[9] "The large majority of our friends maintain the superiority of the Prophets over the angels. Some of them admit the possibility of the superiority of some of the Faithful as compared with the angels; they do not, however, mention anyone individually. The followers of Tradition do not teach the superiority of the angels over the Prophets,

1 Cf. especially Fakhr al-Dīn al-Rāzī, i. 263–75.
2 Cf. D. B. Macdonald, art. *Malā'ika* in the *Encyclopaedia of Islām*.
3 *Supra*, p. 199, note 11.
4 P. 4.
5 *amr*; cf. *supra*, p. 198, note 5.
6 *Supra*, pp. 108, 129, 162.
7 P. 11.
8 I cannot identify this work.
9 *Usūl al-Dīn*, p. 295 *sq.*; cf. p. 166 *sq.*

except al-Ḥasan ibn al-Faḍl al-Badjalī.[1] The Mu'tazilites are divided on this point. The majority of them are of opinion that the angels are more excellent than the Prophets, they even consider the guardian angels of the fire as being superior to every Prophet. Others, however, say that those angels who have committed no sin are more excellent than the Prophets, whereas those who have committed even the slightest sin, such as Hārūt and Mārūt,[2] are inferior to the Prophets. This is the opinion of al-Aṣamm.[3] According to the Imāmites[4] the *imāms* are more excellent than the angels. And the extreme Shī'ites say that they themselves are more excellent than the angels. This is the opinion of the Bazīghīya who belong to the Khaṭṭābīya. Those who teach the superiority of the angels over the Prophets refer to the verse from the Kuran:[5] 'The Messiah by no means disdaineth to be a servant of God, nor do the angels who are nigh unto Him'. But this verse is no argument, for similar juxtapositions may be used in the case of equality.... We do not say regarding any of the Prophets that he is more excellent than all the angels; but we say that he is more excellent than every single one.... Our friends connect the thesis of the superiority of the Prophets over the angels with Ibn 'Abbās and other illustrious Companions. So we need not take notice of the dissension of the Mu'tazilites".

It may be taken as the common orthodox opinion that the Faithful are more excellent than the angels in general.[6] So it appears that the first place in this hierarchic scale is taken by the Apostles, the second by the Faithful and the

1 Arnold, *al-Mu'tazilah*, p. 44. Sam'ānī, fol. 66 *a*, mentions one Abū 'Alī al-Ḥusain b. al-Faḍl al-Badjalī from Baghdād, who lived at Nīsābūr and was one of the later *mutakallimūn*.

2 *Supra*, p. 199.

3 Abū Bakr al-Aṣamm.

4 The "twelvers" of the Shī'a.

5 Sura iv. 170.

6 Commentary on the Fikh Akbar I, p. 27; for the Christian view cf. John of Damascus, Migne, vol. XCIV. col. 865 *sqq*.

third by the angels.[1] Side by side with the angels are mentioned Allah's books, *i.e.* the Kuran and the books revealed to the predecessors of Muhammad. Of the latter category of books those mentioned in the Kuran are the *Tawrāt* (the Tora), revealed after the time of Ibrāhīm and Isrā'īl, and afterwards confirmed by 'Īsā;[2] the *Zabūr* (Psalms), revealed to David;[3] the *Indjīl* (the Gospel), revealed to 'Īsā;[4] further, the scrolls of Mūsā and Ibrāhīm[5] and the books in general.[6]

The Kuran itself[7] is mentioned in this book as Allah's revelation[8] to Muhammad, either as a whole[9] or as single revelations.[10]

The dogmatic position of later Islam towards the books may be summarized here from the chief commentaries. Abu'l-Muntahā says:[11] "Belief in the books means an absolute belief that they exist and that they are the speech of Allah. The totality of the books revealed to the Apostles amounts to one hundred and four; of these ten scrolls were revealed to Adam, fifty to Shīth,[12] thirty to Idrīs,[13] ten to Ibrāhīm".

The following passage is from al-Taftāzānī's commentary on al-Nasafī's *'aḳīda*: "All of them are the speech of

1 On the scholastic doctrine of the angels cf. further al-Baiḍāwī on sura ii. 32; al-Īdjī, *Mawāḳif*, pp. 237–43; Ḳazwīnī, *'Adjā'ib al-makhlūḳāt*, pp. 55–63; al-Nasafī, *'Aḳā'id*, with the commentaries by al-Taftāzānī, al-Khayālī and al-Isfarā'inī, p. 137; 'Abd Allāh ibn Aḥmad ibn Ḥanbal, *Kitāb al-Sunna*, p. 168 *sq.*; Ibn Ḥazm, *Kitāb al-Fiṣal*, iii. 259 *sqq.*

2 Sura iii. 44, 58, 87; v. 50; lxi. 6. On the *Tawrāt* see the article by Horovitz in the *Encyclopaedia of Islām*.

3 Sura iv. 161; xvii. 57.

4 Sura v. 50 *sq.*, 110; lvii. 27.

5 Sura liii. 37; lxxxvii. 18.

6 Sura ii. 205; iii. 181; iv. 135; xvi. 46; xxvi. 196; xxxv. 23; lxvi. 12; xcviii. 2. See Horovitz, *Koranische Untersuchungen*, p. 68 *sq.*

7 Cf. Buhl's article in the *Encyclopaedia of Islām*.

8 Sura xl. 1; xliv. 1 *sqq.*; xlv. 1.

9 Sura xvii. 107; xx. 1; lxxvi. 23.

10 Sura x. 16; lxxii. 1.

11 P. 4.

12 Seth.

13 Enoch.

Allah and this is one; the difference is in the sequence of the text recited and heard. And from this point of view the Kuran is the most excellent; next comes the *Tawrāt*, then the *Indjīl*, then the *Zabūr*....These books, that is, the reciting and writing of them, as well as some of their precepts, have been abrogated by the Kuran. According to some theologians it is preferable not to fix their number, for, the latter not being absolutely certain, some might be included in the number which do not belong to it, and others which belong to it might be excluded".[1]

The same argument, as we shall see later, is used against specifying the number of the Prophets. In our article it is not the Prophets but the Apostles who are mentioned. What is the difference between the two terms?

In the Kuran Muhammad calls himself Prophet as well as Apostle; in canonical Tradition Apostles are not frequently mentioned; apparently they form one class with the Prophets, to whom full weight is given.

Still, in the Kuran a difference is made between the Apostle and the Prophet, in so far as the former is representative of a community or people (*umma*) to which God has sent him.[2] In canonical Tradition there are descriptions of how, on the day of resurrection, the *umma*'s and their leaders will have to pass the bridge;[3] in this fearful moment the Apostles will make use of a pass-word or cry.

The idea of the Apostles as missionaries each to a different people may have reached Muhammad through Christian channels, as this is the scheme underlying the tradition of the preaching of Christianity throughout the world.[4] The difference lies in the fact that neither Muhammad nor Muslim Tradition knows anything of twelve Apostles. The Kuranic series comprises Nūḥ (Noah), Lūṭ

1 al-Isfarā'inī on Nasafī's '*Aḳā'id*, p. 138, at the top; 'Alī al-Ḳārī on Fiḳh Akbar II, p. 11.

2 Sura x. 48; xvi. 38; xxiii. 46; xl. 5. In sura iv. 45; xxviii. 75 "witness" is apparently connected with the same idea.

3 Bukhārī, *Adhān*, b. 129; *Riḳāḳ*, b. 52.

4 *E.g.* in the Apocryphal Acts of the Apostles.

(Lot), Ismā'īl, Mūsā, Shu'aib (Jethro), Hūd, Ṣāliḥ and 'Īsā (Jesus).

The number of the Prophets mentioned in the Kuran is larger. Apart from the Apostles who reappear in the list of the Prophets, we find Idrīs (Enoch), the Patriarchs, Hārūn (Aaron), Dāwūd, Sulaimān, Elijah, Elisha, Job, Jonah, John the Baptist and his father Zakārīyā'. They are not sent each to a different people, but they walk in the footsteps of the Apostles, their predecessors.

Consequently, according to the doctrine of the Kuran, every Apostle is as such also a Prophet; but not every Prophet is at the same time an Apostle. This is also the view of early Christianity; Chrysostom expresses it in the following way:[1] *καὶ ὁ μὲν προφήτης οὐ δύναται εἶναι καὶ ἀπόστολος καὶ προφήτης ὁ δὲ ἀπόστολος καὶ προφήτης ἐστι πάντως*·

Post-canonical Tradition shows a perpetual tendency to enlarge the number of the Prophets as well as that of the Apostles. The latter do not exceed the number of 315,[2] whereas that of the Prophets varies between 1000[3] and 224,000.[4] Owing to this lack of precision, Abū Ḥafṣ 'Umar al-Nasafī († 537/1142) thinks it safer not to fix the number: "In fixing a number", he says, "we might include someone who does not belong to them, or exclude someone who belongs to them".[5]

According to later dogmatics[6] the difference between the Apostle and the Prophet is this, that the former was sent with a law and a book special to him, whereas the latter was only to preach and utter warnings. Sometimes, however, the two words are said to be synonymous.

On the decree cf. General Register in voce *Predestination*; on the computation of sins cf. *supra*, p. 174 *sqq.*; on the balance cf. *supra*, p. 169 *sqq.*

1 Ed. Migne, vol. LI. col. 92.
2 Ibn Sa'd, I/I, 10 and the catechism edited by Reland.
3 Ibn Sa'd, I/I, 128.
4 Reland, *De religione mohammedanica*, p. 40 *sq.*
5 Ed. Cureton, p. 4.
6 *E.g.* Abu'l-Muntahā, p. 4.

Ad art. 2. This is the orthodox view of the difficult question of the essence of Allah and His qualities; the historical background has been sketched above.[1] The present version lays stress on the eternity of the divine qualities[2], in contradistinction to the Mu'tazilites. The formula "knowing through His knowledge..." is ascribed by tradition to al-Ash'ārī.[3] It must be remarked that the short creed "of the adherents of tradition and the people of the *sunna*", which is reproduced by al-Ash'arī in his *Maḳālāt*,[4] is still far from explicit on the question of the divine qualities: "It must not be said that the names of Allah are other than Himself, as the Mu'tazilites and Khāridjites do. They[5] confess that Allah has knowledge. Likewise they affirm Allah's hearing and sight, which they do not deny as the Mu'tazilites do. And they affirm Allah's power...".

So much for the general position of this article. We now turn to some special points. "Allah is one, not in the sense of number, but in the sense that He has no partner; He begetteth not and He is not begotten and there is none like unto Him." It is curious to observe that, nearly the whole of sura cxii being cited here, the word *aḥad*, which in the text of the Kuran expresses the unity of Allah, has been replaced by *wāḥid*, with the remark that this term must not be taken in the numerical sense "so that it might be presumed that there would follow a second".[6]

Apparently the commentators have not understood the true significance of the phrase used in the article. The reason why it seemed advisable to avoid the expression *Allāh aḥad* may have been that the Mu'tazilites emphasized their confession of the unity of Allah, that is, the unity of His essence as opposed to His qualities. When the discus-

1 P. 70 *sqq*.
2 *Infra*, pp. 266, 273.
3 al-Baghdādī, *Uṣūl al-Dīn*, pp. 13 *sqq*.; 90. Further, *infra*, p. 266 *sq*.
4 P. 87.
5 The orthodox.
6 This is the explanation by 'Alī al-Ḳārī. That of Abu'l-Muntahā is to the same effect.

sions with the Mu'tazilites had lost their sharp edge, the orthodox could no longer take objection to a reference to the unity of Allah in their creed. As a matter of fact in later creeds[1] we find the confession of Allah's unity side by side with that of His being unique. In the commentary on the Fiḳh Akbar I[2] *aḥadīya* is declared to be a quality of essence (*ṣifat al-dhāt*), whereas *wāḥidīya* is called a quality of action (*ṣifat al-fi'l*).

The divine qualities are admitted to be eternal in the full sense of the term, viz. *azalī* (without beginning) and *abadī* (without end). Orthodox Islam draws the full consequence of the Christian doctrine of the eternal Word of God: "God, the Father, has begotten the Son from eternity, and the Son is being begotten eternally".[3] A similar doctrine is applied by Islam to all the divine qualities. The most cautious expression of the relation between Allah and His qualities is perhaps the formula that they are neither He nor other than He. Later theologians have developed the doctrine of the *ṣifāt* in a very subtle way.[4]

There are two classes of qualities, those which belong to the essence of Allah and those which belong to His action. Later Islam knows more elaborate classifications.[5] How intensely serious the discussions on the qualities were may be seen from the fact that at the end of the present article dissenters are declared to be infidels. Who is not reminded here of the discussions on the ὁμοουσία which aroused such vehement debates among Oriental Christians?

It may be finally remarked that not only the qualities of Allah, but also His names—the Living, the Almighty, etc.—are confessed to belong to Him from eternity.

On the eternity of the creative action of Allah, cf. *infra*, the commentary on art. 5.

1 *E.g.* in the catechism of al-Samarḳandī as edited by Juynboll (cf. the References, s.v.).

2 P. 23.

3 Abū Ḳurra, ed. Migne, vol. XCVII. cols. 1562 *sq.*, 1567.

4 *E.g.* Taftāzānī *apud* Nasafī, p. 69 *sqq.*

5 *Infra*, Chapter IX, the catechism of al-Sanūsī.

Ad art. 3. This article is a special case of the foregoing one, in so far as the general doctrine of the divine qualities is here applied to one of them, namely, speech, the Christian Logos, which, as has been pointed out above, presented special difficulties because of its incarnation in the visible and audible Kuran.[1] One of these difficulties is dealt with at length in the present article, namely, the question of how the speech of Moses, Pharaoh, nay, even of Satan himself, as quoted in the Kuran, could at the same time be the eternal speech of Allah.

A second question is that of the relation between the eternal speech of Allah and the text of the Kuran as it is recited by man. The answer given in the present article is not universally accepted by Muslim orthodoxy.

It may be noted also that in this article the simple *bilā kaifa*, as it was used by Aḥmad ibn Ḥanbal, appears to have developed into the general principle of *tanzīh*, *i.e.* of excluding all human likeness from pronouncements regarding the Godhead. The article itself gives examples at some length. This method has become the orthodox mean between *tas͟hbīh* and *ta'ṭīl*.[2]

Ad art. 4. The article deals with the question of anthropomorphism, on which cf. *supra*, pp. 66 *sqq.*, 85, 92 *sqq.* One of the chief points, namely, that of the divine throne and of Allah's seating Himself on it, is not mentioned in our creed. This fact is significant for its theological position, which is As͟h'arite[3] rather than orthodox in the old sense.

The hand of Allah is declared to be His eternal quality. The addition of "without how" would scarcely have been able to lay the ghost of Aḥmad ibn Ḥanbal.

Whether Allah is or is not "thing"[4] was a much debated question. It was answered in the negative sense

1 P. 78.

2 On *tas͟hbīh* and *ta'ṭīl* cf. the article *Tas͟hbīh* by Strothmann in the *Encyclopaedia of Islām*.

3 I use this term in the sense of scholastic.

4 Cf. *supra*, pp. 69, 121, on the Mu'tazilite description of Allah.

by D̲jahm.[1] Apparently the term "thing" was, in the opinion of some theologians, too materialistic to be applied to the deity. Their opponents may have feared that to abandon the term in its application to Allah might lead to the well-known evaporation (*ta'ṭīl*). Yet they, or at least our As̲h̲'arites, had to avoid what could be denounced as materialism. So they applied to this case also the method of *tanzīh* and confessed that Allah was "thing", but unlike other things. Yet even this cautious formula was mitigated by a clause in which it was declared that "thing" had the meaning of "positively existing". The orthodox position could be supported on its positive as well as on its negative side by a verse from the Kuran, sura vi. 19: "Which thing is weightiest in bearing witness? Say, Allah"; and, as regards the negative position: "There is nothing like Him" (sura xl. 9). The whole question led the theologians who were interested in it to subtle distinctions, as may be seen from the pages which al-As̲h̲'arī has devoted to it.[2]

The negative side of the pronouncement is worked out in the corresponding negative qualities. We shall explain them one by one.

"Without body." It has been seen above[3] how far the anthropomorphists went in the opposite direction. The tendency of orthodoxy, on the other hand, is towards a spiritualized idea of God. So it is denied that God is a body. This denial covered, however, a wider field than that of the older theology. "Body" is one of the technical terms used by scholasticism; that it is used here also in this sense appears from the context; and the explanation of Abu'l-Muntahā is similarly in the scholastic manner. "Every body", he says,[4] "is divisible, all divisible things are composite, all composite things are created, all created

1 *Supra*, p. 121.

2 *Maḳālāt*, i. 181 *sq.*; cf. p. 70; cf. further Fak̲h̲r al-Dīn al-Rāzī, iii. 21 *sqq.*

3 P. 167 *sq.*

4 P. 14; 'Alī al-Ḳārī, p. 34.

things presuppose a creator. Consequently everybody is contingent and presupposes what is necessarily existent." This is the kind of reasoning which we shall find in later forms of the creed.

"Without substance, without *accidens*." Here we are in the very heart of *kalām* on its Aristotelian basis. Orthodox theology, after long hesitation, has joined the highways of antiquity, following the example of Eastern Christianity, which had decisively taken the same direction under the guidance of John of Damascus, who, we may repeat, based his exposition of the orthodox doctrine upon Aristotelian logic (κεφαλαῖα φιλοσοφικά). On many points the Muslim idea of God is in accord with John's description; the negative statement "without substance, without *accidens*" does not, however, occur in his great work on dogmatics. On the contrary, he illustrates the unity of God by the unity of His substance.[1]

Why does Muslim orthodoxy, also in contradistinction to the sect of the Karrāmites,[2] reject this notion? "Because a substance is a substrate (*maḥall*) for *accidentia* and originated properties (*ḥawādiṯẖ*) and this is foreign to the being of God",[3] says Abu'l-Muntahā. 'Alī al-Ḳārī subjoins the idea of substance to that of body of which it is an indivisible part (atom), and, as such, definite (*mutaḥaiyiz*). The idea of God being definite is rejected in Muslim as well as in Christian theology.[4]

It may be useful to translate here the definition of the terms "body", "substance", and so on as they occur in the catechism of Abū Ḥafṣ 'Umar al-Nasafī:[5] "The world with all its parts has originated, for it consists of (*a*) substances (*a'yān*), and (*b*) *accidentia*.

"Substance is that which has an existence of its own. It is either (*a*) composed, in which case it is called body, or

1 Migne, vol. XCIV. col. 792.

2 Cf. the article *Karrāmīya* in the *Encyclopaedia of Islām*.

3 Abu'l-Muntahā, p. 14.

4 John of Damascus, ed. Migne, vol. XCIV. col. 849; *supra*, pp. 69, 73, 115 *sq*.

5 Ed. Cureton, p. 1.

(*b*) not-composed, in which case it cannot be divided and is called atom (*djawhar*).[1]

"*Accidens* is that which has no existence of its own and originates in bodies and atoms, *e.g.* colour, species, taste and smell".

The next negative pronouncement regarding the Godhead, "without limit", is akin to the idea of indefiniteness.[2] A different explanation of the term "limit" (*ḥadd*) is mentioned by Abu'l-Muntahā[3], namely, the definition of the *quidditas* by means of the enumeration of its parts; God being a unity (*fard*), without parts, the idea of limit is excluded from Him.

The remaining negative terms scarcely require any further explanation. It may, however, be remarked that the plain words "without equal", which go back to the Kuran,[4] are transferred by Abu'l-Muntahā to the philosophical field in the following way: "The idea of equality means partnership regarding species. God, having neither *species* nor *genus*, cannot have an equal".

Ad art. 5. This article, as well as arts. 6 and 7, deals with the questions which are bound up with the idea of Allah as the Creator and Governor of the universe and of man. The difficulties from a purely theological point of view have been mentioned above;[5] the present article takes up a position in opposition to the Djabrites, in so far as Allah's writing on the preserved table is of a descriptive, not of a decisive, nature.[6] The tenour of the article as a whole is rather of a philosophical than of a theological nature.

At the outset the *creatio ex nihilo* is taught, in accordance with the tradition: "Allah existed and there was nothing with Him", and in opposition to the Aristotelian doctrine

1 This term is also used to denote substance.
2 'Alī al-Ḳārī, p. 35.
3 P. 14.
4 Sura xl. 9.
5 P. 75 *sq.*
6 Abu'l-Muntahā, p. 16 *sq.*; cf. *supra*, p. 126 *sq.*

of the eternity of the world. The dogma of Allah as the Creator imposed on theologians the difficult task of harmonizing it with the doctrine of Allah's being exempt from change, a doctrine to which our theologians willingly agree, as appears at the end of the present article. The difficulty of this task was lessened to some extent by the doctrine of the eternity of Allah's creative action, as it is expressed in art. 2, where creating is included among the eternal active qualities.

Another way of avoiding the difficulty mentioned, as well as that of a too rigid predestination, was found in the doctrine of God's foreknowledge. "Allah had knowledge concerning things before they existed, from eternity", as the present article expresses it. For there can be little doubt that the introduction of this doctrine[1] was meant to be a kind of mother-conception containing the germs of creation and predestination, but in a milder form which made these dogmas more acceptable to scrupulous minds. As a matter of fact, the foreknowledge of God follows in the present article immediately on the *creatio ex nihilo*, and is followed immediately by the doctrine of the decree. It has two aspects and adequately fulfils its function. Some of the Mu'tazilites rejected the idea of God as the Creator; according to them the creative function consisted rather in forethought;[2] and Oriental Christianity, through its mouthpiece John of Damascus,[3] gave to divine prognosis the place which the decree holds in Muslim dogmatics; it did not give up the idea of predestination; it started from forethought and then approached predestination, trying to harmonize the two: "For", says John, "on account of His forethought God has already established all things, in accordance with His bounty and His justice".[4] As͟h'arite theology, on the other hand, starting from the dogma of

1 Hardly mentioned in the Waṣīya, cf. art. 7.

2 Cf. the article *K͟halḳ* in the *Encyclopaedia of Islām* by Tj. de Boer, and Fiḳh Akbar I, p. 21.

3 Ed. Migne, vol. XCIV. col. 969 *sq.*; cf. also *Kitāb al-Intiṣār*, p. 117.

4 Ed. Migne, vol. XCIV. col. 972.

predestination, approaches that of divine forethought, trying in this way to harmonize the two, and thereby to weaken the Mu'tazilite position.

The appearance of the idea of God's foreknowledge in a prominent place in the present article rests upon one other ground, namely, its connection with the relation between essence and existence. According to some of the Mu'tazilites, as we have seen, the fact that things were thought by God was the ground of their reality, without an intervening act of creation. This notion led them, for example, to deny the creation of Paradise and Hell.[1] It was embodied in the phrase: "The non-existing is thing" (*al-ma'dūm s̲h̲ai'*).

Orthodox Islam and medieval Christianity could not accept this doctrine; they made a real distinction between essence and existence: "Pour adapter l'Aristotélisme à sa destination théologique, il suffit de transformer la distinction purement logique, posée par le Stagirite, entre l'essence et l'existence, en une distinction ontologique ou réelle; puis d'appliquer à cette distinction réelle la théorie péripatéticienne de la puissance et de l'acte et celle de l'analogicité de l'être".[2] As a matter of fact, Islamic as well as medieval Christian theology teaches that in God alone is there coincidence of essence (*d̲h̲āt*) and existence (*wud̲j̲ūd*), in other beings there is separation between the two,[3] God alone being absolutely existent, whereas all other beings are only contingent and require to be created in order to acquire existence. This fundamental use of the term "contingent" gives it, in some contexts, the meaning of "not-really existing"; consequently the term *ma'dūm* denotes things non-created, things not yet created, and things created, in so far as the latter have no reality of their own.

Ad art. 6. This article contains the doctrine of predestination, especially in relation to human nature. How

1 *Supra*, p. 165 *sqq.*; cf. p. 121.
2 Rougier, *La scolastique*, p. 125.
3 Rougier, *La scolastique*, p. 126 *sq.*

much importance was attached to Mu'tazilite objections to rigid predestination appears from its general tenour, which is against the Djabrites rather than against the Mu'tazilites, as well as from the doctrines of abandoning (*khadhlān*) and acquisition (*kasb*).

The term *khadhlān*[1] is based on sura iii. 154: "But if He abandon you to yourselves, who will help you after Him? Let the Faithful therefore trust in God". The idea belongs to Christian dogmatics, where there exists a term which exactly corresponds to *khadhlān*, namely, ἐγκατάλειψις.[2] It is hardly necessary to remark that in Christian dogmatics this term performed the same function as in Muslim theology—that of safeguarding the deity from a direct connection with evil.[3] There is, however, this difference, that while in Christianity it secured at the same time the providential action of God, in Islam it secured rather the freedom of man. On the opposite of *khadhlān*, viz. *tawfīḳ* or *hidāya*, cf. al-Baghdādī, *Uṣūl*, p. 140 *sqq*.

Further, our article, being orthodox in that it declares human acts to be created, willed, decided and decreed by Allah,[4] mitigates this doctrine by that of acquisition. The term *kasb* is based on sura ii. 286: "God will not burden any soul beyond its power. It shall enjoy the good which it has acquired, and shall bear the evil for the acquirement of which it laboured".

Here the verb *kasaba* is used in the first and in the eighth forms; and the terms *kasb* and *iktisāb* are accordingly found side by side. The latter is however preferred by those who desire to emphasize human freedom to some extent. It is clear that the doctrine of *kasb* or *iktisāb* aims at safeguarding a measure of self-government in man, without giving an exact description of it. Hence this doctrine

1 *Supra*, pp. 82, 143; cf. also the article in the *Encyclopaedia of Islām*.

2 John of Damascus, ed. Migne, vol. XCIV. col. 965 *sqq*.

3 *Supra*, p. 142 *sqq*.

4 *Supra*, pp. 128, 142, 152; cf. the commentary by 'Alī al-Ḳārī, p. 48 *sqq*.

has the reputation of being too subtle to be really valuable.[1] The school of dogmatists which is connected with the name of al-Māturīdī, and to which belongs *e.g.* Abū Ḥafṣ 'Umar al-Nasafī, prefers the term *ikhtiyār*, "choice".[2] A century after the death of al-Ash'arī the terms *kasb* and *iktisāb* had acquired a firm footing in dogmatics, as appears, for instance, from their use throughout al-Baghdādī's *Uṣūl*.

The question of predestination is attached in the present article to that of man's nature (*fiṭra*), which in its turn is connected with fundamental points of difference between the schools of dogmatists and philosophers, especially the Mu'tazilites and the orthodox. The question has been touched upon above,[3] in connection with the practical and theoretical attitudes towards children taken by the Khāridjites. It may be remembered that at least some of them went so far as to maintain that children, on reaching the age of discretion, had to be invited to embrace Islam; for man is not born in the state of Islam, but in a state of neutrality.

It may be surmised with some probability that the view of the Khāridjites was combated in the well-known tradition: "Every child is born in the *fiṭra*; it is his parents who make of him a Jew or a Christian or a Parsee".[4] For whether *fiṭra* be taken here in the sense of natural religion or in that of Islam, the tradition at any rate revealed an attitude regarding children and their fate which was in opposition to that of the Khāridjites.

The question in which sense the term *fiṭra* in this tradition should be taken became of primary importance in the debates with the Mu'tazilites. Religion, according to them, was rational; Islam being the true religion, Islam

1 Cf. the article *Kasb* by Professor Macdonald in the *Encyclopaedia of Islām*.

2 Nasafī's *'aḳīda*, ed. Cureton, p. 2. al-Ghazālī has given an exposition of the whole problem, *Iḥyā'*, iv. 220 *sqq*.

3 P. 42.

4 Muslim, *Ḳadar*, trad. 22; cf. Bukhārī, *Tafsīr*, sura 30, b. 1; *Ḳadar*, b. 3, etc.

was rational; every child born was a Muslim, and the law of Islam, being rational, was valid even before it had been promulgated; its obligatory character was universal.[1] In this train of thought the term *fiṭra* was identical with that of Islam. It is curious to see that, even in several canonical traditions, *fiṭra* is used in the sense of Islam.[2]

In other traditions, however, *fiṭra* denotes the pre-Islamic religion, which is not identical with Islam, but closely akin to it. This *fiṭra* differs from the natural religion of the Mu'tazilites, which was based on rational insight. It has its origin in that act of revelation to Adam which is described in the present article and also in a well-known canonical tradition.[3] Both descriptions are based upon sura vii. 171: "And when thy Lord brought forth their descendants from the reins of the sons of Adam and took them to witness against themselves, 'Am I not', said He, 'your Lord?' They said, 'Yea, we witness it'".

In some versions the tradition is also used with a view to predestination.[4] In the present article it serves as the basis of the idea of *fiṭra* as a general recognition and acknowledgment of the sovereignty of Allah, without any special *taklīf*.

In the commentaries this sense of *fiṭra* is supported by a reference to the verb *faṭara*, which in the Kuran means "to create"; *fiṭra* is consequently the original state of things. It may be asked how the story from the Kuran here mentioned can be reconciled with the doctrine, also mentioned in the present article, that God "created the creatures free

1 Cf. the article *Taklīf* by Professor Macdonald in the *Encyclopaedia of Islām*.

2 Bukhārī, *Manāḳib al-Anṣār*, b. 42; Muslim, *Īmān*, trad. 264; *Dhikr wa-Da'awāt*, trad. 56, 58, etc. Even the chief tradition itself ("Every child", etc.) has undergone modifications so as to acquire the Mu'tazilite stamp: ليس من مولود يولد الّا على هذه الفطرة (Muslim, *Ḳadar*, trad. 23).

3 Aḥmad ibn Ḥanbal, i. 272; iii. 127, 129; v. 135; vi. 441; Tirmidhī, *Tafsīr*, sura 7, trad. 2, 3; Mālik, *Muwaṭṭa'*, *Ḳadar*, trad. 2.

4 Aḥmad ibn Ḥanbal, *Musnad*, vi. 441; *Muwaṭṭa'*, *Ḳadar*, trad. 2.

from unbelief and from belief". Abu'l-Muntahā[1] explains belief in the latter phrase by "acquired belief", whereas in the story regarding Adam it is used, according to him, in the sense of "primeval belief", consisting solely in the recognition of Allah's lordship. According to the present article there are, consequently, three stages in the relation between God and mankind: that of primeval belief, that of the recognition of Allah's lordship, and that of being under the bondage of the law (*taklīf*).[2] The last-mentioned period begins with the mission of the first Apostle. Similar questions to those which form the subject of the present article were debated in the Eastern church at the time when Islam had just taken firm root in Syria. It is well known, and has already been remarked, that in regard to the question of predestination it was not orthodox Islam, but Mu'tazilism, which sympathized with the Christian view. The following passage on nature and free will from John of Damascus has a special bearing upon Mu'tazilism:[3] "It must be known that virtue (ἀρετή) has been implanted by God in our nature. So He is the beginning and cause of all good, and without His help and assistance it is impossible for us to will or to do any good. But it depends upon us either to cling to virtue and to follow God's summons, or to abandon virtue, which means adhering to evil and following the devil, who summons man in this direction, without having power to use any compulsion. For evil is nothing but the withdrawal of good, just as darkness is the withdrawal of light. Keeping, therefore, to nature, we keep to virtue; deviating from nature, we come to what is contrary to nature and reach evil".

A Mu'tazilite could scarcely have taken any objection to this passage. In order to estimate the Christian view at its proper value, it must not be forgotten that its pure

1 P. 19 *sq.*

2 On *taklīf* cf. further al-Baghdādī, *Uṣūl al-Dīn*, pp. 149, 205, 207 *sq.*, and *infra*, p. 261 *sqq.*

3 Col. 972 *sq.*

monism is in large part a reaction against the dualism of Manichaeism.[1]

Ad art. 7. This article is less elaborate than the corresponding one in the Waṣīya (art. 7), where three classes of works are distinguished—obligatory, supererogatory and sinful—with a view to God's will, command, desire, and so on. See *supra*, p. 142 *sqq*.

Ad arts. 8 and 9. These are the articles on the impeccability (*'iṣma*) of the Apostles and Prophets in general and of Muhammad in particular, and have nothing corresponding to them in the Waṣīya. Their appearance in the Fiḳh Akbar II may be due to two circumstances. We have already seen that the Fiḳh Akbar II, notwithstanding its resemblance to the Waṣīya, shows signs of a more systematic arrangement. In arts. 1–7 the orthodox position regarding Allah, His being, His qualities and His creatorship, is stated. It is natural that the doctrine regarding the Apostles and Prophets should follow.

There is also another point to be remembered: the Kuran contains a large number of passages on Apostles and Prophets; they are not of a dogmatic nature, any more than are the stories of the Prophets in the Old Testament. Early Tradition shows but faint traces of systematic thought regarding Apostles and Prophets in the chapters which are especially devoted to them (*e.g.* Bukhārī's *Kitāb al-Anbiyā'*, Muslim's *Kitāb al-Faḍā'il*, and al-Tirmidhī's *Kitāb al-Manāḳib*). Here we find the traditions in which the common features of the Prophets are described. These traditions form the nucleus of the later books on the *Dalā'il al-Nubuwwa* (Characteristics of Prophecy). Yet in the collections of canonical traditions there is no trace of the impeccability of the Prophets; on the contrary, several of them are connected with grave sins: Adam is the father of all murder, Abraham did not shun lying, Moses committed manslaughter, and so on.[2] Muhammad, it is true, is

1 Cf. col. 1193 *sq*.

2 Bukhārī, *Tawḥīd*, b. 24.

opposed to them in this respect, and this distinction is the ground of his privilege of intercession. Yet the dogma of Muhammad's impeccability is never mentioned explicitly in canonical *ḥadīth*.[1]

We have already seen that in the Waṣīya no special mention is made of the Prophets; nor are they mentioned in the confession of faith which al-Ash'arī has inserted in his *Maḳālāt*[2] as the confession of "all the people of *ḥadīth* and *sunna*". The dogma of the impeccability of the Prophets was perhaps for the first time formulated in the Fiḳh Akbar II. We must suppose that it arose out of the growing worship of Muhammad. Andrae[3] has pointed to passages in the works of Ibn Sa'd († 845) and al-Ṭabarī († 922) which betray the tendency to keep Muhammad free from any taint of polytheism. In the present article this tendency finds dogmatic expression for the first time. It may be that the development of the '*iṣma* of the Prophets in its dogmatic form was encouraged by the influence of Shī'a circles.[4] At any rate from the Fiḳh Akbar II onwards the impeccability of the Prophets in general and of Muhammad in particular belongs to the accepted dogmas of Islam, though there are differences as to the precise extent of the idea.[5]

Ad art. 10. The position occupied by this article in our document is stronger than in the previous creeds and its dogmatic importance is heightened. The corresponding article in the Fiḳh Akbar I owes its origin entirely to the events which resulted from the murder of 'Uthmān; in the Waṣīya it has the form of a hierarchic sequence; in our document it follows immediately on those concerning the Prophets in general and Muhammad in particular.

1 Cf. Tor Andrae, *Die Person Muhammeds*, p. 124 *sqq*.

2 i. 290 *sqq*.

3 *Die Person Muhammeds*, p. 129.

4 Andrae, *Die Person Muhammeds*, p. 134.

5 Abu'l-Muntahā, p. 23; 'Alī al-Ḳārī, p. 55 *sqq*.; Abu'l-Barakāt al-Nasafī, '*Umda*, p. 17 *sq*.; Taftāzānī on Abū Ḥafṣ 'Umar al-Nasafī, p. 136; al-Īdjī, *Mawāḳif*, p. 218 *sqq*.; Fakhr al-Dīn al-Rāzī, i. 319; Ibn Ḥazm, *Kitāb al-Fiṣal*, iv. 29.

Ad art. 11. This article scarcely requires any elucidation after what has been said above[1] on the relation between faith and sin, on the community and the sinner, and on the punishment of sin in the world to come.

Ad art. 12. On the wiping of sandals cf. *supra*, p. 158 *sqq.* Here it may be sufficient to recall the difference between the present article and art. 16 of the Waṣīya, in so far as in the latter the wiping of sandals is called obligatory, whereas in the present article it is described only as commendable. We have seen that in later theology, when the debates with the Shī'a on this question had lost their keenness, the view became prevalent that the wiping of sandals was no longer commendable, but merely allowed.

The commentators say that the second half of our article, in which the *ṣalāt al-tarāwīḥ* is declared to be commendable, is also directed against the Shī'a; they do not say, however, in what sense the Shī'a differ from other Muslims on this point. As a matter of fact the Shī'a regard a thousand supererogatory *ṣalāt*'s during Ramaḍān as preferable to the ordinary *tarāwīḥ*. We can only guess at what lies behind this attitude. But we must begin by relating the history of this institution according to the Muslim doctors. It is reported in Bukhārī's collection of traditions[2] that, in the middle of the night, Muhammad once entered the mosque in order to perform prayer. A number of men gathered behind him and did likewise. This was repeated on the two following nights by a growing number of people. On the fourth night the mosque could not contain the crowd; but this time Muhammad delayed his coming until the morning *ṣalāt*, when he declared that he had absented himself on purpose, in order to prevent the rite from becoming obligatory. Commentators assume that this happened in Ramaḍān. It does not appear, however, from the wording

1 Pp. 45 *sqq.*, 67, 94, 140, 192.
2 *Kitāb Ṣalāt al-Tarāwīḥ.*

of the report, to which 'Ā'isha was anxious also to add that the number of *rak'a*'s of Muhammad's *tarāwīḥ* never exceeded eleven.

The second report relates that, in the time of the caliphate of 'Umar, great zeal was shown for these *ṣalāt*'s, so that the caliph thought it advisable to arrange people in groups behind one or more reciters.

Moreover it appears from the commentary of Ḳasṭallānī[1] that the number of *rak'a*'s was considerably extended, especially in Makka and Madina;[2] al-Shāfi'ī declared that he had no objection to similar practices; others, however, were of a different opinion, and we can understand why it was thought desirable to state that Muhammad himself was moderate in his zeal for the *tarāwīḥ*. 'Umar's regulation is called a novelty (*bid'a*), although a praiseworthy one. At the present time the common people in Atchin, although assisting at the *tarāwīḥ* in large crowds, do not take an active part in them, except by a too clamorous chiming-in with the *āmīn*.[3] At the time of the consolidation of the law, there seems to have been no serious difficulty on this point, for in the books of *fiḳh* of the different schools the *tarāwīḥ* are reckoned among the supererogatory prayers which are recommended.[4]

All this seems to point to a high estimation of the *tarāwīḥ* in popular piety and, on the other hand, to a tendency on the part of some learned circles to moderate the popular zeal. Perhaps this state of things may be explained by the assumption of a pre-Islamic origin of the rite, to which also other rites of Ramaḍān seem to point.[5]

Ad art. 13. This article also harks back to the difficulties

1 iii. 458 *sq.*

2 This custom explains the pauses (*tarāwīḥ*) which at certain moments were desirable.

3 Snouck Hurgronje, *De Atjèhers*, I. 248 *sqq.*

4 Cf. the literature given in the article *Tarāwīḥ* in the *Encyclopaedia of Islām*.

5 Cf. "Arabic New-Year" in *Verh. d. Kon. Ak. v. Wetenschappen*, Amsterdam, new series, vol. xxv. No. 2.

caused to the community by the Puritanism of the Khāridjites on the one hand, and by the ungodly behaviour of magistrates on the other. Difficulties of the latter kind were the more serious as the same magistrates were, in virtue of their office, the leaders of prayer. Was prayer behind one who drank wine, or was guilty of other grave sins, valid or not? A negative answer to this question would clearly have meant revolution and this would have been in contradiction to the general attitude adopted by the orthodox community towards temporal power.

It is well known that the Murdjites especially went very far in accepting men and things as they were. Abū Ḥanīfa belonged to, or at least sympathized with, this sect. As a matter of fact, the present article occurs among the genuine traditions of Abū Ḥanīfa which are contained in the *Fiḳh Absaṭ.*[1] It is curious to see that this phrase also has obtained a place in canonical Tradition as a saying of Muhammad.[2]

Ad art. 14. The question of the punishment of sins appears in this article in a version of which the former half is negative, the latter positive—a fresh attempt to find a middle way between the latitudinarian attitude of the Murdjites and the rigid view of the Mu'tazilites. With regard to their differing views on this question[3] the former were connected with the promise (*wa'd*) of God, the latter with His threatening (*wa'īd*).

The version in the article is representative of the orthodox view;[4] although the divine decree is not mentioned in the present article, it must be assumed that the article rests upon it. Intercession on behalf of sinners is treated in art. 20.

1 MS. Cairo, *Madjmū'a* 64, fol. 31 *a*.

2 Abū Dāwūd, *Ṣalāt*, b. 63.

3 See also al-Ash'arī, *Maḳālāt*, i. 144 *sqq.*, 248, 266, 270 *sqq.*, 274 *sqq.*; al-Baghdādī, *Uṣūl*, pp. 97, 242 *sqq.*; al-Shahrastānī, i. 29, 31, 85; Fakhr al-Dīn al-Rāzī, *Mafātīḥ al-Ghaib*, i. 407 *sq.*

4 Cf. Abu'l-Muntahā's commentary, p. 28 *sq.*; 'Alī al-Ḳārī, p. 66 *sqq.*; *supra*, pp. 40, 64, 67, 94, 131.

The view propounded in the third paragraph of the article is based on sura iv. 51 and 116: "Verily, God will not forgive the union of other gods with Himself; but other than this will He forgive whom He pleaseth". The emphasis laid by orthodox Islam[1] and also by As͟h'arite scholasticism, on Allah's will being exempt from human standards and principles,[2] is justified by such passages as this from the Kuran.

Ad art. 15. Ostentation and vainglory take away the reward of any good work. The term "ostentation" is the translation of *riyā'*, which corresponds to τὸ θεαθῆναι τοῖς ἀνθρώποις (Matthew vi. 1); the commentaries say that *riyā'* covers also the idea of *sum'a*, *i.e.* what is done in order to be heard. al-G͟hazālī often combines the term *riyā'* with *d̲jāh* which comes near to ambition. The idea that the reward of good works is taken away by ostentation and vainglory has found expression in closely similar terms in the New Testament phrases "to have one's reward" and "to have no reward" (Matthew vi. 1, 2, 5, 16).

So the whole article may be said to illustrate the affinity of Islam and Christianity in an important point. Canonical Tradition abounds with sayings proclaiming similar views. Instead of many examples it may be sufficient to call attention to the fact that al-Buk͟hārī opens his collection of Traditions with the saying: "The value of works is in their intention", a saying which he and the other collectors of Tradition often repeat. By way of illustration of its meaning, it is enough to recall the traditions in which it is said that he who takes part in the holy war "in order to be seen" is not in Allah's way and will be thrown into Hell.[3]

This train of thought is carried on by al-G͟hazālī, who has devoted one of the books of his *Iḥyā'* to the intention

1 See *e.g.* Abū Ḥafṣ 'Umar al-Nasafī's *'aḳīda* on this point.

2 Cf. *supra*, p. 144 *sq.*

3 Buk͟hārī, *Tawḥīd*, b. 28; Muslim, *Imāra*, trad. 152; Nawawī, iv. 311 *sq.*

(*nīya*), and to the practice of religion and good works for their own sake and with selfless devotion (*ik͟hlāṣ*). al-G͟hazālī, though not denying the value of the religious law, is very strong in condemning those who regard religion solely, or mainly, from the juridical side. He often complains that the doctors in his own days paid no attention to that pure devotion to religion to which the fulfilling of the law serves only as a stage of initiation. His attitude in this respect is much like that of the Gospel towards the Jewish law and the scribes.

As a characteristic example of the juridical handling of religion, I translate the following passage from al-Ḳārī's commentary on the present article:[1] "The fact that the greatest *imām*[2]—may Allah have mercy upon him—ascribes this effect to ostentation and vainglory only, not to other sins, shows that other faults do not nullify good works; nay, Allah says: Verily, good deeds drive away evil deeds,[3] and this is based on the tradition in which Allah says: My mercy hath preceded my wrath.[4] One of the commentators disagrees with this view and writes: Likewise other evil features besides ostentation and vainglory nullify the reward of good works. He bases this view on the tradition: 'Five causes nullify fasting: back-biting, lying, abuse, a false oath and the lust of the eyes'. This commentator is not acquainted with the interpretation of this tradition, according to which it is only the completeness and the beauty of fasting that are nullified by the five sins—not fasting itself, for the lust of the eyes is a venial sin which does not nullify a good work; this is the opinion of the *sunna* as well as that of the Mu'tazilites. This commentator's reference to the tradition: 'A bad character spoils good works, as vinegar spoils honey', is useless, as the tradition is interpreted in the sense that

1 P. 68.

2 The commentator takes the Fiḳh Akbar II for a genuine work of Abū Ḥanīfa.

3 Sura xi. 116.

4 Buk͟hārī, *Tawḥīd*, b. 65; Muslim, *Tawba*, trad. 15.

badness of character, in the form of ostentation and vainglory, spoils the reward of work. This interpretation is according to the reconciling method which is accepted by the orthodox community".

Ad art. 16. In this article the reality of the signs of the Prophets as well as that of the miracles of the saints is confessed, the latter in opposition to the Mu'tazilites. The distinction made between signs (*āyāt*) and miracles (*karāmāt*) is explained in the sense that the signs granted to the Prophets are meant to prove their vocation and their sincerity, in such a way that their opponents are silenced. In virtue of the latter function, those signs are also called *mu'djizāt*, *i.e.* acts of an overwhelming nature. This term is used by Abū Ḥafṣ 'Umar al-Nasafī in his creed, by al-Īdjī in his *Mawāḳif*, and so on. The nature of these signs is that they are exceptional, that is, what we call miracles.

Muslims do not make use of a term exactly corresponding to the idea of miracle, which occupies so large a place in the literature of Christianity. This is due to the fact that modern Western discussions usually start from the dogmas of the existence of nature as an entity and of its working according to laws. Orthodox Islam is less dogmatic on this point. The Fiḳh Akbar II does not give a definition of the term *āya*; the commentaries explain it by "facts that infringe upon the customary course of things".[1] The former definition is the current one (*āyāt khawāriḳ li'l-'ādāt*). Instead of the term "laws of nature" we find in Muslim literature the term *'āda*, which I have rendered by "the customary course of things". This rendering has been chosen for the sake of brevity, but it is not a literal one. By *'āda* is meant that activity of Allah which gives human life and the universe its aspect, and this activity consists in the fact that from time-atom to time-atom He creates a series of universes with a certain regularity. Now when it is Allah's will to support His Prophets in a visible way, He abandons His usual way of re-creating the order of

1 Taftāzānī, p. 133 *sq.*; al-Īdjī, p. 175.

things: the dead are quickened, mountains are annihilated, and so forth. The atomistic philosophy on which this theory of miracles is based is usually ascribed to al-Bāḳillānī (†403/1013).[1] A complete scholastic theory of miracles, their conditions and their classification, is given *e.g.* by al-Baghdādī[2] and al-Īdjī.[3]

The *karāma* is of the same nature as the *mu'djiza*, in so far as it is also a deviation from the ordinary course of events; the difference is that it is not meant to silence opponents, but is a sign of the grace of God towards the saint through whom it takes place.[4]

The saints appear here for the first time in the creed,[5] another sign of the relatively late date of the Fiḳh Akbar II. The term *walī*, in the technical sense of saint, is still very rare in the collections of canonical Tradition. It may be assumed that it became popular in the course of the ninth century A.D. al-Ṭaḥāwī protests against a predilection for saints as against Prophets.

The two categories of miracles are called a reality, a term we often meet in the Waṣīya (arts. 19–22, 24, 25) and in the present creed (arts. 20, 21, 23, 29).[6] In the articles mentioned it is applied to eschatological ideas and in opposition to the Mu'tazilites, who denied some of the eschatological representations that had found their way into Islam, or interpreted them in a way (*i'tibār*)[7] which endangered their literal acceptance. A cognate term (*'ibra*) is used by 'Alī al-Ḳārī as the opposite of *ḥaḳḳ*. Yet he does not disclose to us what this well-known term exactly meant in its connection with signs and miracles. He

1 On the atomistic doctrine see also O. Pretzl in *Der Islam*, XIX. 117 *sqq.*

2 *Uṣūl*, p. 169 *sqq.*

3 *Mawāḳif*, p. 175 *sqq.*; cf. also 'Alī al-Ḳārī, p. 69.

4 'Alī al-Ḳārī, p. 69, who combats the slightly deviating opinion of some dogmatists.

5 They are also mentioned in al-Ṭaḥāwī's *'aḳīda*.

6 Cf. *supra*, p. 194 *sqq.*

7 Cf. al-Baghdādī, *Uṣūl*, p. 204, and *supra*, p. 119 *sq.*, on *tanzīh* in connection with eschatological ideas.

merely says that the Mu'tazilites denied the miracles of the saints.[1]

In connection with the signs of the Prophets mentioned in the present article it is worth while recalling that the Makkans refused to believe in Muhammad, because he could not prove his vocation by signs and miracles (sura xiii. 8, 27; xvii. 95; xxv. 8–11), and that he replied that he was but a human messenger and preacher of repentance. Muslim Tradition, as is well known, ascribes to him a great many miracles.

The theory of miracles on which the version of the present article is based was open to the objection that signs and miracles were also ascribed to Pharaoh and to Satan himself as well as to his auxiliary the Anti-Christ.[2] The reports of their miracles are not found explicitly in the Kuran (though in sura xliii. 50 an allusion is found to the miraculous power of Pharaoh), but in historical Tradition (*akhbār*); thus, while they cannot be rejected, they naturally stick in the throats of the dogmatists. Nevertheless, an explanation is found by connecting them with the deluding activity (*istidrādj*, *makr*) of Allah towards His enemies, which is familiar to Muslims from the Kuran (sura vii. 181; x. 22; xiii. 42; lxviii. 44).

As to Satan,[3] his character is complicated in Muslim theology, because in the story of how God commanded the angels to prostrate themselves before Adam,[4] Iblīs did not simply refuse to do so and thereby become guilty of disobedience, but based his refusal on his being bound to

1 P. 69. Cf. von Kremer, *Geschichte der herrschenden Ideen*, p. 171 *sqq.*; Goldziher, *Muh. Studien*, II. 373 *sq.*

2 Margaret Smith, *Rābi'a*, p. 31, cites a saying of Abū Yazīd al-Bisṭāmī according to which he did not attach a high value to the miracles of saints, just because even the Satans were granted "this answering of prayers".

3 Iblīs is the Arabic name which is usually supposed to be a corruption of διάβολος (cf. Horovitz, *Koranische Untersuchungen*, p. 87). Künstlinger (*Rocznik Orjentalistyczny*, VI. 76 *sqq.*) suggests a connection with Belial and cognate forms.

4 Sura vii. 10 *sqq.*

adore God and nothing beside Him—an argument which was not heard from the mouths of the other angels, who, consequently, are considered to be inferior to him in *tawḥīd*. Nay, Iblīs may be looked upon as the most fervent adherent of this doctrine, as he dared to maintain it against the commandment of God Himself. This attitude of Iblīs made a deep impression in the circles of the mystics, as is shown by some portions of the works of al-Ḥallādj.[1]

Notwithstanding the original devotion of Iblīs to monotheistic worship, he seeks to seduce man, tempting him to abandon it and to serve other gods, though not himself. So he appears to act evilly, though his knowledge is not defective. In a tradition on the authority of al-Suddī[2] the archangel Gabriel is represented as giving Muhammad a description of the two beings whom he hated most, Pharaoh and Iblīs; the comparison is unfavourable to the former, in so far as he claimed divine rank and honour.

The features of the Dadjdjāl[3] are well known from the collections of Tradition—his Cyclopean appearance and his reign of forty years, till he perishes in Syria at the hands of Christ. Like Pharaoh he will claim divine rank and honour, as is implied in his name.

'Alī al-Ḳārī's commentary quotes examples of miracles ascribed to each of the three. Satan pervades the earth in a moment so as to be able to impart his evil inspirations to those in East and West; Pharaoh made the Nile flow according to his command; and the Anti-Christ will quicken the dead.

The explanation of the miracles of God's enemies given here is that they are contingent (*mumkin*) and possible or conceivable (*djā'iz*). The term *mumkin* obtains a still greater importance when the tendency of scholasti-

1 *Kitāb al-Ṭawāsīn*, ed. Massignon, p. 41 *sqq*.

2 'Alī al-Ḳārī, p. 71 *sq*.

3 Cf. the *Encyclopaedia of Islām* and *Handbook of Early Muhammadan Tradition*, s.v.

cism to adopt the principles of logic grows stronger, a process which ends in the final triumph of the spirit of Aristotelian logic. More of this will be seen in our next chapter. Here it may be stated that the occurrence of technical terms such as *mumkin* and *djā'iz*[1] in the Fiḳh Akbar II is significant of the direction which Muslim theology was taking at the time when this creed originated.

The article closes with a phrase that belongs rather to art. 2 than to the present one. In art. 2 it was confessed that Allah was creating from eternity, His creative power being an eternal quality.[2] Perhaps the different version of the present article was deemed necessary, because the idea of a creation from eternity was open to misinterpretation, on account of its being akin to the idea of the eternity of the world, which was the chief objection to Aristotelianism. If indeed—so could Aristotelianism argue—God was creating from eternity, He was creating the world from eternity; consequently the world is eternal.[3] Orthodox Islam therefore ought to maintain Allah's eternal, creative function, and at the same time avoid the eternity of the thing created. This is attempted in the phrase: "Allah was creator before He created", a phrase which may seem preferable to detailed scholastic reasoning. The latter is not lacking and can even be appreciated by us. 'Alī al-Ḳārī,[4] for example, compares the relation between the eternal creative function of Allah and the non-eternity of the created world with the relation between His eternal knowledge and the non-eternity of some of the things known by Him. Far more technical are the arguments summed up by al-Taftāzānī.[5] al-Nasafī sought to express the orthodox view in the following way:[6] "Bringing forth is one of the qualities of Allah, eternal; it means His bringing forth of the world and all its parts, not in eternity

1 On a broader use of the term *djā'iz* cf. J. Obermann in *Wiener Zeitschrift*, XXX. 84.

2 *Supra*, pp. 75 *sqq.*, 188 *sq.*, 193.

3 'Alī al-Ḳārī, p. 20.

4 P. 20 *sq.*

5 P. 86 *sq.*

6 Ed. Cureton, p. 2.

but at the time of its coming into existence, in accordance with His knowledge and His will. And this bringing forth is different from the object brought forth, in our opinion". The last phrase is directed against the eternity of the world.

Ad art. 17. This question as a whole has been treated above, pp. 63 *sqq.*, 88 *sq.*, 179. It need only be observed that the well-known tendency to avoid anthropomorphism shows itself in the new phrase "And there will be no distance between Him and His creatures". Abu'l-Muntahā explains distance by *djiha*, that is, direction in the local sense. 'Alī al-Ḳārī gives an elaborate paraphrase in which he not only intends to exclude all idea of direction and distance, but also of attainment, separation, mingling and union. al-Ash'arī's treatment of the question has been quoted above.[1] According to the commentators the dogma itself cannot be doubted, because it is based on Kuran and *sunna*.[2] Details, however, are quite uncertain (*mutashābih*); it is, accordingly, based on Scripture, not on reason (*thābit bi'l-naṣṣ, lā bi'l-'aḳl*). As the uncertainty concerns the descriptive part (*waṣf*) of the dogma only, its integral acceptance (*taslīm al-mutashābih 'alā i'tiḳād al-ḥaḳīḳa*) is obligatory.[3] al-Ṭaḥāwī's corresponding article (9) likewise demands integral acceptance, without allegorical interpretation or anthropomorphism.

Ad art. 18. The description of faith given in this article needs no comment after what has been said in explanation of arts. 1–3 of the Waṣīya.[4] It may be observed that a slight mitigation of the invariable character of faith is given in the text of those MSS.[5] which make a distinction between the objective and the subjective aspects of faith, the former being invariable, whilst the latter are liable to

1 P. 88 *sq.*
2 Sura lxxv. 22; Muslim, *Īmān*, trad. 299, etc.
3 Abu'l-Muntahā, p. 33.
4 *Supra*, p. 131 *sqq.*
5 *Supra*, p. 194, note 1.

differences of certainty and intensity. al-Ghazālī[1] has viewed the question in the light of the relation between faith and works and their mutual influence. As to the relation between faith and Islam,[2] it is clear that to the author it is not the difference between the two which is of interest, but rather their similarity, which finds its expression in the term *dīn*, covering both ideas.

Ad art. 19. A distinction is made between Allah as the object of man's knowledge and as the object of his veneration. In the latter respect Allah does not receive what is due to Him, for there is no one who serves the Creator with the fervour and the devotion due to Him. With regard to man's knowledge of Allah, there is no short-coming on the part of man, who has appropriated to himself what God has revealed concerning His own being. So the expression "adequate knowledge" has the meaning of "adequate to the power of man and to his faculties in any respect, not to God's essence and the encompassing of His qualities",[3] or, according to the definition of Abu'l-Muntahā,[4] "adequate to the obligation imposed on us". In the latter sense we must also interpret the statement that all the Faithful[5] are equal in knowledge, subjective certainty, and so on, a statement which is surprising when compared with the phrase immediately following it, in which it is said that the Faithful are not equal in all these respects, except in faith.

The commentaries agree[6] in referring the equality of the Faithful regarding certainty, and so on, to the obligation apart from mood and degree, whereas the difference lies precisely in mood, degree and all subjective varieties.

"Except in faith." Abu'l-Muntahā, who appears to belong to those who distinguish between subjective and objective faith,[7] here again interprets it in the latter sense, whereas 'Alī al-Ḳārī[8] takes it in the former.

1 *Iḥyā'*, i. 112–14.
2 *Supra*, p. 22 *sqq.*
3 'Alī al-Ḳārī, p. 80.
4 P. 37.
5 Shahrastānī, i. 61[13].
6 Abu'l-Muntahā, p. 39; 'Alī al-Ḳārī, p. 82.
7 *Supra*, p. 194.
8 P. 82 *sq.*

The second part of the article emphasizes Allah's freedom to show His mercy or His justice to His servants, He being the sovereign who fixes even their eternal fate with the same liberty. We need not revert to this idea, which has been discussed several times in the foregoing pages.[1] It will be sufficient to recall the fact that on this point As͟h'arism does not give way to Mu'tazilism. God's justice and His bounty are allowed to exist on equal terms; this is only possible by elevating them to a superhuman rank; this method (*tanzīh*) saves Islam from the strait-jacket of rationalism, which the Mu'tazilites had prepared for it.

Ad art. 20. We need not revert to the doctrine of intercession after what has been said on the subject above.[2] It is sufficient to observe that in the present article the idea of the intercession of the Prophets in general, side by side with that of Muhammad in particular, appears for the first time. We have seen above[3] that the divergent attitudes regarding intercession of the Waṣīya and the Fiḳh Akbar II find a parallel in two groups of traditions.

Ad art. 21. On the balance cf. *supra*, p. 169 *sq.* We meet here the idea of Muhammad's basin as one of the eschatological stations for the first time in the creed. It is called a reality. Its scriptural basis is said to be sura cviii. 1: "Truly we have given thee *al-Kawt͟har*". This term means abundance and the older commentators take it in this sense.[4] The younger generation, however, explain it as one of the rivers of Paradise, or as Muhammad's basin, which was shown him during the time of his ascension.[5] In some descriptions the basin belongs to Paradise, in others it is one of the stations of the last judgment side by side with the bridge and the balance.

1 Cf. the General Register, under *Predestination.*

2 Pp. 61 *sqq.*, 180 *sqq.*

3 P. 181 *sq.*

4 Cf. the article *Kawt͟har* by Horovitz in the *Encyclopaedia of Islām.*

5 Ṭabarī, *Tafsīr*, xxx. 180.

The difficulties arising from these divergent representations are overcome either by efforts at reconciliation or by the conjecture that there are two basins.

In Tradition the basin is a familiar conception. Here, also, two types may be distinguished. One belongs to the desert; it represents Muhammad as the shepherd, who admits to the drinking-place those members of his community who will thereby acquire eternal bliss, whilst others are driven away, and are thereby excluded from that happiness.[1] The other type belongs to the scenery of Paradise. The dimensions of this basin are as the distance between Aden and Aila, its buckets or goblets are as numerous as the stars, its waters as fragrant, sweet and cool as the waters of Paradise, its banks are hyacinth. Whosoever has drunk from its waters shall never thirst.[2] Although some features in these descriptions show traces of their source, there is nothing to indicate the origin of the conception as a whole.

On retaliation between litigants cf. *supra*, p. 178. On Paradise and Hell as abodes which exist at present and are everlasting cf. *supra*, p. 165 *sqq*.

In some texts there follows the phrase: "The street is a reality".[3] The street or bridge has been mentioned above (pp. 169, 203). It belongs to the same order of ideas as the balance or the books; it is rather a kind of ordeal, for the bridge (*ṣirāṭ*), having a very thin ridge, the wicked will fall down into the pit of Hell, whereas the righteous will pass over it without falling.

For the idea of the bridge a scriptural basis is found in sura vii. 44, 46 (*al-ʿarāf*) and in sura xix. 72:[4] "And verily there is no one of you who shall not go down into it".

1 *E.g.* Muslim, *Ṭahāra*, trad. 37; Buḵẖārī, *Riḵāḵ*, b. 52, several traditions.

2 Buḵẖārī, *Riḵāḵ*, b. 52, several traditions; Muslim, *Faḍā'il*, trad. 25–45; Abū Dāwūd, *Sunna*, b. 22; cf. St John iv. 14. For full references see *Handbook of Early Muhammadan Tradition*, under *Basin*.

3 *Supra*, p. 195, note 2–2.

4 Cf. Andrae, *Der Ursprung des Islam*, p. 78.

The reference does not seem very appropriate, however, for in the preceding verses it is not the bridge which is mentioned, but Hell (*dja̲hannam*). "The bridge" is inserted here as the exegetical means to avoid the conclusion that *all* the Faithful shall enter Hell, as is stated in the verse. This appears also from a tradition on the authority of D̲jābir, which runs as follows: "When the inhabitants of Paradise enter it, they will say to one another: Did not our Lord foretell that we should enter Hell? Then it will be said to them: You have already entered it, but its heat has abated".[1]

In Tradition the bridge (*ṣirāṭ*, *ḳanṭara*, *d̲jisr*) belongs to the well-known representations. It will be erected over Hell and there will be thorny thongs upon it. These will grasp man and torture him in different degrees, according to his works. Some will be lacerated, yet finally be saved. The Faithful will have no trouble, as they will pass the bridge with the swiftness of lightning. The first to pass will be Muhammad and his community. The cry of the Prophets during this ordeal will be: *Allahumma, sallim, sallim*.[2] According to some traditions the redress of griefs will take place on the bridge.[3] Sale has already pointed to the fact that the idea of the bridge (*sinvat*) occurs also in Persian eschatology.[4] It is said that the majority of the Mu'tazilites rejected the idea of the bridge.[5] On later developments of the doctrine, see *Kitāb Aḥwāl al-Ḳiyāma*, p. 82 *sqq*.

The phrase on the black-eyed ones is likewise lacking in the text of 'Alī al-Ḳārī. It is at any rate in accordance with the everlastingness of Paradise and Hell and the immortality of their inhabitants.[6]

1 al-Baiḍāwī on sura xix. 72.

2 *E.g.* Buk̲hārī, *Riḳāḳ*, b. 52; Muslim, *Īmān*, trad. 302; Ibn Mād̲ja, *Zuhd*, b. 33, etc.

3 *Supra*, p. 178.

4 *Preliminary Discourse*, p. 120 *sq*.; cf. Söderblom, *La vie future*, p. 92 *sqq*.

5 'Alī al-Ḳārī, p. 88.

6 Waṣīya, art. 20.

The conception of the black-eyed girls in Paradise goes back to several passages from the Kuran, in which the delights of Paradise are described (sura lv. 72; lvi. 22); in some of these it is said that they are given as wives to its inhabitants (sura xliv. 54; lii. 20); in others that they are free from all impurity (sura ii. 23; iii. 13; iv. 60); that they have never been touched by men or *djinn* (sura lv. 56). Tradition[1] and later literature[2] have worked out these pictures, the prototype of which is unknown; Sale and Berthels[3] have again thought of a Parsi origin; de Vaux[4] has conjectured that Muhammad may have seen in churches the pictures of angels, which he took for beautiful girls and boys.

The commentators are not very explicit on the black-eyed ones.[5] Perhaps they did not desire to speak their mind on questions of *tanzīh* and allegorical interpretation, which were applied to sensual conceptions of this kind.[6]

On everlasting punishment and reward cf. the Waṣīyat Abī Ḥanīfa, arts. 27, 20, and *supra*, pp. 40 *sq.*, 180 *sqq.*, 221.

Ad art. 22. This article is an exposition of art. 6, in so far as it develops the ideas of grace and abandonment.[7] It is worth while to observe that the former is called an outflow of God's justice, *'adl*, precisely the term which was one of the catchwords of the Mu'tazilites. It is as if, by the use and explanation of *'adl*, the author means to say to these opponents of orthodoxy: "This is our idea of God's justice". He goes so far as to define justice as God's punishing the abandoned for the sins committed by him.

1 Cf. Bukhārī, *Djihād*, b. 6; *Riḳāḳ*, b. 51, trad. 18; Muslim, *Djanna*, trad. 23 *sq.*; Tirmidhī, *Faḍā'il al-Djihād*, b. 17; *Djanna*, b. 5, cf. b. 6, 24; Dārimī, *Riḳāḳ*, b. 108; Aḥmad ibn Ḥanbal, *Musnad*, i. 156; ii. 247, 345, 385, 420, 422; iii. 16, 27, 75, 141, 147; iv. 14.

2 *Kitāb Aḥwāl al-Ḳiyāma*, p. 111 *sqq.*

3 *Islamica*, i. 263 *sqq.*

4 Art. *Ḥūr* in the *Encyclopaedia of Islām*.

5 Abu'l-Muntahā, p. 42; 'Alī al-Ḳārī, p. 88.

6 Cf. al-Baiḍāwī on sura ii. 23 and xliv. 54, and Berthels, in *Islamica*, i. 263 *sqq.*

7 *Supra*, pp. 82, 143, 212.

Now what the Muʿtazilites most abhorred in the orthodox doctrine of predestination was that God punishes the sinner for sins committed on divine compulsion.[1] For this reason the present article, like art. 6, declares that there is no compulsion, either on the part of God or on the part of Satan. The process of perdition is that God abandons man by withdrawing His guidance; thereupon man abandons his faith and the *tertius gaudens*, Satan, is at hand to rob him of it. ʿAlī al-Ḳārī cites, in support of this concatenation, sura xv, which contains (verse 28 to verse 50) the well-known description of how Satan, on account of his refusal to worship Adam, was accursed and driven from Heaven; and how respite was given him till the Resurrection, during which interval he proposed to beguile all the children of man. In verse 39 he says: "My Lord! because Thou hast beguiled me, I will surely make all fair-seeming to them on the earth; and I will surely beguile them all; (40) except such of them as shall be Thy sincere servants". Whereupon Allah answers: "(41) This is the right way with Me; verily over none of My servants shalt thou have power, save those beguiled ones who shall follow thee".[2]

Ad art. 23. On the interrogation of the dead by Munkar and Nakīr cf. *supra*, p. 164 *sq.*; on the punishment in the tomb, of which the pressure is a detail only, cf. pp. 117 *sqq.*, 163; on the reunion of body and spirit in the tomb cf. p. 164.

It has been seen above, p. 195, note 3, that some texts call the punishment of the infidels "a reality which will take place", whereas they call the punishment of the Faithful "a reality which may take place". In this pronouncement they express the idea that there are neither theological nor logical objections to the idea that some of the Faithful will be punished in the tomb, but that it may be that God will spare them.

The term *ḥaḳḳ*, "reality", in the two combinations *ḥaḳḳ kā'in* and *ḥaḳḳ djā'iz*, seems to exclude allegorical

1 *Supra*, p. 81 *sq.*

2 Cf. also sura vii. 10 *sqq.*

explanation. It may, however, be that in other articles of this creed such an intention is not in the background. See further, *supra*, p. 225 *sq.*

Ad art. 24. Abu'l-Muntahā[1] is probably in agreement with the tenour of the article in assuming that "Persian" means "non-Arabic". Probably the author of our creed mentions Persian alone, because in his time this was the only language in which, apart from Arabic, a Muslim literature was likely to originate; whereas al-G͟hazālī, when discussing the question, mentions also Turkish and other languages.[2]

Apparently, the reason why the author thought it desirable to formulate the present article, and to give it a place in the creed, was his fear lest an unlimited permission to dwell upon God's names and qualities in foreign languages might endanger the adopted principle of *tanzīh*, either in the direction of anthropomorphism, or in that of allegorical interpretation; on account of this fear he adds "without comparison or modality" and makes an exception for "the hand of God". 'Alī al-Ḳārī,[3] in contradistinction to Abu'l-Muntahā, who does not touch upon this question, asks why this exception is made. His answer does not seem very satisfactory; I translate it because I am not acquainted with a better one. "The distinction", he says, "which is made here between the hand of God and His face is so subtle that it seemed to require a verification. As a matter of fact, I have found that the theological fathers unanimously say that it is not allowed to interpret the hand of God allegorically, in contradistinction to His other qualities, and that al-As͟h'arī shares their opinion. On this point they make a distinction between allegorical interpretation (*ta'wīl*) and *tafwīḍ*".[4] A similar attitude regarding *ta'wīl* and *tafwīḍ* is

1 P. 44.

2 M. Asín Palacios, *El Justo Medio*, p. 387 *sq.*

3 P. 93.

4 *I.e.* leaving the interpretation of anthropomorphic expressions to Allah (cf. Goldziher in *Zeitschrift d. Deutschen Morgenl. Gesellschaft*, XLI. 60).

taken by al-Sanūsī[1] on the question of the interpretation of Allah's sitting on His throne. An illustration of our article is found in a corresponding passage in Abu'l-Barakāt al-Nasafī's *'Umda*,[2] running as follows: "It is permitted to apply concrete terms to God, in Arabic and in Persian. Yet it is not allowed to use Persian words for 'light', 'face', 'hand', 'eye', 'side' and similar terms without allegorical application. Some terms may be applied to God in connection with others only, *e.g.* 'the elevated in rank', 'the fulfiller of wants', 'the scatterer of armies', 'the destroyer of care', 'the severe punisher'. It is not allowed to apply the term 'the veiled' to God, though some scholars declare the use of the term 'who veils Himself' allowed. Some terms may not be used, nor may their opposites, *e.g.* 'the resting' and 'the waking', 'the intelligent'. Likewise it is not allowed to apply to God such terms as 'He who enters the world' or 'He who leaves the world'. Nor may the term 'the absent' be applied to Him; but it is allowed to say that He is hidden from the creatures".

Apparently, what the author of this passage fears is that the free application to God of Arabic or Persian terms denoting human faculties might involve the danger of anthropomorphism and, in consequence, of lack of reverence.

Ad art. 25. The aim of this article is likewise to keep all anthropomorphic associations at a distance. That the author expressly mentions the idea of God's being near or far may be due to the fact that in his time these terms had become popular through mysticism. As a matter of fact, al-Ghazālī[3] uses the terms "near" and "far" in their mystic sense, in a context which seems to betray acquaintance with the present article. On the other hand, it must not be forgotten that they belonged from of old to the religious language of Islam. It may be sufficient to

1 *'Umdat Ahl al-Tawfīḳ*, p. 221 *sq.*
2 Ed. Cureton, p. 28.
3 *Iḥyā'*, iii. 8^{26}.

recall here the well-known verse from the Kuran:[1] "But of old We created man: and We know what his soul whispereth within him, and We are closer to him than his neck-vein". It goes without saying that the present article does not seek to exclude the idea of the omnipresence of God, to which the ideas of distance and nearness cannot be applied.

The question how the ideas of "near" and "far" in this train of thought are to be understood is not answered quite unanimously, as appears from the various readings of the text.[2] There is unanimity, however, on the main points. The chief condition for a correct understanding is, as is said also in the text itself, the method of *balkafa*. Under cover of this it may be said that the sinner is far from God, but that His obedient servants are near to Him, as well as those who are in mystic intercourse (*munādjāt*) with Him; similarly, the idea of nearness may be applied to man's standing before God on the day of resurrection and to his approaching the Lord in Paradise.

The texts and the commentaries differ on the question whether the ideas of nearness and distance also correspond to the rank of honour or dishonour which man may occupy in God's eyes. "Yes," says Abu'l-Muntahā,[3] "the text mentions the effect (nearness, distance) instead of the cause (God's honouring man or the opposite)." "No," says ʿAlī al-Ḳārī,[4] "for these are ideas referring to the ranks of the mystics, whereas the author of the present creed applies them to differences of subjective certainty (*īḳān*) only."

Ad art. 26. This article, as referring to the position of the Kuran in dogmatics, belongs to art. 3, to which it forms a supplement. It states that, although the Kuran was revealed piecemeal to Muhammad and afterwards written down in single copies, yet it is Allah's speech and, as such, its parts are all alike as to their importance. Yet

1 Sura l. 15.
2 *Supra*, p. 196, notes 3 and 5.
3 P. 45.
4 P. 93.

its single verses vary as regards the value of their recitation. So it is also with God's names, which are of equal importance in so far as all of them refer to His being, yet differ in loftiness. In canonical Tradition the value of the different suras of the Kuran is expressed without any reference to its uniformity in respect of dogma.[1]

Such utterances of popular theology are in accordance with the very different degrees of reward which are connected with the recitation of different parts of the Kuran; these also are expressed in the form of traditions, and al-Baiḍāwī mentions such traditions at the end of every sura.

Ad art. 27. It has been seen above[2] that some texts open this article with the statement that Muhammad's parents, as well as his uncle Abū Ṭālib, died as infidels. The same statement is to be found in canonical Tradition in the story of how Muhammad visited Abū Ṭālib on his death-bed and admonished him to confess the unity of Allah, but without success, with the result that he died as an infidel.[3] Such traditions are intended to describe the historical background of sura ix. 114: "It is not for the Prophet or the Faithful to pray for the forgiveness of those who, though they be near of kin, associate other gods with God, after it hath been made clear to them that they are to be the inmates of Hell".

It is, however, well known that later Islam first abandoned such data and finally adopted the doctrine that nearly all Muhammad's relatives ultimately accepted Islam.[4] It may be that this change of attitude was influenced by the very outspoken feelings of the S͟hīʿa regarding this point, and the statement expressed in the first part of the present article may have been a Sunni protest against

1 Cf. *Handbook of Early Muhammadan Tradition*, p. 130 *b*.

2 P. 197, note 1.

3 Buk͟hārī, *D̲janā'iz*, b. 81; Muslim, *Īmān*, trad. 39–42, etc.

4 Cf. Snouck Hurgronje, *Een rector der Mekkaansche universitei*, p. 351 *sq.* (*Verspreide Geschriften*, III. 74 *sq.*); *Mekka*, II. 217, 239,

such exaggerations, a protest which fell into oblivion in the course of time.

Less evident is the dogmatic background of the second part. Abu'l-Muntahā[1] in his commentary remarks that the enumeration of Muhammad's children was simply directed against those who pretended that their number was larger or smaller. What we may conjecture as to the dogmatic background of such differences is again the Shī'a tendency to reconstruct history in favour of Fāṭima, as well as the common Muslim tendency to efface reminiscences of Muhammad's polytheistic period, such as appeared, for example, in the name of 'Abd Manāf borne by one of his sons. An anti-Shī'a tendency, similarly connected with the person of Fāṭima, we have seen to exist also in the corresponding article of the Waṣīyat Abī Ḥanīfa.[2] The discrepancies between the historical traditions on the children of Muhammad have been clearly demonstrated by Lammens in his book on Fāṭima and the daughters of Muhammad, as well as in his article *Fāṭima* in the *Encyclopaedia of Islām*. Apart from perfectly comprehensible ignorance, the difference may be mainly due to the following circumstances. Khadīdja being already of middle years when Muhammad married her, the six children must have been born within a short time after the marriage. On the other hand, there is a tendency to represent Fāṭima as being at her best age (according to Oriental opinion) when she married; owing to this tendency some sources say that she was born in Muhammad's forty-first year, *i.e.* sixteen years after his marriage.[3] As a result of these divergent tendencies, there is no unanimity of opinion as to which of Muhammad's daughters was the eldest.

Still, trustworthy historical facts concerning each of them are not lacking. It would be out of place to mention details and sources here, and it will be sufficient to recall the following facts, which can easily be supplemented by full information from Arabic sources, such as the works of

1 P. 47. 2 Art. 26; cf. *supra*, p. 183 *sq.*

3 *E.g.* 'Alī al-Ḳārī, p. 98.

Ibn Sa'd, Ibn Isḥāḳ and later biographies, as well as from European historians such as Sprenger, Lammens, Caetani and Buhl.

Zainab married Abu'l 'Āṣ, who fought against the Muslims at the battle of Badr and afterwards embraced Islam; Ruḳaiya, and after her death Umm Kulthūm, was married to the later caliph 'Uthmān, Fāṭima to 'Alī. The last named is the only one of Muhammad's daughters who survived in her descendants, the Saiyids and Sharīfs, and these up to the present day are very numerous. Notwithstanding this, she has received the epithet of *al-batūl*, the virgin, "because of her standing aloof from the women of her age as to excellence, religion, rank and genealogy" or "because of her standing aloof from the world".[1]

Less is known with certainty of Muhammad's sons.[2] The eldest, from whom his *kunya* is derived, apparently died before his vocation, for in sura cviii. 3 Muhammad relates that his opponents called him *abtar*, *i.e.* without male descendants.

Some particulars are known concerning Ibrāhīm, the son of the Egyptian handmaid Māriya, who had been presented to Muhammad by the Muḳawḳis. He was born, according to the Arabic sources, in Dhu'l-Ḥidjdja 8 A.H., and died seventeen or eighteen months later.[3] Popular belief connected his death with an eclipse of the sun, which, however, must have occurred at least half a year later.[4]

The place between al-Ḳāsim and Ibrāhīm is taken by Ṭāhir "the Pure". Other names given to this son are 'Abd Allāh, 'Abd Manāf and al-Ṭayib "the Good". According to some sources, however, al-Ṭayib and Ṭāhir were different persons. Our historical information is too

1 'Alī al-Ḳārī, p. 98 *ult.*

2 Buhl, *Das Leben Muhammeds*, p. 120 *sq.*

3 Cf. Caetani, *Annali*, index at the end of vol. II, tomo 2, in voce *Ibrāhīm*.

4 For the data of canonical Tradition, see *Handbook*, in voce *Ibrāhīm, Muhammad's son.*

scanty to decide this question. All that can be said is that it may scarcely be supposed that Muslim Tradition invented the pagan name ʿAbd Manāf. Sprenger[1] has conjectured that ʿAbd Allāh, Ṭāhir, al-Ṭayib and other epithets were later substituted for the name ʿAbd Manāf.

Ad art. 28. This article belongs to those on faith (18 *sq.*) and is intimately connected with the question of *fides explicita* and *fides implicita.*[2] In the light of the extracts quoted above it will be clear that the present article, in accordance with the general tenour of the Fiḳh Akbar II, is a step in the direction of the Muʿtazilite view, which did not recognize the *fides implicita*, and, accordingly, did not admit *taḳlīd*[3] in matters of dogmatics. The question of the *fides implicita* for the ordinary Muslim (*al-ʿāmmī*) goes back to that of the value of *kalām* in general for this category of the Faithful, a question which has been treated in an incomparable manner by al-G͟hazālī in the second book of his *Iḥyā*ʾ.

The "hesitation" mentioned in the article is expressed in Arabic by *waḳafa* and *tawaḳḳafa*, terms which mean "standing aloof, without taking a firm attitude"; they denote a slight degree of doubt.

Ad art. 29. It would be out of place to repeat here the story of Muhammad's ascension (*miʿrād͟j*) which is related in canonical Tradition[4] as well as in the biographies of Muhammad, and on which there exist several critical studies by European scholars.[5] As is well known, the

1 *Das Leben und die Lehre des Mohammad*, I. 199 *sq.*

2 *Supra*, p. 135 *sqq.* and *infra*, p. 265. ʿAlī al-Ḳārī, p. 100, expresses the latter idea by the phrase "believing *bi-tarīḳ al-id͟jmāl*"; cf. also *Le Monde Oriental*, XXV. 38, note 11.

3 Cf. *infra*, p. 265.

4 Cf. *Handbook*, s.v. *Ascension.*

5 Cf. A. A. Bevan, "Mohammed's Ascension to Heaven", in *Studien...J. Wellhausen...gewidmet*, Giessen, 1914, p. 51 *sqq.*; B. Schrieke in *Der Islam*, VI. 1 *sqq.*; Horovitz, *Der Islam*, IX. 161 *sqq.*; *Koranische Untersuchungen*, p. 140.

ascension is usually connected with the night-journey (*isrā'*) to which an allusion may be found in the Kuran (sura xvii. 1).

The difference between the foundations[1] on which the ascension and those on which the night-journey is based—"well-known reports"[2] in the former case and Kuran in the latter—causes a corresponding difference with regard to the denial of these dogmas; whosoever rejects the ascension is an erring schismatic, as the present article expresses it; whosoever rejects the night-journey is a *kāfir*.[3]

Finally, the article comes back to eschatology (cf. also art. 21). The signs of the approaching Hour enumerated here differ from the group mentioned above;[4] they have been selected as being fitted to serve as dogmatic material, which cannot be said of other items such as the handmaid's giving birth to her lord, and so forth. Traditions enumerating the ten eschatological signs, or some of them, are too numerous to be treated here.[5] On those mentioned in this article a few words may be said.

On the Anti-Christ cf. *supra*, p. 227, and the references given there.

Yādjūdj and Mādjūdj are the Gog and Magog of Ezekiel and the Apocalypse, who will make war upon the civilized peoples in the last days. In the Kuran they are not only the warriors of the eschatological period,[6] but also the contemporaries of Alexander the Two-horned.[7] They are often mentioned in canonical Tradition,[8] as is also the rising of the sun in the West.[5]

The appearance of Jesus in the last days is based by the commentator on sura xliii. 61: "And He verily shall be a sign of the last hour". Rodwell observes, in a note, that some refer this to the Kuran as revealing the last hour.

1 On the foundations of dogmatics see the following chapter.
2 Abu'l-Muntahā, p. 49.
3 Abu'l-Muntahā, p. 49; 'Alī al-Ḳārī, p. 100.
4 *Supra*, p. 23 *sqq*.
5 *Handbook*, s.v. *Hour*.
6 Sura xxi. 96.
7 Sura xviii. 93.
8 *Handbook*, s.v. *Yādjūdj*.

Moreover, the word rendered by "sign" (*'alam*) is also read *'ilm*, "a means of knowing", so that the connection between Jesus and the last hour is not an established one in this verse. This lack of certainty does not, however, affect the place of Jesus' reappearance in dogmatics, which is based on numerous traditions.[1] The data afforded by this source of information are summarized by al-Baiḍāwī[2] as follows: "Jesus will descend on a hill in the holy land, called Afīḳ;[3] in His hand He will hold a lance with which He will slay the Anti-Christ. Then He will enter Jerusalem at the time of morning prayer. The leader of this prayer will make way for Him, but He will refuse and perform prayer behind him, following the rites of the law of Muhammad. Thereupon He will kill the swine, break the cross, destroy chapels and churches and kill the Christians, except those who believe in Him".

The last clause may be elucidated by sura iv. 157: "And there shall not be one of the people of the book but shall believe in Him before His death". The last "His" may refer to Jesus and His death, and so this verse may also be considered as a Kuranic basis for the reappearance of Jesus.

It goes without saying that those who believe in Jesus in the last days will be the true Muslims. Finally, it must be observed that in the present article no mention is made of the Mahdī, who in later Muslim eschatology becomes more conspicuous than Jesus. It is said[4] that right up to the present day the Ḥanafites cling to the old view of Jesus as the vicegerent of God on earth in the last days, to the exclusion of the Mahdī, whom they do not expect. The fact that the Mahdī is not mentioned in the Fiḳh Akbar II may be due to the Ḥanafite origin of this creed.

1 *Handbook*, s.v. *'Īsā*.

2 Ad sura xxiii. 61.

3 I cannot decide which of the Biblical localities of this name is meant here.

4 Snouck Hurgronje, *Der Mahdi*, p. 27 (*Verspreide Geschriften*, I. 148).

Having finished our comment on the single articles of the Fiḳh Akbar II, we may proceed to sum up those features which contain indications of its general position.

On the whole, the arrangement of the Fiḳh Akbar II is better than that of the Waṣīya. It opens with a general outline of faith, based on Tradition; whereas the Fiḳh Akbar I and the Waṣīya plunge into the questions which divided the community. On this opening follow the different articles (2–7) in which the idea of God, His being and qualities, His decree, and His relation to man are treated. The following articles (8–10) quite naturally are devoted to the Prophets in general, to Muhammad in particular and to the hierarchic sequence.

At this point, however, the signs of a good version come to an end; the other articles are not only badly arranged, but some are even intended as supplements to those in the first half of the creed; art. 26, on the Kuran, belongs to art. 3; art. 27, on the children of Muhammad, is misplaced between art. 26, which treats of the Kuran, and art. 28, which treats of the *fides implicita*; art. 29, on eschatology, belongs to arts. 20, 21 and 23; art. 22, on the guidance of Allah, belongs to art. 6.

As regards its relation to the sects, the most important difference between this creed and the Waṣīya is its less hostile attitude towards the tenets of the Muʿtazilites. This appears in the doctrine of *kasb* (art. 6), in the introduction of *tanzīh* as a general principle with which to combat the horrors of anthropomorphism (arts. 3, 17, 24, 25), and in the obligation incumbent on every man to examine the details of dogmatics (art. 28). It appears in a striking way in the general attitude of this creed, which is the earliest scholastic creed of rational theology or *kalām*. In this creed *kalām* takes possession of the domain which has ever since remained its special property, namely, the doctrine of God and His qualities (arts. 2–5, to which there is no counterpart in the Waṣīya); we have seen that the way had been shown by Christian theology. A curious symptom of this process of rationalization of theology is found in terms such as "substance", *accidens* (art. 4) and "contingent" (arts. 16, 23), in which the beginnings of Aristotelian influence are manifestly seen.

Notwithstanding all this, it must not be forgotten that the fundamental Islamic idea of God as superhuman sovereign, who gives no account of His acts and decisions, persists in this creed. It may be repeated here[1] that, in the conflict between the rationalistic attitude of the Mu'tazilites and the purely religious attitude of old Islam, the Fiḳh Akbar II and its adherents were ultimately with the latter. Rationalism was admitted by the *mutakallimūn*, but it had to remain in the shadow of theology. With the Mu'tazilites the relation between the two was inverted.

Taking into account the features of the Fiḳh Akbar II as we have endeavoured to expound them, the general position of this creed in the history of Islamic ideas is perfectly clear. We have seen above[2] that the Waṣīyat Abī Ḥanīfa bears the stamp of Ḥanbalite theology. The Fiḳh Akbar II belongs to a later period. It is the embodiment of the final position of the community in relation to Mu'tazilism. It is well known that this position was reached mainly through the efforts of one man, viz. Abu'l-Ḥasan 'Alī b. Ismā'īl al-As͟h'arī († 324/935). We cannot but assume a close connection between the ideas of this man and the author of the Fiḳh Akbar II. To the general arguments in favour of this view we may add that the Fiḳh Akbar II is, so far as we know, the oldest document to use terms such as "knowing through knowledge" (art. 2) and "acquisition" (*kasb*) (art. 6), the introduction of which is ascribed by tradition to al-As͟h'arī.

So we may call the time of al-As͟h'arī the *terminus a quo* for the dating of this document. It would appear that we do not possess sufficient data to ascribe it to himself. Nor can a *terminus ad quem* be given with absolute certainty. Yet we are on safe ground in assuming a date not later than the tenth century A.D.: first, because of the polemics

1 Cf. *supra*, pp. 53 *sq.*, 83 *sqq.*
2 *Supra*, p. 187.

against the Mu'tazilites which lie directly beneath the surface of the document; secondly, because of the absence of a more systematic treatment of dogmatics, such as appears for the first time in writings originating after A.D. 1000. The justification of the latter assertion will be given in the following chapter.

CHAPTER IX

The later development of the creed

Our explanation of the Fiḳh Akbar II may have made it clear that this form of the creed, like Ash'arite theology in general, has a double aspect. On the one hand, it is a new edition of the Waṣīyat Abī Ḥanīfa, and connected with the name and the views of that great *imām*; on the other, it shows an intimate acquaintance with *kalām*.

Apart from isolated efforts, the development of Muslim dogmatics from the age of al-Ash'arī to the present day follows a course which can be characterized as that of a growing intellectualism. Theology, having once called *kalām* to its aid, ends in a state of utter dependence upon its benefactor. al-Sanūsī's short catechism or *Umm al-Barāhīn* ("Mother of arguments") deduces God and His qualities, the universe, the Prophets and their mission, as well as the last things, from a simple logical premise. Muhammad is overshadowed by Aristotle. Allah is no longer the God of the Kuran, of the pious ancestors and of man's own religious experience; He is a logical deduction from the existence of the universe. In my view, al-Ghazālī's crisis and later position can only be fully understood in connection with, and as a protest against, this kind of theological intellectualism.

We shall not endeavour to follow the intellectualizing process of Muslim dogmatics step by step, but concentrate our interest successively on the most prominent points, namely, *the doctrine of the roots (asbāb) of knowledge*, and *the change in the composition of the creed.*

The mention of the term "roots" makes us think at once of the "roots of the law" (*uṣūl al-fiḳh*), well known since Snouck Hurgronje laid them bare,[1] and it might be natural to suppose that the roots of dogmatics were the same. This supposition would, however, be wrong; the

1 In his *Le droit musulman.*

roots of dogmatics are identical with those on which knowledge in general is based, namely: (1) *the sound senses*; (2) *reliable reports*; (3) *reason.*

We shall discuss the meaning of these roots in due course. Here we may state at once that they represent a new stage of dogmatics. We have seen above[1] that al-Ash'arī in his *Ibāna* describes his position and method as "adhering to the book of our Lord, to the *sunna* of our Prophet, and to what is handed down on the authority of the Companions, the generation that succeeded them and the masters of *ḥadīth*,...and to the views of Aḥmad ibn Ḥanbal". We have also seen that al-Ash'arī, after first being a strict adherent of Ibn Ḥanbal, became the first propagator of *kalām* in orthodox Islam. Yet he never seems to have propounded a doctrine of the roots of the creed such as we have just mentioned. The question therefore arises: When did this doctrine originate?

The earliest printed work in which we find it in a summarized, technical form is the '*aḳīda* by Abū Ḥafṣ 'Umar al-Nasafī († 537/1142). Here it appears in concise and well-knit phrasing, which necessarily presupposes a previous development of some kind. As a matter of fact, we can trace back its origins for more than a century. The evidence may be sketched briefly as follows:

Abū Ḥafṣ' concise doctrine of the roots of dogmatics goes back to an almost identical formula in a work[2] by Abu'l-Mu'īn al-Nasafī († 508/1114). In this work, as well as in another by the same author,[3] an exposition is given of the foundations on which the doctrine is based; and in a work[4] by a contemporary of the last-mentioned Nasafī, viz. 'Alī b. Muhammad b. 'Alī al-Kiyā al-Harāsī al-Ṭabarī († 504/1110), we find an elaborate discussion of the foundations of knowledge and their value.

1 *Supra*, p. 90 *sq.*, where al-Ash'arī's *Ibāna*, p. 8, is cited.

2 *Kitāb al-Tamhīd fī Uṣūl al-Dīn*, MS. Cairo 2417, fol. 1 v.

3 In *Tabṣirat al-adilla*, MS. Cairo 2287, fols. 2–14, a more elaborate exposition is to be found.

4 *Uṣūl al-Dīn*, MS. Cairo 17,753, fol. 4 *sqq.*

Of a similar nature, though less elaborate, are the chapters which open the work on dogmatics by al-Djuwainī, the Imām al-Ḥaramain (†478/1085), a work[1] which further deserves attention since its author was the teacher of al-Ghazālī.[2] These chapters deal with the categories of reason (*aḥkām al-naẓar*) and with the question of adequate knowledge (*ḥaḳīḳat al-ʿilm*). Perhaps it would have been better from the point of view of method to treat the latter subject first, as is done by the earliest authority on the subject with whom we are acquainted, ʿAbd al-Ḳāhir al-Baghdādī (†429 = 1037/38), a writer whose name has frequently been mentioned in the foregoing pages.

As a matter of fact, the first chapter of his book on the roots of religion is devoted to the roots in the special sense which we are at present considering. It must be remembered that by the "roots of religion" the outlines of dogmatics are meant, whilst the roots of dogmatics are called the "roots of knowledge". To the "roots of religion" are opposed its branches; the former are matters of a dogmatic, the latter of a practical, nature; to the former consequently belong dogmatics, to the latter the law.[3]

In the work of al-Baghdādī we find, if not a systematic treatment of the roots of dogmatics, at any rate a systematic arrangement of the subject. So far as I can see we have not sufficient material at our disposal to enable us to decide whether al-Baghdādī may claim priority in this method of arrangement. Certainly he was not the first of mediaeval thinkers to engage in the problem of human cognition. Before him, Saʿadya al-Faiyūmī (†942), the Jewish philosopher, in his work on theology,[4] had reduced the roots of human knowledge to three. The man who is credited with being the Kant of Muslim philosophy is al-Bāḳillānī[5] (†403/1013), a pupil of a pupil of al-Ashʿarī. Even earlier scholars who discussed these problems are

1 *Kitāb al-Irshād fī Uṣūl al-Iʿtiḳād*, MS. Leiden, Golius, No. 146.
2 *Supra*, p. 92 *sq*.
3 al-Shahrastānī, i. 28.
4 *Kitāb al-Amānāt waʾl-Iʿtiḳādāt*, p. 12 *sqq*.
5 Macdonald, *Development*, p. 201.

mentioned by al-Baghdādī in his first chapter. These authorities, however, were generally heretics or schismatics, and the fact remains that to our knowledge al-Baghdādī was the first to give an exposition of the roots of knowledge which was taken over by his successors.

al-Baghdādī's first chapter, like each of the following fourteen, consists of fifteen sections. The first section deals with the definition and essence of knowledge.

Of greater importance for our present subject is the second section,[1] on the affirmation of knowledge and *realia*. It appears that the question whether man possesses adequate knowledge was one of the topics of Muslim philosophy. Here we come upon the Sophists, who gave a negative answer to this question, but it does not appear, either here or in any of the subsequent works on dogmatics, who they were; al-Baghdādī does not mention the name of a single individual who shared their views. Although we know these views from a short exposition on the part of their opponents only, they are highly interesting to us. al-Baghdādī mentions three categories of Sophists. The first and most radical denies the reality of things and the possibility of knowledge. Its attitude may be refuted by a practical and by a theoretical argument. The former is of the same nature as that used by some opponents of Fichte, who saw in the fact that his windows were smashed by the mob an argument which might convince him of the existence of a non-ego, which he doubted philosophically. In the same way al-Baghdādī advises that the Sophists should be scourged, in order to convince them of existing realities, or at least to reduce them to silence. However, he is not content with this argument, but gives a second which does credit to his sagacity, if indeed it be the product of his own brain. Ask the Sophists, he says, the following question: Is the negation of real knowledge real or not? If they give an affirmative answer they admit thereby some reality. If they give a negative answer they must be asked: If the negation of reality is not real, then

1 P. 6 *sq.*

the affirmation of it must necessarily be real. Likewise the question must be put to them: Do you know that there is no knowledge? If they answer affirmatively, they acknowledge knowledge, its subject and its object. If they answer: We do not know that there is no knowledge, they are refuted by the question: Why then do you pretend that there is no knowledge?

Akin to the Sophists, who were agnostics, are the sceptics, who do not deny the reality of knowledge, but doubt it. Their opinions may be refuted in a similar way. A third group does not acknowledge the objective reality of things; the reality they acknowledge is wholly subjective, and this attitude involves the consequence that all beliefs are sound and equal in value. They must be refuted, says al-Baghdādī, by the argument that the consequence of their position is that the belief of their opponents is right. If they admit this, further refutation is superfluous; if they do not admit it, they contradict their own thesis, that all beliefs are sound.

So far al-Baghdādī. His view that adequate knowledge is within the reach of man is representative of Muslim orthodoxy[1] and therefore, if for no other reason, of considerable importance. According to the Muslim view, it may be said that adequate knowledge of objective reality is possible for man.

We now turn to al-Baghdādī's fourth section, in which he expounds a general system of knowledge.

There are two kinds of knowledge: (*a*) divine knowledge, which is absolute, and (*b*) animal knowledge, which is of two kinds: natural, primary (*ḍarūrī*), and acquired, secondary (*muktasab*).

Natural knowledge again is of two kinds: direct and sensual. The former is again of two kinds: positive, such as self-consciousness and consciousness of feelings of pain, delight, hunger, etc.; and negative, such as the knowledge

1 With some variations al-Baghdādī's arguments reappear in the works of Ibn Ḥazm, *Kitāb al-Fiṣal*, i. 8 *sq.*, al-Djuwainī, al-Harāsī, and the three Nasafī's.

that the absurd is absurd, that one thing cannot be eternal and temporal, that one person cannot be dead and alive at the same time. Sensual knowledge is that which is supplied by the senses.

Acquired knowledge (also called *naẓarī*, *i.e.* based on discursive reason, *naẓar*) is also of two kinds: the first is based on reason (*ʿaḳl*), the second on the law (*sharʿ*). A bird's-eye view of the kinds of knowledge according to al-Baghdādī may be set out in the following table:

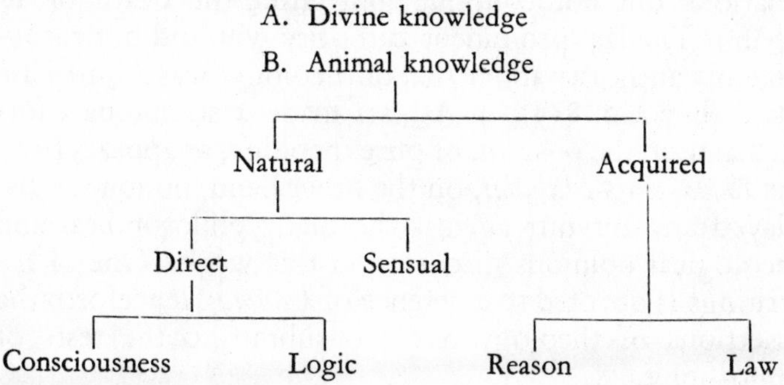

In the fifth and following sections al-Baghdādī turns to the roots or sources of knowledge, though he does not actually use this term himself. Later dogmatics[1] call the roots of knowledge the *asbāb*, *i.e.* the channels which supply knowledge. I have adopted the term "roots" because it is familiar to students of Muslim law. A glance at the table of the kinds of knowledge, and the place which legal knowledge occupies in it, supplies us with an answer to the question raised by a comparison between the system of *fiḳh* and that of dogmatics, I mean the question why the roots of dogmatics are not the same as those of the law and why legal knowledge is only one kind out of many.

The doctrine of the roots of *fiḳh* was a subject of discussion towards the close of the eighth century A.D.; the first to establish this doctrine on a large scale was al-Shāfiʿī[2] († 204/820). In his age philosophy had begun to

1 *E.g.* the Nasafī's.

2 In his *Risāla fī Uṣūl al-Fiḳh*.

exert its influence in the circles of educated Muslims in Syria and Mesopotamia; but it was still far from occupying a leading position. This explains the absence in the theory of the roots of the law of a doctrine of cognition or any other philosophical outlook. At the time when this doctrine originated, jurisprudence was under the tutelage of theology and the latter was indisputably the highest authority.

We have seen above how it came about that these happy relations did not continue long after the death of al-Shāfi'ī. The last prominent authority who did not recognize any authority above that of theology[1] was Aḥmad ibn Ḥanbal († A.D. 855). al-Ash'arī made a strenuous effort to maintain the position of pure theology, as appears from his *Ibāna*. His *Maḳālāt*, on the other hand, no longer displayed any fervour against the many philosophical and theological opinions discussed in this work. One of his writings is devoted to a defence of *kalām*. Henceforth the assertions of theology have to submit to the tests of philosophy.

In his orthodox period al-Ash'arī could still emphatically refer to Kuran and *sunna* as the roots of theology.[2] Probably this point of view may no longer have been deemed sufficient by himself in his later period. However this may be, al-Baghdādī shows that in his time an attitude had become prevalent towards theology which differed largely from that of the early generations. The Mu'tazilites had transferred theology to the common basis of human reason, and theologians saw themselves obliged to follow them at least so far as to establish the theoretical relation between their system and that world-wide basis. So the nature of human knowledge was investigated and expounded; within this scheme religion and law take their place.

A second stage in this process, the development of

1 Apart from Ibn Ḥazm and later Ḥanbalites such as Ibn Taimīya, who stood aloof from the main current of Muslim thought.

2 In his *Ibāna*.

which may have occupied the main part of the fourth century A.H., consisted in determining the roots or channels of knowledge. We have seen that in al-Baghdādī's work the theory is still *in statu nascendi*, just as is the doctrine of the roots of the law in al-Shāfi'ī's *Risāla*. We may now take up the thread of al-Baghdādī's chapter on knowledge from the point where we dropped it.

Although al-Baghdādī does not say so expressly, he is dealing from his fifth section onward with the roots of knowledge. We need not follow the author in his exposition of the value ascribed to each of the five senses by different philosophical schools. It may only be said that there is a difference of opinion as to which of the kinds of knowledge is superior to the other, that which is supplied by the senses or that which is based on judgment, the *'ulūm ḥissīya* or the *'ulūm naẓarīya*. al-Ash'arī is said to have taught the superiority of the former in so far as it is the basis of the latter.

Further, we learn that there was one sect or philosophical school, the Summanīya,[1] who did not recognize any knowledge except that which is supplied by the senses. The sixth section is devoted to the refutation of their thesis and a defence of the *'ulūm naẓarīya*.

The seventh section deals with the second of the roots and bears the following superscription: "On the establishing of reliable reports as a means of knowledge". The Arabic term here translated by "reliable" is *mutawātir*, *i.e.* supplied by so many persons that either their number or their trustworthiness excludes any doubt of its truth.[2] According to another definition, it is a report supplied by a multitude of people, which in itself is a proof of its truth.[3]

1 Horten, *Die philosophischen Systeme*, p. 93 *sqq*.

2 This is the definition given by al-Djurdjānī in his *Kitāb al-Ta'rīfāt*, as cited by Silvestre de Sacy, *Chrestomathie arabe*, 2nd ed., I. 461.

3 *Dictionary of Technical Terms*, p. 1471; cf. also Goldziher, *Le livre d'Ibn Toumert*, p. 47 *sqq*.

Here it appears afresh that theology no longer holds its old position; for the category of reliable reports not only covers the Kuran and those traditions which are *mutawātir*, but also history in general. This is a feature of some importance, as it induces our author to take up a position towards historical facts such as the crucifixion of Jesus.

The seventh section consists in a refutation of two categories of adversaries. The first comprises (*a*) the Summanīya, who deny the value of all knowledge, except that which is supplied by the senses; (*b*) the Brahmans,[1] who reject historical knowledge in general; (*c*) the adherents of al-Naẓẓām,[2] who reject "reliable report", for they admit the possibility that the community should agree in an error, a possibility which is denied in the well-known tradition: "My community will not agree in an error".[3]

The objections of the Summanīya are treated by al-Baghdādī in his section on the senses. Those of the Brahmans are refuted by the argument that they themselves believe in the existence of countries they have never seen and in that of kings and empires of olden times, nay, even in the existence of the Prophets whose reliability they deny; yet this belief cannot have any other basis than "reliable report". The objections of the Naẓẓāmites are refuted by the argument that they involve dishonesty and untruth in the Companions of Muhammad, which cannot be admitted.

The other category of opponents consists of those who, although admitting reliable report as a root of knowledge, deny its primary nature; they consider it to be secondary (*muktasab*), not *ḍarūrī*. According to al-Baghdādī, on the other hand, the category of knowledge based upon

1 Horten, *Die philosophischen Systeme*, p. 90 *sqq*.

2 Abū Isḥāḳ Ibrāhīm b. Saiyār; cf. Arnold, *al-Muʿtazilah*, p. 28 *sqq*.; Horten, *op. cit*., p. 189 *sqq*.; de Boer, *Geschichte der Philosophie im Islam*, pp. 51–3.

3 Abū Dāwūd, *Fitan*, b. 1; Tirmidhī, *Djahannam*, b. 7; Ibn Mādja, *Fitan*, b. 8; Dārimī, *Introduction*, b. 7.

reliable report is *ḍarūrī*. His argument is that no doubt of this knowledge is possible, any more than direct and sensual knowledge can be doubted.

In his eighth section al-Bag̲h̲dādī deals with historical knowledge in general, which he divides into three categories: (*a*) reliable report, based on abundant evidence, so that it cannot be doubted; (*b*) report based upon limited evidence (*āḥād*); (*c*) report which lies midway between (*a*) and (*b*) as to the evidence on which it is based.

This division is followed by an elucidation of categories (*b*) and (*c*):

(*b*) Report based upon limited evidence is admitted on two conditions: its *isnād*[1] must be sound and its *matn*[2] must not be in contradiction with reason (*g̲h̲air mustaḥīla fi'l-'aḳl*). It will be remembered that, according to the doctrine of the roots of *fiḳh*, the only test of a tradition is its *isnād*. The fact that al-Bag̲h̲dādī adds that its contents must not contradict reason is a fresh indication of the phase of rationalism into which religion has entered.

When the two conditions mentioned are fulfilled, such a report has practical effect, but does not afford sure knowledge. It stands on the same footing as the reports of reliable witnesses; their report is valid and has practical effect, but this does not prove that they have spoken the truth. Consequently this kind of report has no place among the roots of knowledge.

(*c*) This kind of report is similar to (*a*) in that it has theoretical as well as practical value; it differs from (*a*) in that it does not afford primary knowledge, but secondary only. al-Bag̲h̲dādī enumerates four species of reports belonging to this kind. The first consists of the reports of the Prophets, whose honesty is proved by their miracles. The second consists of the reports of those persons whose honesty is attested by the Prophets. The third consists of

1 The *catena* of authorities who have handed them down.

2 The text.

reports which have been handed down on the authority of trustworthy persons (*thiḳāt*), and after their death have become so widespread that they come into the category of *mutawātir*. To this species belong *e.g.* the traditions on seeing God in Paradise,[1] on intercession,[2] on the basin,[3] the balance,[4] stoning,[5] the moistening of shoes,[6] the punishment in the tomb,[7] and so on. The fourth species is formed by reports belonging to the class of *āḥād* (*b*), which are agreed upon by the consensus of the community as the basis of practice, for example, the traditions concerning the rule that legacies may not be bequeathed to heirs, that a man may not be married to his wife and her paternal or maternal aunt at the same time, that the hand or foot of a thief must not be cut off, if the object stolen by him does not amount to a certain value or has not been sufficiently guarded.

In his ninth section al-Baghdādī turns to the third root of knowledge, namely, Reason.

He divides the knowledge derived from this root into four species. The first is acquired "through deduction by means of analogy and judgment". This species is of eminent importance, for it not only comprises the elements of all higher religion, but it becomes in the course of time the main starting-point for Muslim dogmatics, eclipsing all other roots, as we shall have occasion to observe later. It already occupies a prominent place in the work of al-Baghdādī, for in his view it is from this species that we deduce our knowledge of the non-eternity of the world, of the eternity of its Maker, of His unity, His qualities, His justice, His wisdom; of the contingency of lawgiving; of the truth of the mission of His Apostles as

1 *Supra*, pp. 63 *sqq.*, 179 *sq.*, 229.

2 Cf. *supra*, pp. 61, 180 *sqq.*

3 *Supra*, p. 231 *sq.*

4 *Supra*, p. 169 *sqq.*

5 The stoning of adulterers, a practice which was based on the so-called *āyat al-radjm*, which is not in the Kuran.

6 *Supra*, p. 158 *sqq.*

7 *Supra*, pp. 117 *sqq.*, 163 *sq.*

proved by their miracles, and so on. The second species of this root consists of knowledge acquired through experience and routine, such as the knowledge of medicines, the skill of artisans, etc. The third species is connected with the law; it is the knowledge of the five categories of works: obligatory, recommended, etc. The fourth species belongs to the region of inspiration (*ilhām*), *e.g.* the taste for poetry, the knowledge of metre, the composition of melodies. al-Baghdādī is well aware of the fact that all this is not knowledge in the proper sense of the word, and that it cannot be acquired in the way of knowledge, but is rather a special gift of God to single individuals.[1]

Just as in the case of the first and the second root, al-Baghdādī asks (and we may repeat the question) to which of the two kinds of knowledge—the primary or the secondary—the *'ulūm naẓarīya* belong.

A glance at the table of the kinds of knowledge[2] shows that reason and law appear under the heading of acquired knowledge, whereas consciousness and logic belong to the category of natural knowledge. al-Baghdādī[3] relates that his friends are of divergent opinions concerning this point, and that the prevalent opinion is that such kinds of rational knowledge as self-consciousness and the exclusively logical function do not stand on the same footing as the other species of rational knowledge, but are prior to them and belong to the group of natural knowledge. All the other species of the third root which we have enumerated—namely, knowledge based on deduction, experience, law, inspiration—belong to the category of acquired knowledge. Yet this whole group occupies a particular place, which may be illustrated by the nature of knowledge based on inspiration. Just as this is often not a matter of knowledge, but of endowment, so all the species belonging to the group of rational knowledge may be transferred

1 al-Ghazālī regards *ilhām* as the channel through which the mystics acquire their knowledge (*Risāla ladunnīya*).

2 *Supra*, p. 253.

3 *Uṣūl al-Dīn*, p. 15, line 15.

from the secondary to the primary group by divine grace.[1] The following table shows[2] the three roots of knowledge in connection with the class to which they belong:

Roots of Knowledge		Kinds of Knowledge	
I. The senses		Primary	
II. Report	A. *Mutawātir*	Primary	
	B. Near to *mutawātir*		Secondary
	(C. *Āḥād*, no root)		
III. Reason	A. Self-consciousness	Primary	
	B. Logic	Primary	
	C. Deduction		Secondary[3]
	D. Experience and routine		Secondary[3]
	E. Legal knowledge		Secondary[3]
	F. Inspiration		Secondary[3]

The place of Muslim law in this system may seem to be subordinate. As a matter of fact al-Baghdādī[4] acknowledges that legal knowledge falls under the category of judgment, its position being based on prophecy and the claims of the latter upon judgment and deduction. It may also be observed that in this system even theology is to a large extent based upon reason. These facts raise the question as to the difference between this system—which may claim the title of orthodoxy—and the abhorred rationalism of the Mu'tazilites.

Muslim theologians have not neglected to give an answer to this question. It is threefold, but there is a close connection between the single parts.

According to the orthodox doctrine, the contents of the preaching of the Prophet, upon which the law is based, are themselves based exclusively upon the sovereign will of God, in this sense, that, if God had willed, He would

1 This recalls the anecdote of Franz Schubert's master who used to say: "The boy does not learn from me, God Himself teaches him".

2 Cf. also *supra*, p. 253, the table of the kinds of knowledge.

3 May become primary.

4 *Uṣūl al-Dīn*, p. 14 *sq*.

have inspired His Prophets with quite a different preaching and a different law.[1] It is in accordance with this conception that, in the system of logic, prophecy and law belong to the contingent things only. The Mu'tazilites, on the other hand, start from the principle that reason (*'aḳl*) is sound[2] and that even the will of God and His decisions are subordinate to it.[3] The orthodox, although giving reason an important place in their system, acknowledge its fallibility as a guide.[4] This is a fundamental difference between the two systems.

From this fundamental difference there arises another, which is hardly less important in the train of ideas which we are considering. The sound reason with which man is gifted enables him, say the Mu'tazilites, to acquire a perfect knowledge of God; this is the Mu'tazilite doctrine of natural religion (*fiṭra*).[5] The law is an outflow of this natural religion only; it is dictated by reason and by the will of God, in so far as the latter is similarly based upon reason. Therefore it cannot be supposed that God should have given either no law or a different one. According to the orthodox view, on the other hand, there would be no obligation (*taklīf*) if there were no law, and it is conceivable (*djā'iz*) that God should have imposed on man either a different law or no law at all.[6] "The Brahmans and the Ḳadarites maintain that it is impossible that God should have left His servants free from the obligation of the law, for thereby He would have brought them to sin. This argument", says al-Baghdādī, "is devoid of reason, for permission and prohibition are based upon the law, and where there is no law, there is no sin."[7] From the numerous passages on *taklīf* in al-Baghdādī's work[8] we may translate

1 Baghdādī, *Uṣūl*, p. 213^{10}. Obermann in *Wiener Zeitschrift*, xxx. 83 *sqq*.

2 Commentary on Fiḳh Akbar I, p. 31.

3 al-Shahrastānī, i. 31^{6} *sq*.

4 Commentary on Fiḳh Akbar I, p. 19.

5 *Supra*, pp. 42, 214 *sqq*.

6 Baghdādī, *Uṣūl*, p. 213^{10}.

7 Baghdādī, *Uṣūl*, p. 149.

8 The fifteenth chapter of his *Uṣūl* (pp. 207–28) is wholly devoted to *taklīf*.

the following, which, though concise, covers the whole orthodox position regarding the roots: "Reason teaches us that the reasonable is reasonable and the absurd is absurd; that the world has originated and is finite; that it is possible[1] that it will vanish, in a general and in a special sense. Moreover, reason teaches us that there is a Maker of the world, that He is one and that He has qualities. The mission of Prophets as well as *taklīf* are contingent with the exclusion of all necessity. From this it must be concluded that there is no obligation anterior to the promulgation of the law. Let it be supposed that before the promulgation of the law someone has proved by deduction that the world has been originated, that its Maker is one and that He possesses qualities; he would not on account of this knowledge be entitled to claim any reward and, if God bestowed on him many signs of favour, they would be a gift of grace on His part. Likewise, if a man should be an infidel before the promulgation of the law, he would not thereby be liable to punishment; if God should punish him, this would be justice on His part, comparable with His making children and animals to suffer though they are not guilty of sin.[2]

"As to the legal categories of prohibition, obligation, and so on, the root of our knowledge of them is report and divine command either by revelation[3] or by order of the Apostle, whose honesty is attested by miracles. Likewise the root of our knowledge of eternal reward and punishment[4] is not reason but report. But reason points to the contingency of these dogmas. Similarly, law, not reason, is the root of our knowledge of the names that may be applied to God.

"But the root of our knowledge concerning God is judgment which makes use of the deductions of reason.

1 Contingent from the point of view of reason; cf. *supra*, p. 235 *sq.*, where we have seen that in the language of the creed this may be called *ḥakk*. 2 *Supra*, p. 81.

3 *khiṭāb* is a term denoting direct commands in the Kuran.

4 *Supra*, p. 221.

The obligation, however, becomes valid only through the law".[1]

It would take us too far to return to al-Baghdādī's first chapter and to follow him through the remaining sections (10–15), which contain only explanations of his exposition of the kinds and roots of knowledge, which are at the basis of the orthodox dogmatic system. Instead of doing so we may translate the doctrine of knowledge and its roots from the well-known catechism of Abū Ḥafṣ 'Umar al-Nasafī:[2]

"The reality of things is established, and adequate knowledge concerning them is possible. This doctrine is contradicted by the Sophists.[3] The roots[4] of human knowledge are three in number: the senses, trustworthy report and reason.

"The senses are five in number: hearing, sight, smell, taste and touch. Each of them is the channel of the knowledge for which it is specially designed.

"Trustworthy reports are of two kinds. The first comprises the *mutawātir*. These are reports which are handed down without deviation by persons who cannot be supposed to have agreed to lie. They are the source of primary knowledge, such as knowledge concerning kings who have lived in the past and concerning countries far away. The second comprises reports derived from an Apostle who is fortified by miracles. They are the source of deductive knowledge; yet the knowledge based upon them is equal to primary knowledge as regards certainty and trustworthiness.

"Reason is also a root of knowledge. The knowledge which is supplied by it immediately is primary, for example, the knowledge that everything is larger than its parts. The knowledge, on the other hand, which is supplied by it through deduction is acquired.

1 Baghdādī, *Uṣūl*, p. 202 *sq*.
2 Ed. Cureton, p. 1.
3 *Supra*, p. 251.
4 *asbāb*.

"Inspiration is not a root of true knowledge in the opinion of the people of truth".[1]

We now turn to the second feature which is characteristic of the development of the Muslim creed from the fourth century A.H. onward, namely, the change in its composition.[2] It will be remembered that the three forms of the creed with which we have dealt in Chapters VI–VIII owe their origin to the inner necessity of the orthodox community to justify its position in face of the conflicting doctrines of the sects. The Fiḳh Akbar I opens with an article directed against the Khāridjites. The Waṣīyat Abī Ḥanīfa, which was composed about a century later, combats the Ḳadarites and the older Mu'tazilites. The Fiḳh Akbar II, which may date from the middle of the tenth century A.D., makes use of *kalām*, combats the Mu'tazilites by their own subtle method, but chooses its position so as to give the least offence to them. It may be called an effort to harmonize the orthodox with the Mu'tazilite point of view. Henceforth the task of vigorous controversy with this sect was left to die-hards such as Ibn Ḥazm and Ibn Taimīya, who did not shrink even from dealing hard blows to al-Ash'arī and the spokesmen of the new orthodoxy. This attitude exercises an influence on the subsequent forms of the creed. In these the old points of difference are not lacking; they, or at least some of them, continue to find expression in articles of the creed, but these articles no longer occupy a prominent place; they have become an almost undisputed possession of the community; besides, there are other points of greater importance.

As an example dating possibly from the beginning of the eleventh century A.D. we may take the so-called Fiḳh Akbar of al-Shāfi'ī. This catechism has in reality nothing to do with the celebrated *Imām*; it bears the clear stamp of a later origin and may be regarded as a direct descend-

1 al-Baghdādī's opinion on inspiration has not been accepted by his successors; it is rejected by Abu'l-Barakāt al-Nasafī.

2 Cf. *supra*, p. 248.

ant of the Fiḳh Akbar II; for this reason I denote it by Fiḳh Akbar III.[1]

As to its form, it is no longer a creed, nor is it a treatise of dogmatics, for, being designed for beginners, it purposely refrains from argument. We may therefore call it a catechism, a type of composition which has become popular in the Muhammadan world and has become known even in the West through specimens such as those of al-Samarḳandī,[2] the Nasafī's, al-Sanūsī, Faḍālī,[2] etc. The following summary will give an idea of this little work:

THE FIḲH AKBAR III

Art. 1. Every one who is under the obligation of the law is bound to acquire knowledge of Allah. Knowledge means to know its object, so that none of its qualities remains unknown. Knowledge cannot be acquired through opinion or *taḳlīd*.[3]

Art. 2. Knowledge is of two kinds, primary and secondary.[4] The former is independent of the special faculty of the knowing subject. The latter is dependent upon his judgments, opinion, and so forth.

Art. 3. A definition of *taklīf* and of the five categories of legal acts (obligatory, etc.).

Art. 4. Obligation to know Allah applies only to him who possesses full mental capacities, has attained his majority, and has been reached, directly or indirectly, by the preaching of a Prophet. Cf. sura xvii. 16.[5]

Art. 5. The definition of judgment or

1 The work is preserved in the Cairene Library in *Madjmū'a* 23, fols. 45–58. Notwithstanding many inquiries I have not been able to procure a copy of the printed text (Cairo, Maṭba'a adabīya, 1900).

2 See References, s.v.

3 Cf. *supra*, pp. 136, 242.

4 *ḍarūrī* or *muktasab*, *supra*, p. 252.

5 This article is directed against the Mu'tazilites, whose *taklīf* is based on reason, independently of the preaching of a Prophet; cf. *supra*, p. 261.

PARALLEL ARTICLES IN OTHER CREEDS

insight (*naẓar*) as "thought of the heart". This is superior to primary knowledge.

Art. 6. World is all that exists, besides Allah. The world is not eternal, but has come into being.

Art. 7. What exists and is not eternal presupposes an originator, Allah.

Art. 8. Allah is from eternity, without end and one. "One" means without parts.

Art. 9. Allah is neither substance nor *accidens*.

Art. 10. Allah is not composed and has no form.

Art. 11. Allah has no colour, taste, smell, warmth, cold.

Art. 12. Allah has no place. The question of His sitting on the throne is subtle. It is better not to engage in discussions regarding this subject.

Art. 13. Allah is living, knowing, mighty, hearing, seeing, willing, speaking, subsisting.

Fiḳh Akbar II, art. 2

Art. 14. Allah is living through life, knowing through knowledge, etc.

Art. 15. The life of Allah is an eternal quality.

Art. 16. The speech is of Allah, eternal and uncreated.[1]

Art. 17. Allah sees Himself eternally, in an immaterial way. It is possible (*d̲jā'iẓ 'aḳlan*) for creatures to see Him.[2]

Fiḳh Akbar II, art. 6

Art. 18 All that happens, happens through the will of Allah. Allah creates the faculty of acquisition in man and makes it His.

Art. 19. Human faculty in general is called *istiṭā'a*. It is the ground of the single acts of acquisition. *Istiṭā'a*, which is valid for faith, is not valid for unbelief.

Art. 20. Allah was free to create the

1 The old question of the created or uncreated Kuran.

2 The old question of the *visio beatifica*. al-Nasafī (p. 2[12]) calls it *d̲jā'iẓa bi'l-'aḳl, wād̲jiba bi'l-naḳl.*

world as well as not to create it. Allah has not created the world either with a view to what is salutary to man,[1] or on any other ground; but He knew from eternity that He would create. Allah is free to make the whole world vanish and to make it return.[2]

Art. 21. It would be absurd to suppose that Allah should wrong anyone. He is free to impose suffering on innocent children and animals, without indemnifying them.[3]

Allaḥ has fixed the terms of the life of man and beast.

The term "sustenance" (*rizḳ*) has a general meaning, without being limited to what is allowed, as the Mu'tazilites pretend.[4]

Fiḳh Akbar II, art. 16

Art. 22. Allah has sent Prophets with commandments and prohibitions. The nature of their signs and of the miracles of saints.

The number of the Prophets is about 120,000; among them were 313 Apostles. The difference between Apostle and Prophet.[5] They are free from sins after their vocation.

Fiḳh Akbar II, art. 9

Art. 23. Muhammad as a Prophet and Apostle. His exemption from sin. His eminence.

Fiḳh Akbar II, art. 18

Art. 24. Faith is knowing with the heart, confessing with the tongue and performing the chief works. There is no objection to saying: We are faithful, if Allah will.[6]

Fiḳh Akbar II, art. 20

Art. 25. Allah is free to punish all the Faithful, whether they be guilty of grave

1 This is directed against the theodicy of the Mu'tazilites. See *supra*, p. 79 *sqq*.

2 This is directed against the Karrāmīya, who taught the eternity of the world. See the article *Karrāmīya* in the *Encyclopaedia of Islām*.

3 This article is likewise directed against the theodicy of the Mu'tazilites. See *supra*, p. 81.

4 Cf. 'Umar al-Nasafī, ed. Cureton, p. 3[3], and *infra*, art. 32.

5 Cf. *supra*, p. 203 *sq*.

6 This proves that the author is an As̲h̲'arite; the Māturīdites rejected the clause. See *supra*, p. 138 *sq*.

sins or not, or to grant them forgiveness. All sins, venial or grave, may be punished. Intercession of the Apostle of Allah on behalf of those who are guilty of grave sins. Whosoever dies without being guilty of a grave sin belongs to those to whom Allah has given His promises[1] and will enter Paradise.

Fiḳh Akbar II, art. 21 — Art. 26. Everlasting reward and punishment in Paradise and in Hell. The latter are created.

Fiḳh Akbar II, arts. 21, 23 — Art. 27. The punishment in the tomb. Munkar and Nakīr. The balance, the bridge, the basin.

Fiḳh Akbar II, art. 28 — Art. 28. No deviation from the *i*d*jmā*ʿ or from the *d*jamāʿ*a* allowed. In cases of doubt an authority must be consulted.

Fiḳh Akbar II, art. 10 — Art. 29. The hierarchic sequence, Abū Bakr, ʿUmar, ʿUthmān, ʿAlī.

Art. 30. Conditions that must be fulfilled by the *imām*. There is only one *imām* at one time.

Art. 31. The Companions of Muhammad as a body must be regarded as pious.

Art. 32. On the question of "sustenance" (*riẓḳ*).[2]

Art. 33. The catechism closes with a kind of anthropology.

The composition of the Fiḳh Akbar III may be called characteristic of the new type of creed, or catechism. A comparison with the Fiḳh Akbar II shows its superiority as a composition, as may be seen from the following review.

Art. 1, the obligation of acquiring personal knowledge, is an indication of the intellectualist current of dogmatics. Art. 2, on the kinds of knowledge, does not yet mention the three roots. Arts. 3 and 4, the definition of *taklīf* and the sphere of its power, would not be out of place in a juridical tract. Art. 5, the definition of *naẓar*, counter-

1 *ahl al-waʿd*, cf. *supra*, p. 221.
2 Cf. *supra*, p. 267, art. 21.

balances, to a certain extent, the intellectualism of the foregoing articles.

The definition of knowledge having been established in arts. 1–5, the catechism proceeds to apply this newly acquired tool to the world and at once there arises not only the world, but its Maker, His unity, His qualities, His eternal speech (arts. 6–16). It must have been with a feeling of the triumph of theology that this was written down for the first time. This we conclude not only from the certitude and conviction of a composition like the Fiḳh Akbar III, but also from the fact that either it or possibly a similar catechism became the model of many later works, such as those of al-Djuwainī († 478/1085),[1] al-Harāsī († 504/1110),[2] Abu'l-Mu'īn al-Nasafī († 508/1114),[3] Abū Ḥafṣ 'Umar al-Nasafī († 537/1142),[4] Abu'l-Barakāt al-Nasafī († 710/1310),[5] Muhammad ibn 'Umar al-Rāzī († 606/1209).[6] After art. 17, which deals with the *visio beatifica*, there follow, quite systematically, a series of articles establishing the relation between Allah as sovereign and man (arts. 18–22). Here the difference between the orthodox and the Mu'tazilite position is still clearly seen. It is again an indication of the methodical composition of the Fiḳh Akbar III that arts. 22 and 23 deal with Prophets, art. 24 with faith as a consequence of their preaching, arts. 25–27 with reward and punishment in the tomb and on the last day. Arts. 28–31 deal with the community. Art. 30, on the conditions of the *imāmate*, is new. There is no trace of such a doctrine in the Fiḳh Akbar II. Yet we know that ever since the rise of the Khāridjites and the Shī'a the question of the *imāmate* was a much debated one. Traces of these discussions are to be found in canonical

1 *Kitāb al-Irshād fī Uṣūl al-I'tiḳād*, MS. Leiden, Golius, No. 146.

2 *Kitāb Uṣūl al-Dīn*, MS. Cairo 17,753.

3 *Kitāb al-Tamhīd fī Uṣūl al-Dīn*, MS. Cairo 2417; *Tabṣirat al-adilla*, MS. Cairo 2287.

4 *'Aḳīda*, ed. Cureton.

5 *'Umda*, ed. Cureton.

6 *Kitāb al-Arba'īn fī Uṣūl al-Dīn*, MSS. Cairo 2249, 6667.

Tradition[1] and faint echoes of them in some forms of the creed. An elaborate doctrine appears for the first time, so far as I know, in al-Ba<u>gh</u>dādī's *Uṣūl*;[2] henceforth it is never omitted in catechisms and treatises on dogmatics. Arts. 32 and 33 are appendices; the latter, which contains a kind of anthropology, is placed at the end, probably because the author could not find a suitable place for it at the beginning; in a similar way Muhammad ibn 'Umar al-Rāzī[3] has placed the *Muḳaddimāt* at the end of his work on *Uṣūl*.

It would appear unnecessary, in taking leave of the Fiḳh Akbar III, to give examples of cognate works such as the well-known *'aḳīda* of Abū Ḥafṣ 'Umar al-Nasafī,[4] since they would reveal little that was new. Yet our survey of the characteristic phenomena in this field[5] would be incomplete without a further glance at the increasingly intellectualist and systematizing tendencies that show themselves in several forms of the creed from al-Ba<u>gh</u>dādī's time onward. We have already observed some indications of these tendencies in the foregoing pages. I connect them with al-Ba<u>gh</u>dādī, not because I regard him as their author, but because the doctrine of the roots of dogmatics appears for the first time in his *Uṣūl al-Dīn*.

The tendency towards a systematic treatment of dogmatics finds a characteristic expression in those catechisms which call themselves explanations of the "two phrases". This type represents a return to the *<u>sh</u>ahāda*. This means two things: first, that their authors have attained to the rational insight that the Muslim creed must not be a polemical tract but the expression of the positive con-

1 Cf. *Handbook*, s.v. *Imam(s)*.
2 P. 270 *sqq.*   3 *Supra*, p. 269, note 6.
4 Translation in Macdonald, *Development*.
5 Apart from forms such as catechisms in questions and answers and metrical compositions which are remarkable for their form only.

viction of the community. This conviction could scarcely find a more dignified expression than in a return to the *shahāda*, the watchword of ancient, undivided Islam; secondly, it must be remarked that this return to the old formula was facilitated by the feeling that the danger of sects and schisms was over; it was consequently no longer the centre of interest.

The first writer in whose work we observe a deliberate return to the *shahāda* is no less a person than al-Ghazālī († 505/1111), who inaugurated the new form of the creed in the first period of his life. But even after the crisis of his life, which changed the self-confident intellectualist into a humble seeker after God, who could no longer ascribe high religious value to *kalām*, he retained this form as often as he thought it desirable to give a short account of the faith. As a matter of fact al-Ghazālī composed a summary of the faith at least three times. The first is his *Iktiṣād fi'l I'tikād*, a complete system of *kalām*, which betrays the pupil of al-Djuwainī. The second is the succinct *Risāla Kudsīya*, the "Letter from Jerusalem", which he wrote after his crisis and before he composed his *Iḥyā'*, into which he afterwards inserted it.[1] The third is the short catechism which opens the second book of the *Iḥyā'*,[2] and is described by him as an explanation of the two sentences of the *shahāda*.

This catechism naturally consists of two parts: the first, in accordance with the first phrase of the *shahāda*, deals with Allah; the second, in accordance with the second phrase, with Muhammad. In order to judge of the difference between this form of the creed and, say, the Waṣīyat Abī Ḥanīfa, it will be sufficient to recall the fact that the latter contains no article on Allah or Muhammad.

The first part of the catechism describes (*a*) the essence of Allah positively (unity, eternity) and negatively (neither body, nor substance, nor *accidens*, nor form, etc.); (*b*) the qualities of Allah (life, power, knowledge, will, hearing, sight, speech); (*c*) the acts of Allah (Allah as the author of

1 *Iḥyā'*, i. 97–108.

2 *Iḥyā'*, i. 83–6.

all that exists and happens; *taklīf* on account of the preaching of the Prophets).

The second part deals with prophecy in general, with Muhammad as a Prophet and as an Apostle in particular, with his preaching, especially with regard to eschatology, with his Companions, and with the hierarchic sequence.

This division forms also the frame of the *Iḳtiṣād*[1] and, with a slight difference, of the *Risāla Ḳudsīya*. It can easily be seen from the scheme just given that al-Ghazālī, by supplementing the scheme of the *shahāda* with the results of *kalām*, has introduced a new form of the creed. Side by side with it, the form of the Waṣīyat Abī Ḥanīfa and the Fiḳh Akbar II continued to be followed in popular works, such as those of the Nasafī's, but only to a certain extent, for even in the latter works the doctrine of God, His essence and qualities, has become the centre of interest. Moreover, these works deal, on a smaller or larger scale, with the roots of knowledge and dogmatics.

It has been seen from the summary of al-Ghazālī's catechism that the doctrine of the roots does not occur in it. Nor was a place given to it in the *Risāla Ḳudsīya*. In the *Iḳtiṣād*, on the other hand, it forms an important part of the introduction.[2] Here we find, as a matter of fact, the three roots of knowledge (senses, reason, reliable reports), and in addition three others, which are to a certain extent derived from the first three and therefore do not require further discussion; moreover, this division was not accepted by later dogmatists.

al-Ghazālī's return to the *shahāda*, on the other hand, was accepted at least by such considerable theologians as Ḳāḍī 'Iyāḍ b. Mūsā († 544/1149, the author of the *Kitāb al-Shifā'*), Muḥyi 'l-Dīn Muhammad b. Sa'd b. Mas'ūd al-Rūmī al-Kafīdjī[3] and 'Ubaid Allāh b. Muhammad b. 'Abd al-'Azīz al-Samarḳandī.[4] Ḳāḍī 'Iyāḍ wrote an '*aḳīda*[5]

1 *Supra*, p. 96. 2 Pp. 9–12.

3 The author of *Kitāb al-Anwār*, MS. Cairo 2259.

4 In his *Sharḥ lā ilāha illa 'llāh*, MS. Cairo 2240, fols. 11–35.

5 MS. Cairo, *Madjmū'a* 250, fols. 1–28.

which he calls an explanation of the two *shahāda*'s (*i.e.* the two phrases of the *shahāda*); it is divided into four parts, each of which consists of ten propositions; this is exactly the same division as that of al-Ghazālī's *Risāla Ḳudsīya*; al-Ghazālī's influence is unmistakable.

The first part (*a*) enumerates ten propositions concerning the essence and the qualities of God, which are *wādjib* to belief, namely, His being one, living, the God of all things, their Creator, almighty, who willeth all things existing or happening, good and evil, His being hearing, seeing, speaking, without bodily organs.

The second part (*b*) enumerates ten propositions concerning God which are *mustaḥīl* to belief, namely, that He should have originated, or that He should not exist; that there should be any God beside Him; that He should stand in need of His creatures in any respect; that He should not be free in His decree; that He should be encompassed by any place; that He should be substance or body or *accidens*; that He should have shape, size, equal or likeness; that He should be subject to change or the like; that He should wrong anyone; that His creatures should act without His decree and will; that He should be obliged to give account.

The third part (*c*) enumerates ten propositions which are established facts in relation to belief, namely, the mission of Prophets and Apostles; the revelation of signs and books, Muhammad being the last of the Prophets and Apostles; the revelation of the Kuran which is the speech of God, neither created nor creating;[1] the trustworthiness of Muhammad in his reports; the reality of Paradise and Hell; the reality of the angels.

The fourth part (*d*) enumerates ten propositions which, in relation to belief, are indubitable facts of the future, namely, that the world shall vanish; that people shall be tried in their tombs, enjoy happiness and receive punish-

1 This is to be understood in the sense of the orthodox doctrine of the *ṣifāt*; they are neither God (Creator) nor other than He (created) (Abū Ḥafṣ ʿUmar al-Nasafī, p. 25).

ment; that God shall gather mankind on the day of resurrection in their former state; that the computation of sin is a reality; that the balance is a reality; that the bridge is a reality; that the basin is a reality; that the faithful shall see God; that God shall punish in the fire whomsoever He pleaseth of those who are guilty of grave sins, and that He shall forgive whom He pleaseth, and shall take them from the fire to Paradise through His superabundant mercy and the intercession of His pious servants, so that only the infidels shall remain in Hell.

There is in the contents of this *'aḵīda* scarcely anything which requires elucidation, except the fact that the first and the second parts appear under the categories of what is compulsory or, on the contrary, absurd in a logical sense. We meet here this pair of categories for the first time. Yet they were known long before the age of Ḳāḍī 'Iyāḍ, as may be seen from the fact that the third term belonging to the scheme, namely *d̲jā'iz*, "contingent", occurs as early as the middle of the tenth century A.D.[1]

The introduction of this logical triad, *wād̲jib*, *mustaḥīl* and *d̲jā'iz* or *mumkin*, means the final triumph of Aristotelianism in the field of Muslim dogmatics. It enabled the *mutakallimūn* to give their system a more strictly logical form, as will be seen below. We must, however, first pay attention to another fact. We have seen[2] that orthodox Islam, on account of its maintaining God as the Creator, had been obliged to make a real distinction between essence and existence, the latter becoming manifest through the creative action of God. God alone, who exists without having been created, must possess essence as well as existence in Himself and through Himself, *ase*. Consequently God is necessarily existing, *wād̲jib al-wud̲jūd*.

This train of thought is also the quintessence of the philosophy of medieval Christianity.[3] It adds a new proof of the existence of God to the so-called cosmological one.

1 *Supra*, p. 227 *sq*. 2 *Supra*, p. 166 *sq*.
3 Rougier, p. 127 *sqq*.

In the course of time other proofs were added to these two.[1]

As a final example of the outcome of the tendency to systematize the Muslim creed, we may consider a summary of al-Sanūsī's short catechism,[2] which in itself is a summary, the printed text occupying only eight pages octavo.

Umm al-Barāhīn

There are three logical categories: (*a*) what is compulsory (*wādjib*); (*b*) what is absurd (*mustaḥīl*); (*c*) what is contingent (*djā'iz*).

Wādjib is that whose non-existence cannot be conceived by reason; *mustaḥīl* is that whose existence cannot be conceived by reason; *djā'iz* is that whose existence and non-existence are equally conceivable by reason.

Every *mukallaf*[3] is obliged to know (*a*) what is compulsory (*wādjib*) with regard to Allah; (*b*) what is absurd (*mustaḥīl*) with regard to Allah; (*c*) what is contingent (*djā'iz*) with regard to Allah.

He is obliged to know the same with regard to the Apostles.

I. (*a*) *Wādjib* with regard to Allah are twenty qualities. The first belongs to His self (*nafsīya*); of the others five are negative (*salabīya*),[4] namely, His existence; His being from eternity and His subsisting for ever; His being different from things originated; His being independent of substrate or termination; His being one.[5]

The following seven qualities are called *ṣifāt al-ma'ānī*:[6] His power, will, knowledge, life, hearing, sight, speech.

The following seven qualities are called *ma'nawīya*:[7] His being mighty, willing, knowing, living, hearing, seeing, speaking.

(*b*) *Mustaḥīl* with regard to Allah are twenty qualities which are the counterparts of the twenty foregoing ones: non-existence,

1 al-Īdjī, *Mawāḳif*, p. 1 *sqq.*; Fakhr al-Dīn al-Rāzī, i. 221, 584 *sqq.*; v. 487.

2 *Umm al-Barāhīn* or *Risāla fī Ma'ānī Kalimatai al-Shahāda.*

3 *I.e.* whoever is under the obligation of the law.

4 Cf. John of Damascus, ed. Migne, vol. XCIV. col. 846 *sqq.*

5 "There being no second to Him, either in essence or in qualities"; cf. *supra*, pp. 188, 205 *sq.*

6 *Ma'ānī* means ideas; here it is used in a special, technical sense.

7 *I.e.* relative to *ma'nā*, cf. note 6.

originating, becoming non-existent, resemblance to things originated,[1] not being independent, not being one, etc.[2]

(*c*) *Djā'iz* with regard to Allah is that He creates all that is contingent, or omits to create it.

The proof of the existence of Allah is the originating of the world.[3] For if it had no originator but had originated through itself, one of two equal elements must necessarily outweigh its partner, without apparent cause; and this is absurd.

Next follow the arguments proving the eternity of Allah and all the other qualities successively. They are all of a similar scholastic character and have nothing to do with belief, except the arguments for the hearing, sight and speech of Allah, which are based upon Kuran, *sunna*, and *idjmā'*, as well as upon purely intellectual reasoning.

II. (*a*) *Wādjib* with regard to the Apostles is their honesty in transmitting the divine ordinances to mankind.

(*b*) *Mustaḥīl* is that they should be untrustworthy, etc.

(*c*) *Djā'iz* with regard to them are human *accidentia* such as sickness, etc.

The arguments for (*a*) and (*b*) are of a scholastic character; that for (*c*) is based upon experience.

III. There follows a passage in which the author seeks to prove by the scholastic method that the whole doctrine regarding God is contained in the first phrase of the *shahāda*.

IV. Likewise in the fourth section the author seeks to prove that the whole doctrine regarding the Apostles is contained in the second phrase of the *shahāda*.

V. The fifth section is of quite a different nature. It points to the importance of the *shahāda*, not only for scholasticism, but for religion in general.

The catechism closes with the usual benedictions.

1 No body, *accidens*, etc.

2 The remaining fourteen negative ones can easily be derived from the list of positive qualities as given above.

3 Cf. also Fakhr al-Dīn al-Rāzī, iii. 47, 99, 102, 229, 546; iv. 3, 50, 68, 90, 95, 119, 123.

Citations from the Kuran

References

'Abd Allāh ibn Aḥmad ibn Ḥanbal, *Kitāb al-Sunna*, Makka, 1349.
'Abd al-Ḳāhir al-Baghdādī, *Kitāb Uṣūl al-Dīn*, Stambul, 1928.
—— *Kitāb al-Farḳ bain al-Firaḳ*, ed. Muh. Badr, Cairo, 1328.
Abū Dāwūd, *Sunan*, Cairo, 1292, 2 vols.
Abū Ḥanīfa, *al-Fiḳh al-Absaṭ*, MS. Cairo, *Madjmū'a* 64, fol. 24 *sqq.*
—— Letter to 'Uthmān al-Battī, MS. Cairo, *Madjmū'a* 64, fols. 20–3.
—— *al-Fiḳh al-Akbar* (I), with a (spurious) commentary by al-Māturīdī, Ḥaidarābād, 1321.
—— German translation by J. Schacht, in *Religionsgeschichtliches Lesebuch*..., p. 35 *sq.*
—— *al-Fiḳh al-Akbar* (II) (spurious), with a commentary by Abu'l-Muntahā, Ḥaidarābād, 1321, *see also* 'Alī al-Ḳārī.
—— German translation by J. Hell, *Von Mohammed bis Ghazâlî*, Jena, 1915, p. 29 *sqq.* Cf. also v. Kremer, *Geschichte der herrschenden Ideen*, pp. 40–3.
—— *Kitāb al-Waṣīya* (spurious), with a commentary by Molla Ḥusain ibn Iskandar al-Ḥanafī, Ḥaidarābād, 1321.
Abū Ḳurra, ed. Migne, *Patrologia*, series graeca, vol. XCVII.
Abu'l-Laith, *see* al-Samarḳandī.
Abu'l-Mu'īn Maimūn, *see* al-Nasafī.
Abu'l-Muntahā, *see* Abū Ḥanīfa.
Aḥmad ibn Dja'far, *see* al-Ṭaḥāwī.
Aḥmad ibn Ḥanbal, *Mosnad*, Cairo, 1313, 6 vols.
'Alī al-Ḳārī, *Sharḥ al-Fiḳh al-Akbar*, Cairo, 1327.
Andrae, Tor, "Die Person Muhammeds in Lehre und Glauben seiner Gemeinde", *Archives d'études orientales*, Stockholm, 1918.
—— "Der Ursprung des Islam und das Christentum", Sonderabdruck aus *Kyrkohistorisk Årsskrift*, 1923–5.
Arnold, T. W., *al Mu'tazilah: being an extract from the Kitābu-l Milal wa-n Niḥal by al Mahdī lidīn Allāh Aḥmad b. Yaḥya b. al Murtaḍā*, vol. I. Leipzig, 1902.
—— *The Preaching of Islam*, 2nd ed. London, 1913.
—— *The Islamic Faith*, London, 1928.
al-Ash'arī (Abu'l-Ḥasan), *Kitāb al-Ibāna 'an Uṣūl al-Diyāna*, Ḥaidarābād, 1321.
—— *Maḳālāt al-Islāmīyīn*, i, Stambul, 1928; ed. Ritter, Stambul, 1929–30, 2 vols. (the latter ed. is the one referred to in this book).
—— *Risāla fi'istihsān al-Khawḍ fi'l-Kalām*, Ḥaidarābād, 1323.
Asín Palacios, M., *El Justo Medio en la creencia*, Madrid, 1929.
—— *La escatologia musulmana en la Divina Comedia*, Madrid, 1919.
al-Baghdādī, *see* 'Abd al-Ḳāhir.

al-Balādhurī, *Futūḥ*, ed. de Goeje, Leiden, 1866.
Bauer, H., *Die Dogmatik al-Ghazālī's, nach dem II. Buche seines Hauptwerkes*, Halle, 1912.
Bell, R., "The men on the A'rāf", *The Moslem World*, XXII. 43 *sqq.*
Bodenschatz, J. C. G., *Kirchliche Verfassung der heutigen Juden*, Erlangen, 1748.
Boer, T. J. de, *Geschichte der Philosophie im Islam*, Stuttgart, 1901.
Buhl, F., *Das Leben Muhammeds*, Leipzig, 1930.
—— "Fasste Muhammed seine Verkündigung als eine universale, auch für Nichtaraber bestimmte Religion auf?" Festschrift für A. Fischer, *Islamica*, II.
Caetani, L., *Annali dell' Islām*, Milano, 1905 *sqq.*, vol. I– .
—— *Studi di storia orientale*, Milano, 1914, 3 vols.
Corpus Iuris Zaiditicum, ed. Griffini, Milano, 1919.
Dedering, Sven, "Ein Kommentar der Tradition über die 73 Sekten", *Le Monde Oriental*, XXV. 35 *sqq.*
Diffelen, R. W. van, *De leer der Wahhabieten*, Thesis, Leiden University, Leiden, 1927.
Dionysius Areopagita, *Opera*, ed. Migne, *Patrologia*, series graeca, vols. III, IV.
al-Faḍālī, *Risāla fī lā ilāha illa 'llāh*, with the *ḥāshiya* of Ibrāhīm al-Bādjūrī, Cairo, 1320; translated by M. Horten, in *Kleine Texte für Vorlesungen und Übungen*, No. 139, Bonn.
Fakhr al-Dīn al-Rāzī, *Mafātīḥ al-Ghaib*, Cairo, 1278, 6 vols.
Fiḳh Akbar, *see* Abū Ḥanīfa *and* al-Shāfi'ī.
al-Ghazālī, *Iḥyā' 'Ulūm al-Dīn*, Cairo, 1302, 4 vols.
—— *Mishkāt al-Anwār*, Cairo, 1332.
—— *Kitāb al-Iḳtiṣād fi'l-I'tiḳād*, Cairo, 1327. *See also under* Asín.
—— *al-Durra al-Fākhira*, ed. and transl. L. Gautier, Geneva-Basle-Lyons, 1878.
Goldziher, I., *Vorlesungen über den Islam*, Heidelberg, 1910.
—— *Muhammedanische Studien*, Halle, 1889–90, 2 vols.
—— *Le livre de Mohammed ibn Toumert*, Algiers, 1903.
—— *Die Ẓâhiriten*, Leipzig, 1884.
Guidi, Michelangelo, *La lotta tra l' Islām e il Manicheismo*, Rome, 1927.
al-Ḥallādj, *Kitāb al-Ṭawāsīn*, ed. Massignon, Paris, 1913.
Horovitz, J., *Koranische Untersuchungen*, Berlin and Leipzig, 1926.
—— "Ueber den Einfluss der griechischen Philosophie auf die Entwicklung des Kalam", *Jahresbericht des jud.-theol. Seminars "Fraenckl'scher Stiftung"*, Breslau, 1909.
Horten, M., *Die philosophischen Systeme der spekulativen Theologen im Islam*, Bonn, 1912. *See also under* al-Faḍālī.
Houtsma, M. Th., *De strijd over het dogma in den Islâm tot op el-Ash'ari*, Leiden, 1875.
Hurgronje, C. Snouck, *Verspreide Geschriften*, Leipzig-Bonn, Leiden, 1923– , 6 vols.
—— *Mohammedanism*, New York and London, 1916.
—— *The Achehnese*, Leyden, 1906, 2 vols.
—— *Mekka*, The Hague, 1888–9, 2 vols.

Ibn Ḥadjar al-ʻAsḳalānī, *Tahdhīb al-Tahdhīb*, Ḥaidarābād, 1325–7, 12 vols.

Ibn Ḥazm, *Kitāb al-Fiṣal fi'l-Milal wa'l-Ahwā' wa'l-Niḥal*, Cairo, 1320, 5 vols.

Ibn Isḥāḳ, *Sīrat Rasūl Allāh*, ed. Wüstenfeld, Göttingen, 1859–60, 2 vols.

Ibn Mādja, *Sunan*, Cairo, 1313, 2 vols.

Ibn Saʻd, ed. Sachau, Leiden, 1904 *sqq.*, 9 vols.

al-Idjī, *Mawāḳif*, ed. Sörensen, Leipzig, 1848.

Isḥāḳ b. Muḥ. b. Ismāʻīl, *see* al-Samarḳandī.

John of Damascus, *Opera*, ed. Migne, *Patrologia*, series graeca, vols. XCIV–XCVI.

al-Ḳāsim b. Ibrāhīm, *see* Guidi.

al-Ḳazwīnī, *ʻAdjā'ib al-Makhlūḳāt*, ed. Wüstenfeld, Göttingen, 1848.

al-Khaiyāṭ, Abu'l-Husain ʻAbd al-Raḥīm b. Muh. b. ʻUthmān, *Kitāb al-Intiṣār*, Cairo, 1925.

Kitāb Aḥwāl al-Ḳiyāma, *Muhammedanische Eschatologie*, ed. and transl. M. Wolff, Leipzig, 1872.

Kremer, A. v., *Geschichte der herrschenden Ideen des Islams*, Leipzig, 1868. (Contains a translation of the Fiḳh Akbar II, pp. 40–3.)

Lammens, "Le 'Triumvirat' Aboû Bakr, ʻOmar et Aboû ʻObaida", *Mélanges de la Faculté Orientale*, Beyrouth, IV. 113–45.

Lewin, B., "Zur Sunnitischen Polemik gegen die Šīʻa", *Le Monde Oriental*, XXV. 85 *sqq.*

Macdonald, D. B., *Development of Muslim Theology, Jurisprudence and Constitutional Theory*, New York, 1903.

Maḳrīzī, *Khiṭaṭ*, Cairo, 1270, 2 vols.

Mālik b. Anas, *Muwaṭṭa'*, Cairo, 1279, 4 vols.

Mehren, A. F., *Exposé de la réforme de l'islamisme, commencée au troisième siècle de l'hégire par Abou'l-Hasan Ali el-Ashari. Travaux de la troisième session du congrès international des orientalistes*, St Pétersbourg, 1876, II. 167 *sqq.*

Muh. Aʻlā b. ʻAlī al-Tahānawī, *Kitāb Kashshāf Iṣṭilāḥāt al-Funūn*, Calcutta, 1862.

Muslim, *Ṣaḥīḥ*, with the commentary of al-Nawawī, Cairo, 1283, 5 vols.

Nadjm al-Dīn Abū Ḥafṣ ʻUmar, *see* al-Nasafī.

Nallino, C. A., "Sull' origine del nome dei Muʻtaziliti", *Rivista degli Studi Orientali*, VII. 429 *sqq.*

al-Nasafī, Abu'l-Muʻīn Maimūn b. Muḥ. († 508/1114), author of *ʻAḳā'id*, MS. Berlin, No. 1941; *Munādjāt*, MS. Leiden, No. 661, Warner, No. 862; *Tamhīd*, MSS. Cairo, Nos. 2286, 2417; *Tabṣirat al-Adilla*, MS. Cairo, Nos. 2287, 6673; *Baḥr al-Kalām*, printed at Cairo, 1329.

al-Nasafī, Ḥāfiẓ al-Dīn Abu'l-Barakāt ʻAbd Allāh († 710/1310), author of *ʻUmda*, ed. Cureton, London, 1843, No. 1.

al-Nasafī, Nadjm al-Dīn Abū Ḥafṣ ʻUmar b. Muḥ. b. Aḥmad b. Ismāʻīl b. Muḥ. b. Luḳmān († 537/1142), author of *ʻAkīda*, ed. Cureton, London, 1843, No. 2; Commentary of al-Ṭaftāzānī, with Supercommentary of al-Isfarā'inī and *ḥāshiya* of al-Khayālī, Cairo, 1335.

al-Nawawī, *Sharḥ 'alā Ṣaḥīḥ Muslim*, Cairo, 1283, 5 vols.

Nyberg, H. S., *see* al-Khaiyāṭ.

Obermann, J., *W.Z.K.M.* vol. xxx.

Patton, W. M., *Aḥmad ibn Ḥanbal and the Miḥna*, Leiden, 1897.

Reland, H., *De religione Mohammedanica*, Utrecht, 1704.

Rodwell, J. M., *The Ḳorân*, transl. from the Arabic, 2nd ed. London, 1876.

Rougier, L., *La scolastique et le Thomisme*, Paris, 1925.

Sa'adya al-Faiyūmī, *Kitāb al-Amānāt wa'l-I'tiḳādāt*, ed. Landauer, Leiden, 1881.

Sachau, E., "Zur ältesten Geschichte des muhammedanischen Rechtes", *Sitzungsberichte der Akad. der Wissenschaften in Wien*, vol. LXV.

Sale, G., *The Koran...to which is prefixed a preliminary discourse*, London, 1821, 2 vols.

al-Samarḳandī, Isḥāḳ b. Muḥ. b. Ismā'īl Abu'l-Ḳāsim al-Ḥakīm († 342/953), *al-Sawād al-A'ẓam*, Būlāḳ, 1253.

al-Samarḳandī, Abu'l-Laith Naṣr b. Muḥ. b. Aḥmad b. Ibrāhīm († 373/993), *'Aḳīda*, ed. A. W. Th. Juynboll in *Tijdschr. voor de Taal-, Land- en Volkenkunde v. Ned.-Indie*, 4th series, vol. v (1881), pp. 215–31, 267–74.

—— *Uṣūl al-Dīn*, MS. Cairo, No. 6686. (This is an early work on dogmatics, but in the MS. there is no trace of the authorship of Samarḳandī.)

—— *Sharḥ al-Fiḳh al-Akbar*, MS. Cairo, *Madjmū'a* 349, fols. 7–23. (This is the commentary on Fiḳh Akbar I, printed at Ḥaidarābād, 1321, author unknown, *see supra*, p. 122.) See further Brockelmann, *G.A.L.* I. 170 *sq.*

al-Samarḳandī, 'Ubaid Allāh b. Muḥ. b. 'Abd al-'Azīz, *Sharḥ lā ilāha illa 'llāh*, MS. Cairo, No. 2440, fols. 11–35.

al-Sanūsī, *'Umdat Ahl al-Tawfīḳ*, Cairo, 1306.

—— *Umm al-Barāhīn* or *Risāla fī Ma'ānī Kalimatai al-Shahāda*, ed. and transl. M. Wolff, Leipzig, 1848.

Schacht, Joseph, *Der Islam* in *Religionsgeschichtliches Lesebuch...*, von Alfred Bertholet, 2nd ed. Tübingen, 1931, p. 35 *sqq.*

Sell, E., *The Faith of Islam*, London and Madras, 1880, esp. chap. IV, pp. 116–80: The Creed of Islam.

al-Shāfi'ī, *Risāla fī Uṣūl al-Fiḳh*, Cairo, 1321.

—— *Fiḳh Akbar* (III), MS. Cairo, *Madjmū'a* 23, fols. 45–58 (spurious).

al-Shahrastānī, *Kitāb al-Milal wa'l-Niḥal*, ed. Cureton, London, 1846, 2 vols.

Smith, Margaret, *Rābi'a the Mystic*, Cambridge, 1928.

Söderblom, N., "La vie future d'après le Mazdéisme", Paris, 1901, *Annales du Musée Guimet. Bibliothèque d'études*, tome IX.

Spitta, W., *Zur Geschichte Abu'l-Ḥasan al-Aš'ari's*, Leipzig, 1876.
Sprenger, A., *Das Leben und die Lehre des Moḥammed*, Berlin, 1861–5, 3 vols.
Strothmann, "Islamische Konfessionskunde", *Der Islam*, XIX. 193 *sqq*.
al-Ṭabarī, *Tafsīr al-Ḳur'ān*, Cairo, 1901–3, 31 vols.
al-Taftāzānī († 791/1389), Sa'd al-Dīn Mas'ūd b. 'Umar, *see* Nadjm al-Dīn, al-Nasafī.
al-Ṭaḥāwī, Aḥmad b. Dja'far, *Bayān al-Sunna wa'l-Djamā'a*, Ḥalab, 1344. With an explicit commentary: Makka, 1349 (*Kitāb Sharḥ al-Ṭaḥāwīya fi'l-'Aḳīda al-Salafīya*). German translation by J. Hell, *Von Mohammed bis Ghazâlî*, Jena, 1915, p. 39 *sqq*.
al-Ṭayālisī, *Musnad*, Ḥaidarābād, 1321.
Theodorus Abū Ḳurra, *see* Abū Ḳurra.
al-Tirmidhī, *Ṣaḥīḥ*, Cairo, 1292, 2 vols.
'Ubaid Allāh b. Muḥammad, *see* al-Samarḳandī.
Wellhausen, J., *Skizzen und Vorarbeiten*, vol. IV, No. 3, Berlin, 1889.

General Index

tion of, in the creed, 147 *sqq.*; the position of the Fikh Akbar II towards, 229, 237 *sq.*
Anti-Christ, his signs, 193, 227, 243; his appearing, 197; will be killed by Jesus, 357
Apostles, who does not believe that Moses and Jesus belong to the, is an infidel, 104, art. 8; making difference between the, 113 *sqq.*; excluding none of the, 113 *sq.*; interrogation of the, 176 *sq.*; impeccability of the, 192, 217 *sq.*, 267; belief in the, 203; difference between Apostles and Prophets, 203 *sq.*, 267; with their communities on the bridge, 203; password of the, 203; Kuranic series of, 203; as missionaries to the peoples, 203, 273; names and number of the, 203 *sq.*, 267; knowledge derived from, 263; their honesty, 273, 276; what is *wāḏjib* with regard to the, 276
Aristotle and *kalām*, 78, 209, 248; and the eternity of the world, 86, 87, 210 *sq.*, 228; and the difference between essence and existence, 212; introduction of the triad *wāḏjib*, *mumkin*, *mustaḥīl* in *kalām*, 274
al-Aṣamm, 201
Asbāb al-ʿilm, 253, 263
Ascension, explained away by the Muʿtazilites, 100; Muhammad's, a reality, 197, 242 *sq.*
Aseitas, 274
al-As̲h̲ʿarī, his *Ibāna* and his *Maḳālāt al-Islāmīyīn*, 2 *sq.*, 87; his leading position, 87; and al-Ḏjubbāʾī, 87; his conversion, 87; his attitude towards *kalām*, 87 *sqq.*, 254; on the *visio beatifica*, 88 *sqq.*; on Allah's sitting on His throne, 90, 116; his ambiguous position, 90 *sq.*, 254; detested by Ibn Ḥazm, 91, cf. 264; and anthropomorphism, 88, 91, 92; description of his position by al-Ḏjuwainī, 92; and *tanzīh*, 92; and *kasb*, 92; his works, 95; al-G̲h̲azālī and As̲h̲ʿaritic dogmatics, 94; the As̲h̲ʿarites in a middle position between allegorical interpretation and anthropomorphism, 100; on faith, 134, 136; the question whether one may declare himself to be faithful, 138 *sq.*; and *k̲h̲aḏ̲h̲lān*, 143; on the author of sin, 144 *sq.*; the As̲h̲ʿarites on the relation between Allah's speech and the Kuran, 151; on the hierarchic sequence, 152; differences between the As̲h̲ʿarites and the Māturīdites regarding *istiṭāʿa*, 157; seems to prefer Fāṭima to ʿĀʾis̲h̲a, 184; is said to have admitted the possibility of the faithful in Hell and of the infidels in Paradise for ever, 184; his doctrine of the eternal attributes of Allah, 205; on predestination, 211 *sq.*; and the Fiḳh Akbar II, 246; on sensual knowledge, 250; and theology, 254
Āsiya, 184
Aṣlaḥ, see Ṣalāḥ
Atomism, atoms, 210, 224
Attributes, similarity between Christianity and orthodox Islam regarding the doctrine of, 70, 73, 275, note 4; described in a negative way, 71 *sq.*; eternal, rejected by the Muʿtazilites, 74; by the Ḏjahmites, 121; of Allah, 74 *sqq.*, 134, 188; the Muʿtazilites cannot wholly reject, 75; the Muʿtazilites and, 75 *sqq.*; eternal, 188, 204, 266, 273; arranged in groups, 188, 27[illegible];

difference between the attributes of man and those of Allah, 189; whether the attributes of Allah may be expressed in Persian or Turkish, 196; Allah's attributes and names equal in excellence, etc., 196; the doctrine of the, in the Fiḳh Akbar II, 204 *sq.*; in the Fiḳh Akbar III, 266; are neither Allah nor other than He, 205, 273, note 1; what names and attributes may be applied to Allah, 236 *sq.*; *see also* Kuran, Speech
al-Awzā'ī, 135
Āyāt, 224 *sq.*

Badr, 241
al-Bāḳillānī, 225, 250
Bakr ibn Akhshab 'Abd al-Wāḥid ibn Zaid, 184
al-Bakrīya, the followers of Bakr, *q.v.*, prefer 'Ā'isha to Fāṭima, 184
Balance confessed to be real, 130, art. 21, 169 *sq.*, 258, 268; *see also* Weighing
al-Balkhī, Abū Muṭī', 115, 123
Barā'a, 109
Barzakh, 119
Basin, the, of the Prophet, 195, 231 *sq.*, 258, 268, 274
Baṣra, *see* Mu'tazilites
Bazīghīya, 201
Bilā kaifa, 86, 116, 190, note 2, 207, 238; the formula is not deemed permanently satisfactory, 86; its place taken by the doctrine of *tanzīh*, 207
Bishr ibn al-Mu'tamir does not reject the idea of *luṭf*, 82
Black-eyed girls, *see* Paradise
Body, Allah without, 210; *see also* Allah
Book, the reading of the, confessed to be a reality, 130, art. 22; in eschatology, 172 *sqq.*
Books, revealed, 202 *sq.*
Brahmans, 256, 261
Bridge in eschatology, 169, 178, 203, 232 *sq.*, 268, 274

Catechisms, 2, 265, 270 *sq.*; metrical, 270, note 5
Children, killing of, proposed by some Khāridjites, 42; this is prohibited in Islam, 42; born in the *fiṭra*, 42, 214; the fate of, who die before reaching the adult age, 43; even children of infidels in Paradise, 43; no *taklīf* of, 43; the difficulty to harmonize the tradition on the fate of children with the dogma of predestination, 43; according to the Khāridjites children are in a state of neutrality, 44, 214; the suffering of, 81, 262, 267
Christianity, and Islam, similar attitude regarding the fate of children who die during minority, 44; regarding the distinction between mortal and venial sins, 47; the relation between faith and works in, 47, 141; and Islam on predestination, 51, 211; and Islam on the *visio beatifica*, 65 *sq.*; teaches free will, 51, 145 *sqq.*, 216; similarity between Christianity and the Mu'tazilites in explaining anthropomorphic expressions, 68 *sq.*; similarity between Christianity and orthodox Islam regarding the attributes of God, 70, 150, 186, 206; prepares for Islam the way to *kalām*, 78, 206; hereditary sin in, 131, note 1; on the connection between God and evil, 145 *sq.*; and intercession, 180, 182; mission of the Apostles to different peoples, 203; difference between Apostles and Prophets, 204; on the relation between essence and

Dja'far ibn Ḥarb, does not reject the idea of *lutf*, 82
Djāh, 222
Djahm ibn Ṣafwān, rejects anthropomorphism, 91; on the punishment in the tomb, 104, art. 10, 119; description of his doctrine, 119 *sqq.*, 132, 165 *sq.*; on Paradise and Hell, 121, 165 *sq.*
Djā'iz, 227 *sq.*, 261, 274 *sqq.*; *see also* Contingent
Djamā'a, no deviation from, allowed, 268
Djawhar, 210
Djibrīl, 199
Djiha, 187, 229
Djisr, 233
al-Djubbā'ī, 'Abd al-Salām b. Muhammad b. 'Abd al-Wahhāb, 137, note 1
al-Djubbā'ī, Abū 'Alī Muhammad b. 'Abd al-Wahhāb, 76, 82, note 3
al-Djuwainī, 92, 250, 269, 271
Dogma, Dogmas, evolution of Muslim, follows the logical line, 37, 52; the dogmatic crisis of Islam, 37; uncertainty regarding, must be repaired as soon as possible, 197; the basis of, 249

ἐγκατάλειψις, 213
Eschatology, 117 *sq.*, 121, 167 *sqq.*, 197, 268; sequence of eschatological scenes, 100, 172; interpretation of, 172; *see also* Balance, Basin, Bridge, Hour, Street, Sun
Essence (*dhāt*) and existence (*wudjūd*), 166 *sq.*, 212, 274
εὐδοκία, 145
Evil, no relation between Allah and, according to Wāsil ibn 'Aṭā, 81; prohibiting what is evil, 103, art. 2, 106 *sq.*; prohibiting what is evil is called a doctrine peculiar to the Mu'tazilites, 107; Allah and, 109, 143 *sqq.*, 186, 216; and the Mu'tazilites, 145; the connection between God and, according to Eastern Christianity, 146, 216
Existence (*wudjūd*), 166 *sq.*, 212, 274
Experience, 260

Faculty, *see* Acts, *Istiṭā'a*
Faith, definition of, in Tradition, 23, 35, cf. 188, 197; discussions on the nature of faith perhaps in the background of the Khāridjī doctrine, 37; impaired by sin according to the Khāridjites, 39, 44; and sin according to the orthodox position, 45 *sqq.*, 125, 138, 140 *sq.*, 156; whether faith is liable to increase or decrease, 45, 125, 138, 194, 229; and works according to the orthodox position, 48, 148; saves from Hell, 48 *sq.*; in *ḥadīth*, 67 *sq.*, 131, 148 *sq.*; the Mu'tazilites do not recognize faith as a divine gift, 82; minimum of, 107; Djahm on, 120, 132; and knowledge, 120, 125, 134 *sq.*; definition of, in the Waṣīyat Abī Ḥanīfa, 125, 131 *sqq.*, 138, 186; and works, 125 *sq.*, 131, 133 *sq.*, 230; according to the Murdjites, 132; according to the Mu'tazilites, 132; according to al-Baghdādī, 134; according to al-Ash'arī, 134; *taklīd* and *fides implicita*, 135, 137, 242; according to Ibn Ḥadjar al-Haitamī, 141; the relation between faith and works in Oriental Christianity, 141; as defined in the Fikh Akbar II, 188, 194, 229; objective and subjective sides of, 194, 230; definition of, in the Fikh Akbar III, 267; *see also* *Īmān*

Tsena!